MW01260202

This is a biography of one of the most undervalued commanders of the Second World War, General Stanisław Maczek, a soldier overlooked by most military historians in the West both because he was Polish and above politics. Unlike most Polish commanders he rocked no boats and after his service was complete in 1947 he retreated into relative obscurity. When he died at the age of 102 he had left a single published book of his war memoirs and little else to the popular imagination. One had to be acquainted with his armoured division, the wartime 1st Polish Armoured Division, in order to know anything of the man or even to have heard of him. This book is an attempt to try to put the historical record right, at least in the English language, and place front and centre into the wartime historiography the story of an extraordinary man. Maczek's story is the story of 20th Century Poland and begins naturally enough with his birth in 1892, into a Poland that hadn't existed since 1795 when it was trisected between the three empires of Austrian, Russia and Prussia (later Germany). Maczek was born in the Austrian sector, which meant in 1914 he was conscripted into the Imperial Austrian Army, with which he served with great credit on the Italian Front, high in the Alps. It was this experience which was to serve Maczek well in his future career in the Polish Army after 1918.

Maczek should be remembered for his pioneering use of mixed armour and infantry units as well as the early use of commando-style units during the Polish border wars of 1918-1920. However his work was ignored despite its obvious success. He should also be recognised as being the saviour of the Normandy Campaign, which by August 1944 was seriously bogged down. It was feared that the German forces in Normandy might be able to flee over the River Seine and head eastwards towards Germany. A magnificent, stubborn and costly stand by the Polish 1st Armoured Division during August 1944 prevented this happening, and the Normandy Campaign was able to succeed. This is yet to be credited to the Poles in the imagination of the West. Maczek's division was later able to advance into Germany, fighting its way through the Low Countries. Maczek's command of the division and its combat service in North-West Europe 1944-45 is fully described, and represents, in particular, an important contribution to our knowledge of the Normandy Campaign. After the war, Maczek, now exiled and stateless and with his homeland seized by the Soviet Union, was stripped of his Polish citizenship by the Communists, and was left to bring up his young family on his wages as a barman. This is the story of a man who changed history, fully researched from archival and printed materials, and with a heavy reliance on original Polish language sources. The text is complemented by over 150 previously unpublished photographs.

Evan McGilvray was born in August 1961 in Winchester, Hampshire. He is a graduate of the School of Slavonic and East European Studies, University of London (UCL). Following this he undertook post-graduate studies at the University of Bradford and the University of Leeds, where he researched the politics of the Polish Army from 1918 to date. He also taught at the two universities. Evan is quite happy to challenge the myths that Poles have created around the Polish Army and the role of Poland during the Second World War. He also has an interest in other militaries and their role in society – quite simply civil-military relations – Poland being one of the most interesting European examples.

Evan has written two previous titles – *The Black Devils' March – A Doomed Odyssey. The 1st Polish Armoured Division 1939-45* (2004) and *A Military Government in Exile. The Polish Government in Exile 1939-45, a Study of Discontent* (2010), both published by Helion.

At present Evan is writing a new history of the 1944 Warsaw Uprising in readiness for its seventieth anniversary in 2014, as well as researching the military politics regarding the involvement of General Sir Ian Hamilton at the Dardanelles during 1915. He is also anticipating the opening of the archives relating to the Falklands War in 2012. To relax he has learnt to ignore the rest of the world, and notes, "Despite what Poles think, I am not a Scot, only in name!"

MAN OF STEEL AND HONOUR

General Stanisław Maczek
Soldier of Poland, Commander of the 1st Polish
Armoured Division in
North-West Europe 1944-45

'The Polish Soldier Fights for the Freedom of
Other Nations but Dies only for Poland'

Helion Studies in Military History Number 18

Evan McGilvray

Helion & Company Ltd

Helion & Company Limited
26 Willow Road
Solihull
West Midlands
B91 1UE
England
Tel. 0121 705 3393
Fax 0121 711 4075
Email: info@helion.co.uk
Website: www.helion.co.uk
Twitter: @helionbooks
Visit our blog http://blog.helion.co.uk

Published by Helion & Company 2012. This paperback reprint 2015.

Designed and typeset by Farr out Publications, Wokingham, Berkshire
Cover designed by Euan Carter, Leicester (www.euancarter.com)
Printed by Lightning Source Ltd, Milton Keynes, Buckinghamshire

Text © Evan McGilvray 2012
Images © as individually credited
Maps pp.33, 71, 87, 135 © Helion & Company Limited. Other maps taken from *10 Pulk Strzelcow Konnych w Kampanii 1944–45* (no imprint, published 1947)

ISBN 978-1-910777-38-1

British Library Cataloguing-in-Publication Data.
A catalogue record for this book is available from the British Library.

All rights reserved. No part of this publication may be reproduced, stored in a retrieval system,or transmitted, in any form, or by any means, electronic, mechanical, photocopying, recording or otherwise, without the express written consent of Helion & Company Limited.

Cover illustrations: Front cover – Maczek in the turret of a Cromwell VII, July 1944. (Narodowe Archiwum Cyfrowe). Rear cover – 26 February 1945, Maczek is awarded the Légion d'Honneur by General Juin at the Arc de Triomphe, Paris. (Narodowe Archiwum Cyfrowe).

For details of other military history titles published by Helion & Company Limited contact the above address, or visit our website: http://www.helion.co.uk.

We always welcome receiving book proposals from prospective authors.

Contents

List of Photographs

List of Maps

1

The Young Maczek, 1892-1914

His Poland and the Years of Peace

G eneral Stanisław Maczek was born in Poland in 1892 and died in exile at the great age of 102 in 1994 in Edinburgh. His long life was, in so many ways, a human example of the travails that Poland suffered between 1795 and 1989.

Maczek was born in Poland, although when he was born Poland did not exist as an independent state and had not done so since 1795, when the country had been divided up for the third time between the Russians, Austrians and Prussians. The concept of Poland only lived on in the hearts of patriots and the arts.

The Poland where Maczek was born was part of the Austrian Empire, which of the imperial powers partitioning Poland was the most lenient towards the Poles.[1] The Russians had proved themselves to be absolutely brutal in their reactions towards any Polish rebellion in their lands. The Germans were less aggressive towards Polish nationalism, but even so Bismarck's policy of *Kulturkampf*, which was aimed principally against Catholics, also felt anti-Polish given that many Poles were fiercely Catholic while Polish language was restricted in German-governed areas of Poland. This had the effect of many Poles feeling aggrieved at German policies which seemed determined to undermine Polish culture and identity.[2]

General Stanisław Maczek was born in Szczerzec, Galicia in Austrian Poland on 31 March 1892; he was a twin. His twin brother, Franciszek, was killed in 1915 fighting in the First World War. Maczek had two younger brothers, Jan and Karol. The First World War also claimed Karol's life while Jan was killed in 1920 during the Polish-Soviet War.[3]

At the time of Maczek's birth Europe was largely at peace and Galicia was very much a backwater of a failing and overburdened empire. Quite simply, over the centuries Austria had acquired more territory than it knew what to do with but like the Soviet empire at the end of the 20th century was reluctant to let any of it go. However as the 20th century dawned, Galicia was beginning to change while the world was already getting smaller owing to more efficient communications, ranging from the spread of the railways to that of the telegraph and the widespread circulation of newspapers and ideas, such things even reaching remote Galicia.

Simultaneously, nations such as the Slavic nations were yearning for independence and sought to remove themselves from the three Central European empires and strike

---

1   Neal Ascherson, *The Struggles for Poland*, London, Michael Joseph, 1987, p. 28.
2   A.J.P. Taylor, *Bismarck. The Man and Statesman*, London, NEL Mentor, 1968, pp. 115-23.
3   Witold A. Deimel, 'The Life and Career of General Stanisław Maczek: An Appreciation' in Peter D. Stachura (ed) *Themes of Modern Polish History – Proceedings of a Symposium on 28 March 1992. In Honour of the Century of General Stanisław Maczek*, Glasgow, The Polish Social and Educational Society, 1992, pp. 11-13.

out alone as independent states. The problem was that there was little chance of doing so quickly; changes between 1892 and 1914 were slow and difficult. Poland was no exception regarding the desire for self-determination and was in the vanguard for nationhood and independence throughout East-Central Europe.

Throughout the 19th century Poland had seen several uprisings following the demise of the Polish state after 1795, or, as the Polish Romantic poets had it, 'descended into the grave'. Most of the rebellions were directed against Russia. At first, during the Napoleonic Wars, many Poles, especially the aristocracy, joined the armies of Napoleon in his doomed invasion of Russia during 1812. After Napoleon's final defeat in 1815 Poles had to re-think how they might retrieve Polish sovereignty. The first rebellion occurred in 1830, was against Russia, and lasted until 1831 with a Russian victory. The next uprisings were in the Austrian and Prussian partitions during 1846 were shortlived and a disaster, as revealed in Polish society in Galicia. In Prussian-occupied Poland Polish leaders were arrested almost immediately and in the Free City of Kraków, Prussian and Russian troops put down the rebellion immediately.

In Galicia however, as soon as the revolt began, the Austrians provoked a peasant revolt against Polish landlords which became a *jacquerie*. Hundreds of landlords and their families were murdered and their estates burnt. In previous rebellions Polish leaders had been able to rely on the support of Polish peasants by promising an end of serfdom in return for military service. The Galician rebellion revealed that Polish peasants had very little interest in Poland but instead wanted individual freedoms which they perceived as the end of serfdom and the adoption of peasant landownership. By 1848 the Austrians abolished serfdom in the Austrian partition of Poland and so at a stroke removed the support of the peasants which Polish nobles had previously depended on.

The failures of the 1846 rebellions so demoralised Poles that during the 1848 Europe-wide rebellions Poland was silent. Throughout the remainder of the 19th century there were no further revolts against rule in Austrian Poland. Indeed Kieniewicz asserts that 'the year 1846 saw a complete defeat of the Polish cause'.[4] The last rebellion of the 19th century against foreign rule in Poland, the 1863 revolt against Russia, also ended in failure. Basically, the Russians adopted the Austrian method and abolished serfdom; once again the Polish nobles lost the support of the peasantry. It would seem that Polish Nationalism was not as popular as it might be claimed and that it was only in the interests of the Polish aristocracy, who would once more rule over Poland but at the expense of the Polish peasantry.

The Russians put down the 1863 revolt so harshly that there was quiet in the Polish lands for two generations. This was the Poland into which Maczek was born. In fact, as we have already observed, Maczek's Poland was even quieter as it had been at peace since the failed revolt of 1846.

What is interesting is that Maczek's family were not actually Polish and this reveals the nature of the multi-nation Austrian empire ruled by the Habsburg dynasty. As Ascherson observes, as it attempted to keep its different people together – Germans, Czechs, Hungarians, Croats, Poles and Ukrainians – to name a few, this multinational empire allowed the Poles in the Austrian partition a considerable amount of autonomy.[5] This was underlined in 1895 when the Austrian Emperor, Franz Joseph, in an attempt to hold his

---

4   Stefan Kieniewicz, *The Emancipation of the Polish Peasantry*, Chicago, University of Chicago, 1969, p. 124.

5   Ascherson, op. cit. p.28. See also Kieniewicz, op. cit. Chapter 9.

empire together, appointed not a German nor a Hungarian, as had always been the case previously, but instead a Pole, Count Kasimir Badeni, as Governor of Galicia. Badeni was considered a 'loyalist' to the Austrian monarchy but he also had a reputation of being a 'liberal'.[6] Neither the Russians nor the Germans would have taken such a risk in their Polish territories.

Maczek was of Croat descent and was the cousin of the Croatian peasant politician Vladko Maček (1879-1964).[7] Both cousins were subjects of the Austrian emperor while to travel directly from modern day Croatia to distant Galicia, now in present day Ukraine, during the 19th century meant that one did not cross any international frontiers if they remained within the bounds of the Austrian Empire. As the empire was so vast this was easily achieved if one was a subject of the Austrian emperor; one did not need a passport, as one had not travelled abroad – a little like travelling within the European Union today. Both cousins were to die in exile many years after the breakup of the Austrian Empire; such were the upheavals of 20th century Europe.

Galicia was very much a backwater, especially once compared with the imperial capital, Vienna, let alone London or Paris, but it did have one great asset – the Polish cultural city of Lwów. This was essentially an oasis of culture in an intellectual desert, which consisted of the ignorance and superstition of the local Polish and Ukrainian peasantry. At the same time it should be realised that Galicia, despite its virtual autonomy, was the poorest part of Europe.[8]

Despite Maczek's Croatian background Majka insists that Maczek was brought up in an atmosphere of patriotism and Polish culture.[9] However this assertion is meaningless as any Pole of the standing of the Maczek family would have been brought up in this manner as it reflected local values of the middle and upper classes in Polish society of that time, while the poor would not have been able to enjoy such a life of leisure, study and reflection. The statement is as worthless as that of noting that a middle or upper class Victorian boy was schooled in the perceived virtues of the British Empire. Such statements reflect beliefs that, it could be argued, caused harm to both cases as the 20th century unfolded. Deimel notes that Maczek did not anticipate a military career but instead intended to study philosophy or psychology – the First World War ended these plans.[10] To study Maczek was ideally placed, as he lived so close in Lwów, with its university as well as it being a centre for Polish culture.

As Maczek was growing up much was changing in Europe and in the Polish lands it was becoming obvious that two of the three ruling powers that divided Poland were on the wane. Since 1867 the Austrians had been obliged to share power with the Hungarians, hence the Austro-Hungarian Empire. This caused friction amongst the other subject nations of the empire, notably the Slavs. Furthermore Maczek's homeland, Galicia, was haemorrhaging people owing to the poverty found there. Indeed in 1913 alone 400,000 people or 5% of the population emigrated. In the 25 years prior to the outbreak of war

6   Robert Bideleux & Ian Jeffries, *A History of Eastern Europe. Crisis and Change*, London, Routledge, 1998, p. 350.
7   Zbigniew Mieczkowski, *The Soldiers of General Maczek in World War II*, Warsaw & London, Foundation for the Commemoration of General Maczek First Polish Armoured Division, 2004, p. 16.
8   Norman Davies, *God's Playground. A History of Poland. Volume II: 1795 to the Present*, Oxford, Oxford University Press, 1983, pp. 143-62.
9   Jerzy Majka, *Generał Stanisław Maczek*, Rzeszów, Libra, 2005, p. 6.
10   Deimel, op. cit. p. 12.

in 1914 over 2,000,000 people emigrated. Some went to other parts of Poland; others to France or Germany but the vast majority went to America.[11]

Russia was also in decline, especially since its defeat at the hands of the Japanese as a result of the Russo-Japanese War, 1904-05. This was the first time in modern history that a European power had been defeated by an Asian people; this led to the 1905 Revolution in Russia and the establishment of a parliament or *Duma*. This was a somewhat limited forum for democracy but the Russian emperor, Tsar Nicholas II, remained an absolute monarch and a demi-god to so many Russian peasants. Nevertheless, it was a tiny step towards democracy in Russia, although nothing like the democracy experienced in western Europe, which in turn was not democracy as recognised throughout Europe today.[12]

The third power, Germany, was under the rule of another absolute monarch, the emperor, Kaiser Wilhelm II, who had ruled since 1890. At times war loomed as the British, French and German empires began to compete for colonies and influence, especially in Africa. A further complication was the slow demise of the Turkish or Ottoman Empire, which did not directly affect Poland although its weakening rule was affecting Europe in the shape of the Balkan Wars of 1912 and 1913. Turkey was also losing territory in North Africa as Italy took advantage of the decline of the Ottoman Empire. The Balkan Wars were to be important as the Slavs of the Balkan region sought to establish their own identities against each other as well as the Turks, including a new state, Albania, established in 1913. These conflicts were seen by the leading Polish rebel, Józef Piłsudski (1867-1935) as a precursor to a larger conflict which he correctly predicted would see the end of the east-central European imperial system and of course the resurrection of Poland.[13]

Piłsudski, even if he is a national hero in Poland, should be seen as a controversial figure as he clearly was not the hero or democrat which many Poles try to make him out to be. It is without doubt that only Piłsudki had, in 1918, the charisma to lead the Poles to independence and maintain it during his lifetime. Zamoyski observes that Piłsudski had had a varied career, having been born a Lithuanian noblemen and by twists and turns enjoyed life as a terrorist, a Socialist, a train robber and finally a self-appointed military commander.[14] Coutouvidis furthers the assessment of Piłsudski: 'Józef Piłsudski had personified independent Poland. Successively convicted terrorist, Socialist agitator, cavalry officer, Commander-in-Chief and vanquisher of Trotsky's Red Army, democratic president and dictator, he became the embodiment of Polish statehood'.[15]

Piłsudski, as early as 1908, had founded a paramilitary organisation with which he sought to establish the re-independence of Poland. This followed a daring mail train robbery by an armed band which included Piłsudski, the future lame duck Polish exiled Prime Minister, Tomasz Arciszewski and incredibly Piłsudski's future wife, Alexandra Szczerbińska. The robbery took place near Wilno (today Vilnius, the Lithuanian capital) complete with a dramatic escape by speedboat down the River Niemen. The robbery realised a fortune in Russian roubles which was enough to buy weapons and printing equipment. Despite this success Piłsudski had already concluded that guerrilla warfare and terrorism

11   Davies, op. cit. p. 107.
12   Ibid. p. 107.
13   Andrzej Garlicki, *Józef Piłsudski, 1867-1935* Warsaw, Czytelnik, 1988, p. 145.
14   Adam Zamoyski, *The Battle of the Marchlands*, New York, Columbia University Press, 1981, p. 4.
15   Andrzej Garlicki, *Józef Piłsudski: 1867-1935* edited and translated by John Coutouvidis, Aldershot, Scolar, 1993, p. xiii.

was getting nowhere as since 1905 the Russians had tightened their grip on their partition of Poland. While the Russians authorities seemed unable to defeat him Piłsudski removed himself to the fairly free Galicia with the view of founding a Polish Army.[16]

Piłsudski had long brooded over the question as to why the Polish people did not believe that they could free themselves from imperial rule: he concluded that this lack of self-believe was because Poland lacked an army, which he considered to be the proudest of all of the Polish institutions. Piłsudski believed that he could provide an army that would return self-confidence to Poles but also claimed that Austria would accept Polish regiments not as cannon fodder but as allies in a future war against Russia.[17]

On 21 February 1914 in a speech in Paris Piłsudski made his case for a Polish Army to a largely Polish audience. He demonstrated that if war between the east European empires did break out, 600,000 Poles would be conscripted into the Russian Army, 200,000 into the German Army and 300,000 into the Austrian Army. These Poles would then more likely fight each other on the behalf of others with no gain for Poland. Piłsudski concluded that the only way that Poles could have any influence on a future war was to have an army itself and that such a force could only be raised in Galicia as the whole administration of the province was in Polish hands. The battle for Polish independence, according to Piłsudski, could only begin from Galicia.[18] And this was Galicia's legacy; without it Polish independence might have been more difficult to achieve once the three empires collapsed in 1918. Because of the liberal attitude of Austrian rule in Galicia, Piłsudski was able to build up a military force which eventually became the Polish Army, which in turn was the only unifying force to be found in Poland during November 1918 when Poland achieved independence. But, that is to get ahead of our story.

Once in Galicia Piłsudski began to build up his forces. At first the origins of the paramilitaries, called 'riflemen' or in Polish 'Strzelcy', were modest, drilling secretly in backyards, but within a few years their numbers grew and their units spread all over Galicia while talk of their use by the Austrian Army in a possible war against Russia had begun.

The Austrians were clearly distrustful of the Polish units as it was inconceivable that the Poles were to be inspired by an undying love for the Habsburg dynasty, so the Strzelcy were kept short of essential equipment, including rifles. However what was interesting was the type of men enlisting in the Strzelcy, men who were to help form the modern Polish Army and state, such names as Kazimierz Sosnkowski and Władysław Sikorski, who were to play their roles in the inter-war Polish Second Republic and the wartime Polish Government-in-Exile.[19] Maczek first met Piłsudski in 1913 when he was an anonymous young student volunteer of the Strzelcy in Lwów.[20] It was not the last time that these two men would meet. It should be noted that Maczek once said that whilst at university in Lwów he became involved with the Rifle Association and that it was only his call-up for the Austrian Army that prevented him from joining the Polish Legions, the military force which grew out of

---

16   Ascherson, op. cit. pp. 45-6.

17   Ibid. p. 46.

18   Wacław Jędrzejewicz, *Piłsudski: A Life for Poland*, New York, Hippocrene, 1982, p. 52. For the original speech see '*O Polskim Ruchu Strzeleckim*' in Józef Piłsudski, *Pisma Zbiorowe*, Volume 3, Warsaw, Krajowa Agencja Wydawnicza, 1937, pp. 250-53, hereafter referred to as *Pisma*. Jędrzejewicz has worked out the figures, as Piłsudski in his speech does not give any.

19   Ascherson, op. cit. p. 46.

20   Stanisław Maczek, *Od Podwody do Czołga: Wspomnienia Wojenne 1918-1945*, Edinburgh, Tomar, 1961, p. 34.

the *Strzelcy*.[21]

On 6 August 1914 Austrian and Russia went to war and Piłsudski, with 3 companies of riflemen, marched out of Kraków and unilaterally 'invaded' the Russian empire. As a result of the Austrian authorities withholding military equipment from Piłsudski's men, the Poles marched with old rifles which fired a bullet 'the size of a potato' while some of the cavalrymen, lacking mounts, carried their saddles across the River Vistula into Russian territory in the hope of finding horses on the other side. Piłsudski had wanted to begin a Polish insurrection. In 1916 he wrote:

> In 1914 I was not concerned with settling the details of the military question in Poland but simply with this – was the Polish soldier to remain a mystical entity deprived of flesh and blood? In a great war fought on Polish soil, when a soldier with his bayonet and uniform would penetrate to every cottage and farm of our countryside, I wanted the Polish soldier to be something more than a pretty picture often looked at secretly in corners by well-brought up children. I wanted Poland, which had forgotten the sword so entirely since 1863, to see it flashing in the air in the hands of her own soldiers.[22]

This obviously futile march, which was to have gone to the town of Dąbrowa, where Piłsudski considered that he had political support from the local population, ran into problems when it was found the town was already occupied by the German Army, as allies of Austria. The Polish force moved towards the town of Kielce, but, again, this was also occupied by German forces. After two weeks the Poles retired back to Kraków having fired only a few shots at a Russian patrol.

Piłsudski had been determined to raise the standard of a Polish Army but nothing happened. At Kielce he had been politely received but few had any inclination to fight on the side of Germany or Austria. Neither side had promised Poles liberty in exchange for loyalty but the Russians, if victorious, had. The concept of an independent Polish Army in 1914 was lost and instead Polish Legions were raised around the riflemen but place firmly under Austrian command.[23]

And what of Maczek? As Lwów was part of the Habsburg Empire he was conscripted into the Austrian Army: the fate that Piłsudski had predicted for thousands of Poles.

21   Mieczkowski, op. cit. p. 16.
22   'List do Prezesa Naczelnego Komitetu Narodowego Władysława Leopolda Jaworskiego', 6 October 1916, *Pisma* (vol.4.), pp. 82-4.
23   Ascherson, op. cit. p. 48.

2

1914-18: Poland, Maczek
and the First World War

The First World War of 1914-18 continues to cast its long shadow over western Europe as the 100th anniversary of that conflict rapidly approaches, but for Poland it is of little consequence until one reaches the last day of the war, 11 November 1918. It was on that day that Poland as an independent state returned to the world map. While it is true that millions of Poles, including Stanisław Maczek, fought in the First World War as a consequence of the east-central European empires conscripting Poles for their own armies (and as an added bitterness, Poles found themselves fighting each other from all sides), there was little reason for Poles to fight. Poles such as Maczek were conscripted to fight in the Austrian Army while others living in the Russian partition of Poland would have been conscripted into the Russian Army and would have fought against Poles serving in the Austrian and German armies. The future commander of the Second World War Polish II Corps, General Władysław Anders, who lived in the Russian partition, served in the Imperial Russian Army, as did the future post-independence Finnish president Karl Gustav Mannerheim (1867-1948) as a consequence of Finland belonging to Russia until 1917. However the First World War has left few marks on the collective Polish psyche.

The First World War was not about Poland, even if Poland proved to be a major battleground on the Eastern Front – Poles had no vested interest in the conflict.

Stanisław Maczek, the subject of our study, as a reserve officer of the Imperial Austrian Army was conscripted once war was declared in July 1914. After training he was destined to fight on the Italian Front from 1915 until the end of the war in November 1918. There are several observations to be made at this point, the principal one being the make-up of the Imperial Austrian Army or the 'Imperial and Royal Army' [K.u.k.] that is the Imperial Austrian Army and the Royal Hungarian Army; Franz Joseph, the Austrian Emperor was also the King of Hungary of the Austro-Hungarian Empire.

Not all of the work of Jaroslav Hašek in *The Good Soldier Švejk* can be taken seriously – it is an excellent book but not an accurate historical account, although it does reflect the problem of the various nationalities of the Austro-Hungarian Army, indicating that in 1914 it was not a unified force owing to the various nationalities, especially the Czechs and Hungarians, who hated one another, while the German-speaking officers were more or less universally despised by their men. Even though the official language of the Austrian Army was German it was obvious that many ordinary soldiers had very little understanding of that language beyond basic commands, which often meant that soldiers also could not understand each other.

An overview of the ethnic makeup of the Imperial Austrian Army at the outbreak of war in 1914 is given by Schindler. Out of 100 soldiers in the Austrian Army in 1914 there were 25 Germans (Austrians), 23 Hungarians, 13 Czechs, 9 Serbs, 8 Poles, 8 Ukrainians, 7 Romanians, 4 Slovaks, 2 Slovenes and a single Italian. Overall 10 'regimental languages' were recognised which reflected the ethnic groups listed above while regiments tended to reflect the various nationalities i.e. Czech regiments, Polish regiments and so on.[1]

Thompson observes that, even so, the whole Austrian Army could not understand itself – in 1914 the Austrian Officer Corps was 72% German-Austrian and the language of command was German, although only 90 (military) expressions were used. Two languages were frequently used in each regiment and officers were expected to learn within 3 years the language of the regiment in which they were serving. However, under wartime conditions, this system broke down, as reserve officers who replaced regular officers in the early years of the war were frequently unable to communicate with their own men.[2] The regimental system based on nationalities was to become a problem after 1917 when the war began to go against Austria and the re-assertion of national consciousness amongst the various subject people of the Austrian Empire led to wholesale desertions from the Italian Front.

In *Švejk* much of the humour is derived from the fact that Švejk cannot understand his Hungarian counterparts while they in turn cannot understand him and other Czechs. One of Švejk's officers, a popular man, before giving a lecture noted that all of those present were Czech; the officer was also Czech and so, against all regulations but saluting common sense, he gave the lecture in Czech. The result was that everybody understood the lecture. This was the very army to which Maczek was delivered up to. In theory he should have found himself in command of fellow Poles but this was not to be the case.

Maczek, as already mentioned, was conscripted as a reserve officer. In fact he was an 'Aspirant' or Cadet Officer with a Non Commissioned Officer's (NCO) rank. Maczek received officer training at III Corps centre in Graz, Austria. After this period of training, Maczek as an Aspirant, received command of a motorized platoon of the 3rd Regiment of the *Landwehr* during the second half of June 1915; Potomski suggests that it was possibly around this time that Maczek might have decided to change his career plans from that of some form of academic approach to being a soldier.[3] There could be two reasons for this: 1) the war had gone beyond the initial 'it will all be over by Christmas' which had been the popular thought six months earlier during August 1914, while 2) Zamoyski noted in Maczek's obituary that Maczek, even though he was clever, was 'no intellectual'.[4] Maczek was more of a practical man and soldiering obviously agreed with him.

The winter of 1914 and spring of 1915 saw Maczek on specialist courses which included 'storm tactics' – the use of automatic weapons as well as skiing and mountaineering in the Alps.[5] These courses were to provide a basis for Maczek's future military career and on 14 June 1915 he joined the elite 2nd Tyrol *Kaiser-Jaeger* Regiment. The speciality of this regiment was high altitude mountain warfare. Maczek as a Pole was an unlikely recruit to the regiment as it generally took men such as Austrians, Croats and Slovenes, who came from mountainous regions. The regiment's function in the Austrian VIII Corps was to fight in the mountains in the south-eastern theatre of the war i.e. the Italian Front.[6]

The war between Italy and Austria was mainly about the question 'who should be

1   John R. Schindler, *Isonzo: The Forgotten Sacrifice of the Great War*, Westport, Praeger, 2001, p. 27.
2   Mark Thompson, *The White War: Life and Death on the Italian Front, 1915-1919*, London, Faber & Faber, 2009, p. 78.
3   Piotr Potomski, *Generał Broni Stanisław Władysław Maczek*, Warsaw, Wydawnictwa Uniwersytetu Warszawa, 2008, pp. 27-31.
4   Adam Zamoyski, *The Independent* (London) 13 December 1994.
5   Potomski, op. cit. pp. 27-31.
6   Ibid.

master of Italy'.[7] Italy declared war on Austria on 23 May 1915 and the fighting between 1915 and 1918 took place over a front of about 500 miles as the two armies squared up to each other. The mastery of Italy was a question which, according to Page, originated from the time of Imperial Rome.[8]

The front between Austrian and Italy was 80% mountainous; several of the mountains on the front were in excess of 3,000 metres, and in winter were covered in snow and ice. This meant that explosions, as always occur in war, led to avalanches.[9] Indeed Thompson notes that in one day alone, 13 December 1916, known as 'White Friday', 10,000 men died in avalanches.[10] A truly terrible Friday 13th. It should be noted that neither Austrian nor Italy were equipped for a war of this type.

On 22 July 1915 the 2nd *Kaiser-Jaeger* Regiment was sent to the south to the Italian Front to defend the River Isonzo Valley. From June 1915 to September 1917 there were 11 battles on the Isonzo and the casualties were dreadful.[11] The Isonzo Front was to become a front of attrition. It was to see 29 months of fighting with 1.1 million Italian dead and wounded whilst the Austrians, 'fighting for every inch of territory', suffered 650,000 dead and wounded. The final Italian victory in the autumn of 1918 was pyrrhic and was only achieved as a result of political collapse in Austria.[12] An early account of the war on the Italian Front noted that in the First Battle of Isonzo, 1,900 Italians were killed including 110 officers while 11,500 were wounded and a further 1,500 had either been captured or were missing. The Austrians suffered a total of 10,400 casualties. The second battle saw 340 Italian officers killed, 860 wounded with 5,400 Italian other ranks (ORs) killed, 26, 850 wounded and 466 Italians missing or captured. The total Austrian losses amounted to 47,000.[13]

By 1917, as conditions began to deteriorate in Austria, the losses on the Italian Front began to even up, but continued to be horrendous, as during the spring and summer offensives of that year the Italian losses amounted to 36,000 killed, 96,000 wounded and 25,000 taken prisoner. The Austrian losses were over 100,000 killed and wounded and 24,000 captured. Villari noted that by 1917 the military and political conditions in Austria were grave and that the Western and Italian fronts had almost destroyed the ability to wage war.[14]

The plan for the Isonzo Front was originally conceived by the Italian Commander-in-Chief, General Luigi Cadorna, whose idea was that the Italians, in a series of swift drives, would be able to cross the River Isonzo and then exploit the territory beyond. The terrain to be crossed was rugged and included Monte Nero, the Bainsizza Plateau and the 'wilderness' of Carso in the south. However, any element of surprise was lost when a French leak regarding the Treaty of London (26 April 1915) alerted the Austrians. The treaty saw

7   Thomas Nelson Page, *Italy and the World War*, (1920) Chapter XIV, 'Conditions When Italy Entered the War' http://net.lib.byu.edu/estu/wwi/comment/Italy/Page05.htm Accessed 22 April 2009. Thomas Nelson (1853-1922) was an authority on Italy during the period as he served as the American Ambassador to Italy between 1913 and 1919. He wrote his account of his time in Italy in 1920.
8   Ibid.
9   Hew Strachan, *The First World War. A New Illustrated History*, London, Simon & Schuster, 2003, p. 150.
10   Thompson, op. cit. p. 204.
11   Potomski, op. cit. pp. 27-31.
12   Schindler, op. cit. p. xii.
13   Luigi Villari, *The War on the Italian Front*, London, Cobden-Sanderson, 1932, p. 44.
14   Ibid. pp. 44, 115, 129.

the Italians, who despite being paper allies of Austria and Germany had yet to declare war, switch their allegiance to the Allies. This led to 14 Austrian divisions facing 35 Italian divisions, falling back to well-prepared defensive positions. Very swiftly this front became one of stalemate, as had been experienced on the Western Front since Ypres and the Race to the Sea in 1914.[15]

Part of the problem as to why the Isonzo Front became such a front of attrition that cost so many lives was the nature of General Cadorna – as was the perception with so many commanders of the First World War, he was described as being overbearing and inflexible.[16] Whether this is fair to the commanders of the 1914-18 War when compared with commanders of other wars is increasingly becoming a matter of opinion. However by the end of 1917 there had been 11 battles along the Isonzo. It was along this static front that Maczek witnessed the misery and military impoverishment of warfare.

Schindler considers the 2nd Battle of Isonzo to have been a loss of innocence and both sides prepared for a long drawn out war. By the autumn of 1915 conditions on the Italian Front had broken down and were as ghastly as the Western Front; cholera had broken out in late October 1915 while Benito Mussolini, the future Fascist Italian dictator but in 1915 an Italian artilleryman, escaped cholera but was infected with typhus.[17]

On 29 June 1916 the Italian Front took a turn for the worse as the Austrians used gas.[18] By the end of 1916, as the threat from Russia faded away, the Isonzo Front became Austria's highest military priority, as it deployed its 854,000 infantrymen as follows:

- 452,000 on the Russian Front
- 74,000 on the Balkan Front
- 328,000 on the Italian Front.[19]

Even though more Austrian troops were deployed on the Russian Front, it was a much longer front compared with the more compact Italian Front, which meant more troops to the square mile.

Schindler notes that the battle along the Isonzo taught some the necessity of a more mobile battle plan and the flaws of such tactics, which relied on co-operation between infantry and artillery units as well as co-ordination between ground and air units. The main flaw could be found in communications, as field telephones and radios were still in their infancy between 1914 and 1918.[20] The Austrians had to become ingenious in their attempts to fend off Italian armoured car attacks, as they had no equivalent vehicles to reply with, thus becoming proficient in anti-armour tactics. To this end the Austrians used mines, vehicle traps, anti-tank rifles and field guns over open sights to destroy Italian armoured vehicles.[21]

No doubt Maczek saw and learnt these lessons and as his consequent history he was quick to understand the lessons of mobile warfare and the necessity of close co-operation between artillery, infantry and armour with a reliable communications network. Maczek, in his autobiography, mentions that throughout his military career he found that his

---

15   John Wittam, *The Politics of the Italian Army, 1861-1918*, London, Croom Held, 1977, p. 193.
16   Mark Cornwall, *The Undermining of Austria-Hungary. The Battle for Hearts and Minds*, Basingstoke, Macmillan, 2000, p. 74.
17   Schindler, op. cit. pp. 81, 106-7.
18   Ibid. p. 152.
19   Ibid. p. 200.
20   Ibid. p. 292.
21   Ibid. p. 293.

grounding in map reading which he learnt in the Austrian Army stood him in good stead for the remainder of his career as he was able to understand a relief map which aided him in future battles. He mentions the Carpathian Campaign (1918-19), the September Campaign (1939) when Maczek defended Polish mountains against the German invasion, and even the Falaise Campaign of August 1944, which saw the Allied breakout from the Normandy peninsular.[22] It is quite obvious that Maczek's ability to read a relief map intelligently led him to order the Poles to seize Hill 262, which dominated the Vimoutiers Road and the German route out of Normandy.[23] The seizure of the hill and the holding of it by armoured regiments of the 1st Polish Armoured Division during August 1944 denied the Germans a free passage out of Normandy.

Maczek was on the Italian Front on 18 June 1915, where he remained until 17 December 1915 when he was taken ill (14 December 1915) and sent to Military Hospital No. 2. in Vienna.[24] The New Year of 1916 started well for Maczek as he was finally commissioned into the Austrian Army as a 2nd Lieutenant following his duties in the field as an 'Aspirant' or Cadet Officer.[25]

After returning from hospital Maczek was sent as an instructor to the XIV Corps Officers' School in Styr, Upper Austria. With his experience of mountain warfare Maczek had a lot to offer to other young officers. Once he returned to his regiment, which was still on the Italian Front, Maczek was given a company, 8th Company, to command from 2 October 1916. It was a company that specialised in ski and mountain warfare and acted as a 'storm' battalion undertaking raids and so on. Maczek was the only Polish officer in his battalion and from the autumn of 1916 until the beginning of 1918 he and 8th Company were involved in many bloody battles in the mountains on the Italian Front. Finally, on 31 January 1918, Maczek was wounded in the leg. He was swiftly transferred to a Viennese hospital and was there for weeks until he was sent on 3 months convalescent leave, which he spent in his native Lwów.[26]

It was while he was on leave that Maczek not only completed his university studies but also noticed that many officers from Piłsudski's Legions and the Austrian Army were in Lwów cafes contemplating the collapse of the Austrian-Hungarian Empire. However Maczek noted that his leave finished before the empire actually collapsed.[27] Maczek must have been aware that Austria could not continue the war for much longer because German reinforcements were required during 1917 to maintain the Austrian positions on the Italian Front and inflict a temporary defeat for the Italians. As Maczek recorded, he did not have the time or opportunity to enter into conspiracies as by the summer of 1918 he was back in the Austrian Alps, 3,000 metres above sea level with a regiment who seemed determined to win the war for Austria. But other agents were at work and by November 1918 the situation was changed, to the extent that owing to a complete lack of faith in

22   Stanisław Maczek, *Od Podwody do Czołga*, Edinburgh, Tomar, 1961, p. 17.
23   Eddy Florentin, *The Battle of the Falaise Gap*, London, Elek Books, 1965, translated by Mervyn Savill, p. 214.
24   See copy of Maczek's service record with the Imperial Austrian Army, 1914-1918, KOL.298/1 (PISM) Polish Institute & Sikorski Museum, Kensington, London, KOL.298 (General Maczek Collection) original held at the Austrian Military Archives, Vienna. Copy supplied by General L. Brosch-Forahem, Austrian Army (letter, Dembinski to Brosch-Forahem, 18 April 1986).
25   PISM, KOL 298/1.
26   Potomski, op. cit. pp. 27-31.
27   Maczek, op. cit. p. 17.

victory and an inability to command the mountainous battlefield of the front, in a single day the line was broken at Trento and an evacuation by train to Vienna was ordered. At the same time vague news about the situation in Maczek's homeland began to reach him with the first news of fighting between Poles and Ukrainians in Lwów.

On hearing rumours that any possibility to leave Vienna for the east was becoming increasingly difficult, Maczek took advice that his best chance to get home was to ditch his Austrian uniform and don civilian *mufti*.[28] All of this was ironic as during November 1918 Maczek had been promoted to lieutenant and had been awarded various campaign and gallantry medals, but the war for Austria was over.[29]

Once Maczek returned to his native Poland he was quick to put the lessons learnt on the Italian Front to use in order to defend Poland against Ukrainian insurgents. This was not the last time that Maczek was to take such drastic action to flee a hostile environment. He was doomed to do so twice more in, in 1939 and 1940.

28   Ibid.
29   Potomski, op. cit. pp. 27-31.

3
Establishing Frontiers: The Polish Wars, 1918-1920

After the collapse of the Austrian Empire and the Allied victory during November 1918 Lieutenant Stanisław Maczek decided to return to his native Poland. As a result of the Allied victory Polish independence was restored on 11 November 1918. This was one of the points which concluded the First World War as far as the Western Allies were concerned, but for the Poles a major concern was just where were the new frontiers going to be?

It was obvious that the victorious Western powers were going to divide up Europe as well as the colonies of the defeated countries in a manner which suited their worldviews and politics. Put simply, the new Polish leadership may have had an idea of where they considered the Polish frontiers should lie, but the Allies had their own view as to where these borders should be. To add to the confusion the eastern frontiers of the proposed Poland were in a state of flux as a result of revolution and civil war in Russia. At the same time the Ukrainians were also striving for independence, which the Poles saw as being at the expense of Poland.

In the British camp, Winston Churchill, the then Secretary State for War, during the time of the Paris Peace Conference held during 1919, was one of the few who realised that the Bolshevik revolution and its aftermath was not as wild and undisciplined as many considered but was actually very regimental and designed to obtain power no matter the cost.[1] As a consequence of Churchill's instinct the British Government regarded Poland as a bulwark against Bolshevism or Communist expansion across Europe. This had the effect of further muddying the waters as far as the question of a final settlement of the Polish eastern frontier was concerned.

Polish independence had been achieved in a fairly unorthodox manner. Not only was it part of the plan for the new Europe as envisaged by the American President, Woodrow Wilson, but the very manner that Polish independence was established was most peculiar. Marshal Józef Piłsudski, to whom the restoration of Polish independence is frequently attributed, arrived in Warsaw from Berlin in a sealed train and took possession of Poland. His charisma as a martyred Polish liberator – he had in the past been imprisoned by the Russian Government and it was from a German prison that he made his journey back to Poland – gave him the necessary kudos and authority with many to Poles to justify taking over the country without any legal qualification.

However at the Paris Peace Conference Piłsudski's political rival, Roman Dmowski, a rabid Nationalist, who had the ear of the West, was negotiating the future Poland and its frontiers. Dmowski wanted a return to the 1772 borders, which would have been at the expense of the newly established independent Lithuania, Belarus and much of Ukraine.

---

1   Margaret Macmillan, *Peacemakers: The Paris Conference of 1919 and Its Attempt to End War*, London, John Murray, 2001, p. 75.

Marshal Józef Piłsudski, 1867-1935. (Private collection)

Piłsudski was more cautious but like Dmowski he also wanted a strong Poland, but he saw its future as some form of federation, working with the Lithuanians and perhaps the Ukrainians.[2] Poland was to dominate any such federation.

Macmillan notes that from early 1919 until late 1920 the greatest struggle for Polish independence was with the Bolsheviks because of the struggle for the eastern frontiers. The Poles, having a history of antipathy towards Russia, merely saw the Bolsheviks as just another form of Russian oppression, while the Bolsheviks regarded Polish Nationalism and Catholicism as not in the interests of the revolution and thus that it was necessary to overcome them.[3]

Norman Davies has noticed that the vacuum which had been created as a result of German troops leaving the borderlands between the proposed Polish state and Russia allowed Polish and Soviet (Bolshevik) units to move spontaneously eastwards and westward.[4] It was obvious that despite the vast emptiness of the border wastelands known locally as the *kresy* that these units would eventually meet and clash. The first clash took place on 14 February 1919 in the township of Bereza Kartuska, and so the Polish-Soviet War began. At first the Poles were triumphant – their progress can be viewed as quite successful, with the capture of the Lithuanian capital, Vilnius, during April 1919, followed by the capture of Minsk, the Belarusian capital, during August 1919. The eastward Polish advance dismayed the Allies in Paris, who had expected a much smaller Poland and not the

---

2   Ibid. p. 221.
3   Ibid. p. 237.
4   Norman Davies, *White Eagle, Red Star: The Polish-Soviet War, 1919-1920 And 'The Miracle on the Vistula'* London, Pimlico, 2003 (Reprint) p. 27.

Symon Petliura (1879-1926), Ukrainian leader, and General Antoni Listowski
(1865-1927) during the 1920 Kiev offensive. (Private collection)

giant 1772 model.[5]

Piłsudski turned his attention to Ukraine in his pursuit of a central European federation, which he saw as a method of securing collective security for the central European states against Germany, albeit principally aimed against Russia. In an alliance with anti-Russian Ukrainians under the leadership of Seymon Petliura, Polish forces invaded Ukraine on 8 May 1920. Piłsudski claimed that the Polish Army had entered Ukraine to liberate the Ukrainian people from foreign invaders. He claimed that the Polish Army would remain in Ukraine until such a time that a Ukrainian government was established and Ukrainian troops were able to secure their own frontiers.[6]

The Polish action was annexation and the Bolsheviks saw it as such, and dealt with it as a threat to the revolution. During the summer of 1920 the Bolsheviks counterattacked in a double offensive. This counterattack was so successful that by August 1920 the Soviet armies were outside of the gates of Warsaw itself. The Polish Army had been pushed all of the way from Kiev while Lenin, the Bolshevik leader, hoped that the Red Army would march westward and bring revolution to the heart of Europe.[7] This interpretation is now disputed and there is an argument that the Soviet offensive against Poland was a deterrent

5   Neal Ascherson, *The Struggles for Poland*, London, Michael Joseph, 1987, p. 58.
6   Peter D. Stachura, *Poland, 1918-1945. An Interpretive and Documentary History of the Second Republic*, London, Routledge, 2004, p. 38. 'Jozef Piłsudski's "Proclamation to the Citizens of the Ukraine", 26 April 1920', quoting T. Kutrzeba, *Wyprawa Kijowska*, Warsaw, Gebethner & Wolff, 1937, p. 107.
7   Ascherson, op. cit. p. 58.

Polish soldiers display captured Soviet flags after the
victory at Warsaw 1920. (Private collection)

to the West against invading Russia.[8] Whatever the motivation of the Red Army in
counterattacking the Polish Army and pursuing it to Warsaw, the Polish victory at Warsaw
on 15 August 1920 was decisive.

The Battle of Warsaw is often accredited to Piłsudski's military brilliance.[9] Piłsudski
himself dismissed the battle as a 'brawl'.[10] It is not clear why he should be so dismissive of
the only Polish victory in 200 years but it may be that he did not want to give too much
credit to the professional officers from the ex-imperial armies for their role in the victory.
Whatever the motivation Piłsudski failed to prevent a myth growing from the battle. For
many Poles, the date, 15 August, was significant as it was the Catholic feast day of the
Assumption of the Virgin Mary and so a myth was born: divine intervention had caused
the godless Bolsheviks who had imperilled Catholic Poland to be scattered. This was the
'miracle on the Vistula'.[11] During the Communist period of Polish history (1944-1989) the
Polish-Soviet War was rarely mentioned but in the post-Communist period it is once more
again on the school history syllabus, although it has become an object of Polish national
mythology again.[12] The reasons behind the Polish-Soviet War and the victory at Warsaw
are yet to be seriously studied.

Maczek recalled some of the chaos in the first days of Polish independence in November
1918. He wanted to do something to aid his newly independent country and was aware that
the greatest threat came from Ukrainians, who were just as determined as the Poles to
establish their state and create frontiers. Part of the problem was that as yet a formal Polish

8   Orlando Figes, *A People Tragedy: The Russian Revolution, 1891-1924*, London, Pimlico, 1996, pp. 700-2.
      See also Davies, op. cit. p. 187, Richard Pipes, *Russia under the Bolsheviks, 1919-1924*, London, Harvill,
      1994, p. 182.
9   Jerzy J. Wiatr, *The Soldier and the Nation. The Role of the Military in Polish Politics, 1918-1985*, Boulder,
      Colorado, Westview, 1988, p. 13-14.
10   Józef Piłsudski, *Rok 1920*, London, Polska Fundacja Kulturna, 1987, 6th Edition, p. 165.
11   Norman Davies, *God's Playground: A History of Poland. Volume II, 1795- to the Present*, Oxford,
      Clarendon Press, 1981, p. 398.
12   I am grateful to Dr. Artur Lipinski, Kazimierz Wielki University, for his observations; e-mail dated 23
      September 2009.

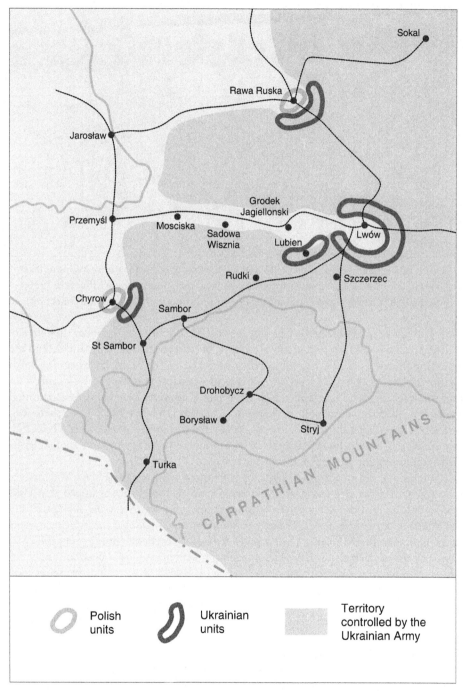

Situation in the Polish-Ukrainian War after the capture of Lwów
and Przemyśl by Polish units, winter 1918-1919.

Polish officers defending Lwów, 1918. Note the mixture of uniforms, including at least two of the former Austrian Army. Compare with the photograph of officers in 1920, demonstrating the greater standardisation of uniforms by 1920. (Private collection)

Army had not been established. There were various Polish military units but they were too widely spread around Europe and into Russia. All were trying to get home and defend their homeland from those trying to establish their own states at the perceived expense of Poland. To illustrate the problem, Maczek mentioned his desire to serve Poland by joining a unit that was guarding a magazine in the Kraków area – no units were being formed to fight at the front because, quite simply, there was a lack of lower ranks. As ever, there was a surfeit of officers but a shortage of lower ranks and non-commissioned officers (NCO).[13] A perennial problem for the Polish Army, it gives cause to wonder why 'non-elite' Poles had little interest in fighting for Polish independence.

Maczek wanted to get to the fighting at Lwów: *his* Lwów. The railway line between Przemyśl and Lwów was under attack from Ukrainian forces. It was hoped that Polish forces could relieve the situation by advancing from the south via the sub-Carpathian Mountains. On 14 November 1918 Maczek found himself in a long queue waiting to report to the Commanding Officer of the Krosno Garrison. Everybody's military capability was judged by the rank that they held; he saw captains, lieutenants; 2nd lieutenants and cadet officers waiting. Maczek rather put himself down by describing himself as 'bringing up the rear' with the rank of *Oberleutnant* (Lieutenant) which he had legally held since November 1918 as a result of the last orders he received whilst still in the Imperial Austrian Army just before the empire irretrievably collapsed; furthermore, he was dressed in civilian clothing, a measure he was forced to take in order to get from Austria and back home.[14]

Quite clearly Maczek was feeling uncomfortable. Through no fault of his own he felt something of a fraud, which he most certainly was not given his experience on the Italian Front and his willingness to serve his own country, the newly resurrected Poland. Maczek

13 Stanisław Maczek, *Od Powozy do Czołga: Wspomnienia Wojenne 1918-1945*, Edinburgh, Tomar, 1961, p. 17.
14 Ibid.

need not have worried because, as he put it, the grizzled Colonel Swoboda was going from one officer to the next listening to an endless litany of requests, about going to Krosno, of leave, and of the revisions of the borders but Maczek earnestly asked Swoboda about his chances of joining a formation for the relief of the besieged Lwów. With a wide smile Swoboda grasped Maczek by the arm and said 'Finally I have a commander for the company for the relief of Lwów; ready to march but at present without a commander'.[15]

The same day Maczek took command of the Krosno Company, as it was called. Over 40 years later he recalled the mixture of those 'first class lads', none of whom seemed have held any rank beyond that of 2nd Lieutenant or Cadet Officer. In his autobiography he recalled various names: Kulczycki from Krosno and Bartosz from Jasła, who were both from the former Austrian Army, and two officers from Piłsudski's Legionnaires, Szczypiórna from Czeriatowicz and Szmidt from Lwów itself. As for the riflemen of the company they were a mixture of veterans from the different fronts of the 1914-18 War, some from the Legions and some from the ex-Austrian Army. There were also a fair number of boys 'straight from school and the skirts of their mothers'; lads from Krosno, Odrzykonia, Potoka and Jasła. These men were enflamed and enthusiastic for the fight ahead and Maczek, the following morning, not really knowing Polish military rules and customs, threw out the challenge: 'Are you lads ready?'

The reply came in unison: 'We are Lieutenant!'

Maczek was very proud and honoured to receive such trust from his men. As he reflected, half of his men had never seen combat or even handled a rifle before. Decades later Maczek considered that to have been part of that force in Poland during November 1918 was a great and unique honour.[16] It was comparable to have been an Englishman at Agincourt with Henry V or a British fighter pilot of the Battle of Britain. It was one of those brief and unique moments of history that it is an honour to have lived through and to be honoured forever.

Several days later, on 20 November 1918, movement orders were received for the relief of Lwów. Moving to the largely Ukrainian town of Sanok, Maczek's men met with Lieutenant Bołesław Czajkowski's company, which was defending the oil-rich area of Borysław. Maczek and his company also linked up with the Sanok Company commanded by Lieutenant Leszek Pragłowski, who was dressed in formal civilian black trousers, as if he had been caught unawares by an enemy attack. From these two companies, as informal as they were, Maczek was later able to raise first class troops and commanders for his first specialist group, the 'Flying Column' and later the first 'Storm Battalion', which were to briefly revolutionise Polish warfare.[17]

The move by the Poles to a more mobile form of warfare using armoured vehicles began in the east during the Polish-Ukrainian War when on the night of 20-21 November 1918 at the Ustrzyki Dolne railway station on the Sanok-Chyrów railway line two trains approaching the station from opposite directions. One, a Polish train, sported improvised armour on its wagons, which were full of Maczek's men. The other train was manned by Ukrainians, namely Zaporogian Cossacks, and contained a battery of field guns. Maczek's men, warned of the danger by Polish railway workers, reacted swiftly, using hand grenades and rifles after a short skirmish, and in their first taste of action captured the Ukrainian

---

15   Ibid.
16   Maczek, op. cit. p. 18.
17   Ibid. p. 19.

train and with it their first 'present' – 4 field guns. This led to the first Polish artillery battery being founded in Maczek's group.

Following this first success and after a succession of skirmishes with the enemy, by the end of November 1918 the Poles had captured the Chyrów railway junction. Maczek's group was reinforced by the 20th Infantry Regiment, which was still known in the area as an Austrian regiment, and prepared to strike out in the direction of Sambor in an attempt to relieve Lwów at the earliest opportunity. However, there were a few obstacles to be overcome before this could be attempted. The main offensive, as proposed, was to be led by 20th Infantry Regiment as it was fresh, supported by the new Polish artillery battery and Maczek's armoured group, which had recently been strengthened with armoured lorries, using improvised armoured made in the railway workshops. The lorries made ideal infantry carriers. However, elements of a newly recruited battalion were halted in the offensive on Felsztyn, the first target on the route to Sambor, owing to Ukrainian artillery fire and long-range heavy machine-gun fire.

The halting of the offensive caused frustration amongst the young Polish officers and so a deputation led by Maczek and supported by Lieutenant Pragłowski went to Colonel Swoboda with a 'first class' proposal and an extraordinary request from very young but confident commanders. Colonel Swoboda was, of course, senior to Maczek and his contemporaries in both age and military rank; he was also qualified for an Austrian Army pension for long service (but who would pay it given that the empire no longer existed?), although he remained a Polish patriot and was very impressed with the young officers of whom it had fallen to his lot to command. He was struck by their enthusiasm that in the face of adversity they still wanted to press on against the Ukrainians and still received the support of the majority of young officers. It was decided that further action should be undertaken. Orders were not to be wild but instead reserved and correct, which meant that not all of the troops available would be thrown into action. Thus, a single company from the Krosno Regiment was kept as a reserve force. This caused a near mutiny but orders were orders and peace prevailed within the Polish force. Maczek reflected that pride caused the near mutiny.

Maczek set about his next operation from an unexpected direction, which totally shocked the Ukrainians. They had not been expecting a night attack immediately after the stalling of the Polish day offensive earlier that day. Maczek wrote that to get to the rear of the railway station was easy, as even though it had been prepared for defence, it had only been readied for an attack from the direction of Chyrów. Maczek took a company and led a single platoon along the railway track; there was to be supporting fire while the remaining troops already covered by the fall of night entered the valley between the hills and from which Ukrainian heavy machine-guns that day had given the Poles such a tough time. With the participation of prisoners of war, 3 heavy machine-guns and a single 75mm artillery piece were made ready to fire directly along the railway line. The battle commenced but both sides were evenly matched; eventually the offensive came to a halt and then to stalemate. The Poles held the town of Chyrów and the nearby Jesuit monastery while the Ukrainians held the hill from which they attacked the Polish positions with machine-guns and artillery. At one point the Poles even temporarily lost Chyrów. Once more the Poles had to fight to recapture it, being reinforced by the Minkiewicz Brigade.

Chyrów was very important for the Poles as it was not only a staging post for the march on Lwów but as the days became weeks and the weeks became months it became the winter garrison and home for Maczek and his men. The war had become one of stalemate with the Ukrainians, and only having a single supply line, the road and railway line between Ustrzyki and Sanok, Maczek considered that their perilous position was something out of a Sienkiewicz novel, which dealt with the wars of the 17th century fought between the Poles and the Ukrainians.

However sometimes the front on which Maczek was serving became so quiet that it could easily be forgotten that there was a war going on. Reality was always swift to reassert itself, such as when Polish infantry trained with heavy weapons, especially machine-guns – the sound of the trainees firing was often in unison with that of machine-gun fire on the fighting front. Another example was that once the hills were covered in snow; Polish volunteers were taught how to ski (something that Maczek had learnt in the Austrian Army) but often Ukrainian artillery fire exploded amongst them. Quite a harsh lesson in warfare! Maczek does not give any account of casualties but does confirm that the Ukrainians were actually shelling the Jesuit monastery near the Polish position.

The evenings enhanced the deceptive idyll which at times was the Polish position, especially when officers relaxed in their quarters at the Bąkowice Monastery to the south of Chyrów. Maczek remarks just how comfortable the monastery was as a billet. This included individual rooms for officers but made no mention of how ordinary soldiers were quartered. It appears that the officers' billet had all of the comforts of an Edwardian gentlemen's club but with an inconvenient war just down the road.

The war against the Ukrainians was beginning to take shape, perhaps the most interesting point being just how the modern Polish Army was being formed during November 1918. Largely the army was formed 'on the hoof', relying on a fusion of the professional traditions of the three former imperial armies (German, Russian and Austrian) with a sprinkling of amateurism from Piłsudski's quasi-paramilitary legions. Maczek related that, probably as a result of the lack of a formal Polish Army but instead acting on his 3 years of combat experience, he had to rely on a feeling in his 'bones' regarding the situation at the front. This would come to serve him well in the future as he had learnt early in his career not to rely solely on intelligence reports but to find out for himself as well as to have a feel for the fighting front. It was during the winter of 1918-19 that Maczek gained his reputation as being a very efficient commander of the heavy machine-gun company and after a series of clashes with the Ukrainians his prestige grew amongst his colleagues.[18] In many ways, this war was a series of small campaigns, with the Poles and Ukrainians trying to assert sovereignty over each other, whilst parties were also trying to stop the westward spread of Bolshevikism, as confirmed by Klimecki.[19]

Maczek was unsure what made November 1918 seemed magical: was it the first days of

---

18   Maczek, op. cit. pp. 20-2.

19   Michał Klimecki, *Polsko-Ukraińska Wojna o Lwów i Galicję Wschonią 1918-1919*, Warsaw, Volumen, 2000, p. 16. Klimecki chronicles the fighting in East Galicia as Ukrainian Uprising, 1-19 November 1918, Relief of Lwów, 1-23 November 1918, Besieged town, 23 November 1918 – 31 March 1919 with victory between 8 June and 17 July 1919. He also gives the demographic breakdown of Galicia: Poles, 47.6%, Ukrainians, 40.3%, Jews, 10.9%, Germans and others, 1.2%. However in Eastern Galicia it is obvious that the Ukrainians were the majority as out of a population of 5,337,000; 3,791,000 were Ukrainians (71%), 777,000 were Poles (14%) while 660,000 (12%) were Jews with up to 82% of the population living in the countryside. Ibid. It is quite obvious why fighting broke out between the Poles and the Ukrainians in late 1918 as both sides tried to expand their frontiers at the expense of each other, whilst the Polish claims on East Galicia seem quite invalid.

independence or was it the common experience of fighting for independence and defending Poland? This, to young men, meant adventure with a capital 'A' or as Maczek wrote in Polish '*Przygoda*' with a capital 'P'. Maczek compared the atmosphere with that of student halls where young people feel that they can conquer anything and everything. However the reality of war tempered this heady setting with an account of the breakdown of one officer who, after Maczek and his men set out ill-equipped for a mission, took casualties and arrived back, late and carrying their wounded. Maczek was met with the grief of his comrades. One of the officers, Lieutenant Zalewski, had had a complete breakdown and kept repeating that 'Maczek was not coming back'. Maczek spoke quietly to Zalewski, as to a child but after a while Zalewski continued to repeat that Maczek was dead and turning to Maczek himself repeated: 'No – it's not you – Maczek is not returning.'[20]

Maczek by now was fine-tuning his method of waging war. One thing that he was determined to avoid was haphazard raids and patrolling. He wanted these activities to be more focussed. Instead he chose to go out on raids with groups of handpicked and trustworthy men, well armed with hand grenades. Maczek preferred grenades as he considered them to be effective weapons which produced rapid shock amongst the enemy and cowed them. This allowed the Poles to take prisoners; the object of the raids in order to gain intelligence of the Ukrainian foe.

During November 1918 the base at Chyrów was manned by two to three infantry battalions supported by two artillery units. The Polish position was rather isolated and dependent on supplies and ammunition via the Chyrów-Zagorz railway line. However this line was vulnerable to Ukrainian attacks, as on the hills which ran along the supply line, groups of Ukrainians periodically attacked the line. The most serious danger was posed by a howitzer battery several kilometres to the west of Chyrów whose shelling threatened the Polish supply line. Maczek was detailed to take out this danger.

For an entire week, night after night, snow fell but Maczek and his men waded through the drifts, patrolling different parts of the hills. For hours they lay in the snow watching because Maczek had sent patrols in an attempt to provoke the Ukrainians into opening fire with their artillery and betray their positions. Finally Maczek was able to fix the whereabouts of the Ukrainian howitzers. He planned his attack: it was to be a night attack from a valley just beyond the village of Smereczna near the forest from which ran steep slopes from the edge of the hills and from there the Poles were to move between two Ukrainian positions and proceed directly onto the Ukrainian howitzer posts.

Maczek had plenty of good soldiers to choose from and so he took 100 men for the mission with Lieutenant Szafran as his deputy. All of the men wore camouflage so that they would not stand out at night against the snowy background. Carefully Maczek and his men approached the Ukrainian positions, avoiding enemy outposts. The march, in deep snow, took most of the night and it was almost dawn when they approached the Ukrainian artillery position. The Polish group used vistas, furrows between carefully planted trees, to recover and to plan. There was no room for mistakes or blunders, no premature shots were to endanger the mission.

Before the Poles were able to attack the guns' positions, Ukrainian heavy machine-guns haphazardly opened fire on them; it was hardly co-ordinated but still dangerous to the Polish operation. Frightened and disorientated Ukrainian gun crews hastened from the

---

20 Maczek, op. cit. p. 22.

village, leading horses for the guns: the horses were kept to the rear for safety. They all ran directly into the hands of Maczek and his men and were taken prisoner.

The mission did not pass without Polish casualties as several were wounded, including Lieutenant Szafran who had been shot in chest. The Poles were deep behind Ukrainian lines but nobody, especially the wounded, could return the way they came as the steep slopes were impassable. It was decided to breakout via the main road which wound through the gorge from the valley of the River Strwiąż and along the railway line. This breakout relied on speed and the disorientation of the Ukrainians as a result of the Polish assaults on the Ukrainian ranks. It was quite a risky strategy and meant sending a group of men, who had already spent the morning fighting Ukrainians at the mouth of nearby gorge, to act as a diversion in an attempt to convince the Ukrainians that the Poles intended to withdraw using the route which they had used to come in.

The Polish luck held, as while attacks were put in against the Ukrainians in the attempt to convince them that they were indeed intending to withdraw via the hill tops, Cadet Officer Zawadowski was able to lead a surprise attack to the rear of the Ukrainian positions and without receiving any casualties captured an entire Ukrainian platoon as well as the howitzers which had been menacing the Polish supply route. The guns and prisoners were taken in triumph to Chyrów.[21]

Maczek began to notice that as a result of regular clashes with the Ukrainians, his 'amateur volunteers' were becoming seasoned campaigners – quite a compliment from a man who had been fighting for over three years. At the same time Maczek, with his fellow officers, became preoccupied with plans for the relief of Lwów. A major complication however arose as two obvious military targets were identified: to the left Lwów and to the right, the oilfields of Borysław. At Borysław, not only lay oil but also thousands of Poles filled with nationalistic fervour that only needed arming in order to rise up against the Ukrainians. Maczek considered this to be a similar conundrum to the one which faced Hitler before Stalingrad: Moscow or the Baku oilfields? In 1918 the Poles faced a similar problem: Lwów or the Borysław oilfields?

It was around this time, the winter of 1918-19, Maczek expressed a certain frustration with staff officers who were planning the eventual relief of Lwów, as he considered that the answer lay with the 'enflamed' young lieutenants and cadet officers sitting in the trenches around Chyrów. This was the first time that Maczek considered, as an antidote to the static warfare he was facing, the use of motorized infantry using farm carts and sleighs as a means of transport, although his plans were to be frustrated during that winter.[22] Despite all of the fighting that was taking place in Galicia at the time it should be noted that veterans of the Western Front from the 1914-18 War were somewhat bemused by what they perceived to be the miniscule scale of the Polish Wars. Indeed General Adrian Carton de Wiart's servant, Holmes, after travelling with his master, who was a Polophile, from Przemysl to Lwów across what they had been assured was a raging battlefield remarked 'The Poles seem to make the 'ell of a fuss about this 'ere war of theirs!'[23] Winston Churchill said at the time 'when the war of the giants is over the wars of the pygmies will begin'. This was the attitude of Western statesmen towards the east-central Europeans as the literally fought for their independence and statehood.

---

21   Maczek, op. cit. pp. 23-4.
22   Ibid. pp. 24-5.
23   Lieutenant-General Sir Adrian Carton de Wiart, *Happy Odyssey*, London, Cape, 1950, p. 98.

During April 1919 Maczek and his men were replaced at Chyrów by the 3rd Legionnaire Division and a battalion from the San Rifles. Maczek reflected on that winter's campaigning and the pleasure that had been derived by the Poles from it, especially the capture of the surrounding hills, the occupation of the neighbouring villages along with the capture of the howitzers and prisoners during the same operation. The young Polish officers were sad to leave the district over which they had skirmished but relief to their unhappiness was at hand as the idea of the use of mobile units was surfacing once more – General Aleksanderwicz, the commander of 4th Infantry Division, and his chief of staff, Colonel Tyszkiewicz, were sympathetic to this idea.

Maczek was ordered to report to divisional headquarters, where a plan was hammered out which was to see the merging of elements of the 10th Infantry Regiment and the 37th Infantry Regiment into Maczek's units, the original 'assault troops' or 'storm troopers' (in Polish *szturmowców*) in order to create motorized units. Maczek is discreet about where the idea for the type of motorized unit to be deployed came from – was it from Colonel Tyszkiewicz, Maczek himself or from an example already known to Tyszkiewicz and Maczek, so-called *Jagdkommandos* of the former Austrian Army? Maczek merely says that it was difficult to pinpoint one man, although he does pay tribute to Colonel Tyszkiewicz and the staff of 4th Infantry Division for their energy and help in the first few weeks of organizing the units that became the 4th Infantry 'Flying Column', and later still the 'Flying Storm Column'.[24] Using such tactics the future commander of the German *Afrika Korps*, Erwin Rommel, as a humble captain in the German Army in November 1917, saw the defeat of the Italian Army at Caporetto.[25] Maczek noted that soldiers loved the terms 'storm' and 'flying' as it made them feel special, a part of an elite unit and having a sense of a mission to fulfil.

The offensive opened in the middle of May 1919. It initially encountered strong Ukrainian resistance. However it was Maczek and his men who were to win the day with their unorthodox tactics, which ensured the success of the operation and the holding of vital hills, which overlooked objectives, against Ukrainian assaults. Maczek reflected, perhaps ruefully, that even if the new Polish Army, which in his eyes shone in their new ex-German Army uniforms, disciplined and ready for action, his men, 'peasant-volunteers', were still kitted out in a mixture of uniforms and civilian clothes, although nonetheless eager to fight for their country.

On the second day of the offensive Maczek was called to staff headquarters, which was operating from railway carriages, and given orders to counter direct Ukrainian attacks on the staff HQ, which were beginning to bog down the Polish offensive. Maczek was directed to extend his company's left flank and then attack and occupy the local railway junction. If this was successful it would ensure the safety of the Polish flanks as well as that of the group staff. It was also made clear to Maczek that the holding of the hill overlooking the valleys towards the local railway line and highway would be decisive for this offensive. So many tasks!

Maczek gathered his men and moved to a position on a high embankment from where he saw the throwing away of lives as raw recruits attacked a position recklessly firing high and blind. 'Careless, raw recruits' Maczek reflected. Maczek's men attacked Ukrainian

---

24   Maczek, op. cit. p. 26.
25   Len Deighton, *Blitzkrieg: From the Rise of Hitler to the Fall of Dunkirk*, London, Triad Granada, 1981, pp. 35 & 156.

positions on the hilltops and swiftly cleared an entire Ukrainian battalion, who fled down the valley leaving behind 5 heavy machine-guns as well as scores of dead and wounded. The operation for the hills was over while the question of holding the hills 'at any price' was already not an issue as a result of the Ukrainian flight into the valley and away from the Poles.

This release enabled Maczek to use a single platoon to attack and capture a nearby position while the rest of the company went into the valley below in pursuit of the fleeing Ukrainians. Maczek used a captured artillery piece to guard the nearby highroad while he and his men 'prowled' during the night along the road ambushing and capturing withdrawing Ukrainians in the Chyrów area. To complete his 'victory', in the morning withdrawing Ukrainians were surprised by heavy Polish attacks using artillery, small arms and grenades (Maczek's favourite weapon at that time) which caused entire Ukrainian formations to be scattered in confusion, unwilling to fight any further. The route to Chyrów was open.

Maczek's thoughts then turned towards his hometown. He advanced his idea for its capture to the chief of staff of 4th Infantry Division, Colonel Tyszkiewicz. Maczek observed that he knew the area like the back of his hand; he had completed his secondary education there and as he put it 'as a boy scout he knew the fields'. Maczek was given orders to capture Drohobycz.

Maczek divided his men into small 'storm' units which were armed with grenades. At nightfall, with two platoons, Maczek passed Drohobycz from the east and taking the shortest route moved towards the main railway line with its gigantic oil terminal. In the distance train whistles could be heard as Ukrainians fled the town. The Poles had been detected and fired on by Ukrainians but nonetheless the Poles kept moving towards the railway station. The tenacity of the Polish assaults paralyzed the Ukrainian reaction and caused confusion in their ranks. Local Poles furthered the Ukrainian confusion as they streamed from their homes to aid their compatriots in the fighting against the Ukrainians. At the same time there was a short but sharp fight at the railway station using hand grenades before it was captured, complete with 3 trains already under steam.

The capture of the station mean that other objectives could be considered, including a march on Borysław and its oilfields. The 3rd Legionnaire Division was to move in the direction of Chyrów-Borysław while 9th Uhlan Regiment was to act as a communications unit. Owing to the confused fighting in the forests between Drohobycz and Borysław, in which Polish units could easily lose contact with each other, it was necessary that there was a formation to try to keep the fighting units together and the operation rolling forward and keeping its shape. Sadly, the movement and momentum of the 9th Uhlan Regiment's operations was slowed when their commander, Major Bartmański, was killed.

Maczek's 'Flying Column' had been deployed the Drohobycz-Borysław road for the purpose of attacking the Ukrainian flanks. Maczek knew every bend of the road as well as every hill and wood. It had been his childhood home.

Furthermore, Borysław held a special sentiment for the Poles, as for months they had been trying to get there, occupy it and take advantage of the fact that local Poles living there and in the surrounding area would assist them in fighting against the Ukrainians. Maczek's column moved to the east of the forest from where 9th Uhlans and the reconnaissance party could already see Drohobycz. The buildings on the outskirts could be seen but they were still 3 kilometres from the town.

Through binoculars movement could be seen and then suddenly a huge mass of civilians moved towards the Polish troops. Silence was broken by the sound of hundreds of sirens from the oil fields and church bells. It suddenly dawned on the Polish soldiers that there were no Ukrainians left in the town; the local Polish population had liberated Drohobycz for themselves, disarming Ukrainians and then coming out to meet the Polish troops.

Maczek always remembered that sunny day during May 1919 on the road to Borysław when ordinary folk welcomed liberation. He reflected that on the way to Lwów, towns, large and small, including Borysław, the capital of the Polish oil basin, asserted their own manifesto, that of 'Polishness'.

Peasants in civilian clothes with improvised red and white armbands (the colour of the Polish national flag), armed with captured rifles, spontaneously assumed the role of guides in reuniting the Polish patrol with the larger Polish body (3rd Division and 9th Uhlans). Meanwhile Maczek made a single demand of the armed civilians – in the event of any alarm or arrival of new orders, he must be notified immediately and he would bring his men to a designated assembly point. The next day new orders arrived; he and his men were to move to Stryj. It was clear that Borysław was being overlooked.

Maczek and his 'Flying Column' swiftly advanced towards the town of Kałusz, via Stryj, which was already occupied by Polish units. The Ukrainians were totally shocked by the speed of the Polish advance. The Ukrainian defence was on the south-eastern banks of the River Łominca. Their defence was based around a bridge which was prepared for demolition using two heaps of combustible material and hand grenades. When Maczek and his men arrived one of the heaps was already alight but the second was yet to catch. The Polish picket ran onto the bridge into a hail of Ukrainian bullets from the opposite bank.

Despite two men wounded, Corporals Wojtuń and Bienia ran to the blazing piles and with supporting fire began to strip the piles, throwing the blazing logs and grenades into the river and out of harm's way. Meanwhile, Cadet Officer Zawadowski's platoon, without receiving any casualties, cleared and captured the bridge. The skirmish was over. The defence of the entire Ukrainian battalion was laid bare, and such was the shock, speed and ferocity of the Polish attack that the Ukrainians gave up any hope of fighting further. The road to Stanisława was open.

Outside of Stanisława members of the Polish military underground movement, *Polska Organizacja Wojskowa* (*POW*), approached Maczek's men. The town centre had already been liberated by *POW* and the local militia but the suburbs remained in Ukrainian hands. A plan was developed using volunteers, some of whom went to the town with sections of the 'Flying Column' while the rest linked up with 9th Infantry Regiment. Quickly the Ukrainians were driven out of town and celebrations began.

Following the complete liberation of Stanisława the Poles pushed further eastward and in the following days were lucky enough to find an intact bridge over the River Dnieper at Niżniow; the crossing was taken and the Ukrainians were driven out of the town and further eastward. After the Polish drive from Stanisława the situation on the front began to settle. The weather continued to be blazing hot; it was a roasting and dry June. Maczek's company was made responsible for the security at the Dnieper crossing and as a consequence was responsible for the safety of the division in the Pokucia region, which was still held by the Ukrainians. Even so Maczek's men were well overdue a period of rest and relaxation. It was decided that this would be granted, with the men taking it in turns.

An Ukrainian counter-attack destroyed this well-earned rest. The Ukrainians had pushed units onto the Żóraw line and as a result orders were received by Maczek's company that they were to return to the front. The first assignment of the Polish troops was the hamlet of Czerniów, which was located at the foot of hills which dominated the area for several kilometres over the plain that ran all of the way to the Dnieper.

The key to the position was 4th Infantry Division, which was close Żóraw; the direction of the Ukrainian push. Maczek remembers that the heat was terrible and that his men were slowly dispersing into huts having just collected their lunches when suddenly a storm broke. It was typical of the summer storms of Eastern Europe: short but very heavy with large, fat raindrops that beat heavily like a tattoo on the hut windows. Then, just as suddenly as the storm had started, it stopped and the sun came out. As the sun rapidly returned and began to bathe the area with its warm rays, shots rang out as the Ukrainians, taking advantage of the storm, had crept into the village and from its eastern side attacked the Polish positions.

Maczek recounted that there was no time for manoeuvres and that only a 'reflex action' would do and so a single 'flying platoon' reacting with maximum violence ejected the Ukrainians from the village and began a pursuit of them out to the outlying Polish positions. By now the platoon was supported by artillery fire from every gun under the command of Lieutenant Walasek. Part of Maczek's company stayed in reserve while the remainder moved swiftly under the cover of a high railway embankment in order to strike the hills from the flanks. The units involved operated only with officers who could work in hand signals rather than spoken orders in order to execute the counter-attack. This was to counter the sloppy soldiers who had failed to notice the Ukrainians slipping into the village during the storm. But it all seemed too late. Then as the skies cleared after the storm Polish tank support, alerted by the fighting on the hills, came to the aid of the Poles. Maczek's 'boys' meanwhile moved towards the smoke of the fighting, interrupting their lunch, which, as Maczek reflected, 'Polak jak głodny to zły' ('a hungry Pole is an angry Pole') only served to add to their fury against the Ukrainians and their attack that day.

Maczek was trying to lead his men into action against Ukrainian positions in the hills. Their rapid reaction had pushed the enemy from the slopes with minimal casualties and once on top of the hills he was trying to decide how best to deal with an Ukrainian artillery battery which was endangering the Polish position. He opted for support from the tanks. Almost immediately he was ordered to report to the High Command. Maczek hastened back down the slopes and with a gun slung across his back, two grenades hanging from his belt, covered in mud and tar, Maczek had to report to the commander who had come to the front in an armoured train. The commander was Marshal Piłsudski himself.

Maczek remembered Piłsudski writing under the nom-de-plume 'Komendant' while Maczek was at university. Later Maczek was involved with Piłsudski's paramilitaries. It was during that time, in 1913, that Maczek first met Piłsudski at the local rifle union in Kadecki Street in Lwów when Maczek reported for sentry duty. The acquaintance was one-sided – Piłsudski did not remember Maczek – and why should he have any recollection of a young student rifleman preparing himself on Sundays and evenings in the 'arts of being a knight'? The concept of 'being a knight' is surely a clue to the collective mentality of the inter-war Polish officer corps.

Maczek made his report, formally and militarily correct: name, rank etc and then gave a report of the fighting. Piłsudski's eyes scrutinised Maczek, searching before finally smiling and then he pronounced, 'it looks threatening, Lieutenant, but from the hills it is settled quickly – hold the position until the units of the division are settled'.

Maczek remembered that he sweated more whilst making his report than he had during all of the fighting for the hills and the liquidation of the Ukrainian positions on them. He left Piłsudski's train and several weeks later received promotion for his outstanding deeds on the battlefield. However, the orders were incorrect, as he had been promoted to the rank of lieutenant – a rank that he had held since November 1918. This mistake was eventually corrected and his promotion to captain was confirmed, backdated to the original promotion by Piłsudski during June 1919. Maczek was also very conscious that a battlefield promotion was a great honour. He was to always wonder just how this meeting and promotion was to influence Piłsudski in Maczek's career – he always remained friendly towards the besmirched lieutenant fresh from the battlefield with hand grenades hanging from his belt.

The 'Flying Column' was the favourite of the Division, which created a sort of rivalry between the various units, although it did not hamper operations. This is illustrated by the fact that units from 9th Uhlans and the divisional reconnaissance unit commanded by Captain Reiss worked in friendly co-operation with the 'Flying Column', especially as the Uhlans moved around in carts rather than their more familiar horses. It was while working with the 9th Uhlans that Maczek got to know and befriend the squadron and platoon commanders of that regiment. This included the commander of the machine-gun squadron, Captain Komorowski, who was later to be known as '*Bor*', Commander of the Polish Home Army (AK) Warsaw during the ill-fated Warsaw Uprising of 1944.

Maczek was honoured when it was proposed that his 'Column' should become a squadron of an infantry regiment, but he refused, as even though he was honoured that infantrymen regarded both he and his men as equals, he did not want to give up the independence that was enjoyed with the 'Flying Column' in its present form. Furthermore confirmation of the Column's reputation was confirmed when a communication was received direct from the 'arms of the division' at the front. It seemed that General Żeligowski had made a special visit to the front. This led to Lieutenant-Colonel Jaruzelski coming from divisional staff headquarters with a request. Maczek was required, owing to his specialist services, to resolve a situation in the nearby Ursuline convent at Jazłow.

The operation was to be very 'ticklish' given the nature of the building and its inhabitants – nuns of the order and several young girls of the landed gentry including Lieutenant-Colonel Jaruzelski's two daughters. Jaruzelski, knowing of a coming offensive, was anxious about the safety of his daughters and that of the others at the convent and so a decision was reached that the convent had to be evacuated, but how?

For this purpose a special unit, expertly led, was to be deployed. The operation called for good intelligence in order to avoid mistakes, given what may be at stake. The overall operation was to remove Ukrainians from two hilltops that were a threat to Polish operations. The operation was vital but the convent with the young women was in the area of the proposed operation. So, the first priority was intelligence, and for this purpose a small reconnaissance party set out, consisting of Cadet Officers Michałewski and Mrowke and Sergeants Kielar and Szponar. They approached the ravine that led towards the Ukrainian positions following a crooked path which took them to the convent from where they were able to take stock of the area and decide how best to get the girls and nuns out from it and to the safety of Polish lines.

It was noticed that the Ukrainian positions embraced the convent from two sides rather like a pair of arms. It was decided to create two small units: one under the command of Lieutenant Czerniatowicz and the other under Cadet Officer Zawadowski. Both groups were to go directly into the hills and begin to engage the Ukrainians if Maczek considered that there was a need to do so. Meanwhile Maczek led the rest of the company directly into the ravine from the convent. The Ukrainians were shocked by the Polish attack as the Ukrainian outlying posts were overrun and did not have time to fire. However, fire was returned by Ukrainians on the hilltops; Maczek's and his men quickly dealt with this and the day went to the Poles.

Meanwhile the Mother Superior with her nuns and the young girls were led to safety, being evacuated in carts. The appearance of these women of faith with their young charges was an incredible sight amongst the young Polish soldiers in the middle of a war and seemed so romantic to the men, and perhaps to the young girls, too, who, it must be assumed, had led quite sheltered lives.

Suddenly reality took a hand and Maczek's men were once more propelled to the fore of the division as renewed fighting broke out. In the area of Buczacz-Czortków-Husiatyn area there were small skirmishes with some successes that took the Division to the River Zburcz.

In the autumn of 1919 the Division moved to Wołyn. Maczek reflected forty years later, in the early 1960s, that he still remembered the pride that he felt for his 'soldier-volunteers' who fought in the first battles for the Polish frontiers and for Polish independence.[26]

26   Maczek, op. cit. pp. 32-6.

4

1920: Maczek and the Polish-Soviet War

The Polish-Soviet War of 1919-1920 is a controversial war. During the Communist years in Poland (1944-89) it was not officially mentioned. It was part of the list of things that could not be mentioned or discussed which led to two generations of Poles not knowing for sure that their grandfathers had defeated the Red Army on the battlefield.

However before the Soviet occupation of Poland in 1944, and after 1989, when the Polish-Soviet War was and is discussed, a great deal of mythology has arisen with little rational thought. It was a feat of arms that defeated the Red Army at the gates of Warsaw during August 1920 and not divine intervention, as Nationalistic and superstitious Poles like to claim. There was 'no miracle on the Vistula' or '*Cud na Wisła*'. The Virgin Mary did not intervene on the behalf of Catholic Poland against the 'godless Bolshevik' and the date, 15 August 1920, the day of victory, was just another day, albeit one generally taken to be the day of the Polish victory over the Red Army and the ending of westward Bolshevik expansion for a generation. Who was really responsible for the victory is yet another controversy.

What is certain is Maczek's role in the Polish-Soviet War during the summer of 1920, as he writes his history of that time and there are other accounts available. We pick up Maczek's story in July 1920, after he had spent time chafing as a staff officer attached to General Iwaszkiewicz's Polish 2nd Army. He finally freed himself from this chore, as he viewed it, and was made available once more for active service – the very existence of the newly reborn Poland was threatened. Indeed, the 2nd Army had suffered defeats in early skirmishes with General Semyon Budyonny's 1st Cavalry Army of the Red Army (the famous *Konarmiia*), which was advancing towards Poland along with the rest of the Red Army.

Captain Benedykt, the Chief of Intelligence of the 2nd Army, had intercepted and deciphered dispatches from Budyonny. The dispatches were revealing as they exposed the weaknesses of the Red Army, especially as Benedykt learnt that Budyonny was virtually out of ammunition, especially artillery shells. Furthermore, the exact location of the Soviet Brigade Headquarters was revealed as being in the Korca area.[1] It should be noted that Benedykt was a brilliant mathematician and code-breaker.[2]

This information allowed the Polish 2nd Army to go on the offensive against Budyonny. The 6th Infantry Division was to strike from the forests to the north while along the Równe-Korzec axis the 3rd Infantry Legionnaire Division, under the command of General Berbecki, was to cover the western flank of the axis, protecting the 9th Uhlans'

---

1   Stanisław Maczek, *Od Podwody do Czołga: Wspomnienia Wojenne, 1918-1945*, Edinburgh, Tomar, 1961, p. 37.
2   Andrzej Pepłonski, *Wywiad w Wojnie Polsko-Bolszewickiej, 1919-1920*, Warsaw, Bellona, 1999, p. 222.

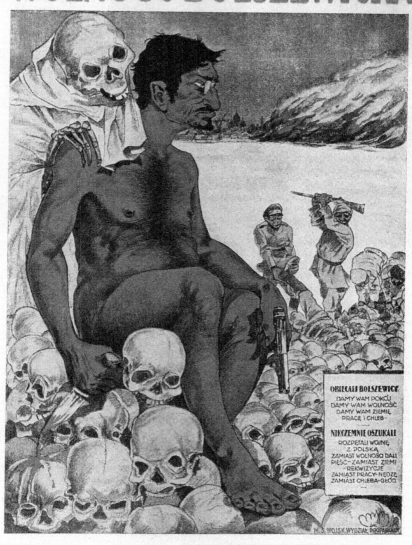

An anti-Soviet Polish poster c.1920, prominently showing Leon Trotsky. The legend
at the top translates as 'Bolshevik Freedom', the panel on the right reads: 'Bolshevik
promises – We will give you peace, We will give you freedom, We will give you land,
work and bread. Shameful deceits – Began war with Poland [not strictly true, as Poland
invaded eastward in a grab for land whilst the Bolsheviks were still fighting the Russian
Civil War], Instead of freedom gave blows, Instead of land – requisition [collectivisation
of agricultural land], Instead of work – destitution, Instead of bread – starvation. This
poster was distributed by the Polish Army's Propaganda Department. (Private collection)

Officers of the Polish Army during the war against the Soviet Union, 1920. (Private collection)

assault from the south. As Maczek recalled, there was an excellent concentration of Polish forces in the area which made it possible for them to consider an offensive directly on Korca via Międzyrzecz Korzecki. As a result of the developing situation Maczek was once more recalled to the front, as his skills and experience were needed and it was his desire to return to the fighting.

At dawn on 1 July 1920 Maczek's communications group moved quickly to Międzyrzecz Korzecki, capturing it after an energetic fight and pushing the defending Cossack units out of the position. Later in the afternoon Maczek and his group came across homesteads and farms in the western part of Korca and they were then able to link up with 6th Infantry Division and 3rd Legionnaire Division. Success was complete.

At the time of the march towards western Korca two running events coloured the situation – enemy artillery fire from the north in the direction of the expected operation of 6th Infantry Division and then afterwards, from the south, the arrival of a patrol of the 9th Uhlans. Cadet Officer Wieleżyński, an acquaintance of Maczek from the days of the Borysław offensive during November 1918, arrived with the next batch of orders. Maczek sent Wieleżyński to Lieutenant Adam Epler, a battery commander of the 3rd Light Artillery Regiment, who knew Maczek from Chyrów, with the advice that General Berbecki was uncertain about attacking Korzec.

This attitude confounded Maczek as he referred to orders of the previous day from Lieutenant-Colonel Bońca-Uzdowski which demanded instant action against any Cossack movements and to return fire at all times – and now suddenly a return to Równe? The latest orders were extremely pessimistic in nature and hardly had Wieleżyński arrived at Maczek's position before it was noticed that Cossacks were already circling in from the south. As Maczek wrote, 'Lovely situation' or in Polish, '*Ładna sytuacja*!'

Thus a battalion already exhausted from a night march and having being at stand to or alert all day now had to react quickly to counter the Cossack threat. It was proposed that the battalion quick march to the forested north to join 6th Infantry Division while reconnaissance was undertaken to try to discover the whereabouts of small Cossack units. From reconnaissance into the forests it was established that there were a number of ways of returning to the relative safety of the River Horyń. The problem was that the local commander, Major Wolf of the General Staff, despite being a staff officer, did not have any prior experience of war and so the withdrawal was conducted as a standard text book exercise of the ex-Austrian Army. This lengthy procedure had the possibility of creating panic amongst inexperienced soldiers and at times caused confusion.

Major Wolf was astute enough to realise that his actions were causing panic and had the sense to take action to prevent it from spreading by sending Maczek with a squadron of heavy machine-guns from the 11th Uhlans directly to a platoon of the 37th Infantry Regiment who were the rearguard of the Polish withdrawal. After an initial exchange of surly attitudes with the rearguard commander Maczek settled down to the task of preventing further panic as well as keeping the Cossacks at bay. Using his experience, Maczek moved into nearby fields of tall wheat and began to move the rearguard towards the lines of the previous day. Orders were given that nobody was to fire until ordered and then Maczek began to check the area in front of the line.

The immensity of Ukraine and Wołyn County left Maczek with the indelible impression as the great fields lay before him and his men – that the greatest enemy of Poland was the towering height of the crops standing in the field. Perhaps this is hyperbole but the vastness of Eurasia has long confounded travellers and invaders, Napoleon and Hitler to name but two.

Maczek contemplated his surroundings; how were they to fight amongst the tall stalks of wheat which blew around so picturesquely? He realised that the crop, even if it acted as cover for the Poles, would easily cause them to lose contact with one another and that they were unsuitable for defence owing to their height. The terrain allowed cavalry to move to hilltops about 600 metres in front of Maczek's position; they waved their swords above their heads as an act of intimidation towards the Poles. While Maczek was considering that the Cossacks did not have too much pep in their ranks, all hell broke loose as the enemy charged the Polish position. It seemed that only Maczek realised that the Cossacks were attacking and he just had enough time to give the general alarm, loosen off a round from his rifle before throwing himself to the ground as horses' hooves splattered earth all around him. He realised, just in time, that during his preoccupation of the defence lines and observations of the Russian cavalry on the hilltops, his comrades had taken the opportunity to melt away and leave him. This only became apparent to him once he had given the alarm and found that his shot was the only Polish shot. He was now quite alone.

Maczek lay quite still amongst the corn that hid him but within earshot of the enemy, who were moving all around him. He could not wait until dusk before attempting to get away. He decided to sneak away before the clear moon betrayed his presence and so with his rifle carefully wound into his uniform and his cap hidden, he made his move. He had chosen to hide the weapon and cap so that he did not give a distinctive silhouette. He moved towards a village but fires there and homesick Cossacks singing on the hills precluded any further movement in that direction.

A wet and filthy Maczek moved from the village and after several hours of avoiding the enemy found himself in a forest. It was whilst he was in the forest that an instinct for self-preservation took him back to Korca. With some caution he began to march to the west and

Polish Renault FT-17 tanks, 1920. (Private collection)

north-west using the moonlight that faintly shone through the forest foliage. There was a strange silence and after the emotions of the day the tension began to leave his body. When dawn rose Maczek was deep in bushes where he slept on and off for several hours, waking from time to time when far off artillery fire awoke him.

By the second night Maczek had learnt that the forest near the River Horyń was full of Polish colonists and so he struck out in that direction. Maczek approached the first isolated cabin and he was well received by the Poles living there. They fed him, gave him drink and rest. Afterwards he was passed from guide to guide as he was directed back towards Polish lines. After three nights he was in Równe, where the staff of the 3rd Division Legionnaires were close to moving owing to the operations of Budyonny's Army. Maczek was sincerely welcomed by the Staff. They were happy as they realised that if Maczek had survived, others surely must have done. Nevertheless, there was no time for pleasantries as the situation at hand was extremely grave.

Maczek was temporarily promoted as commander of two battalions chosen *ad hoc* and given the task of protecting Równe from the west. He was assigned a platoon of armour and three French tanks. Maczek was uncomfortable in this deployment because he had no real way of commanding his troops once he took his place in his tank. He was cut off from the operation and had no faith in this situation. However, he did reflect that the appearance of tanks on the battlefield did deter any further Cossack attacks in that direction. Twenty years later, in 1940, during the retreat across France, Maczek considered that not much had changed; tanks could always intimidate infantry.

Maczek's concerns led to him being appointed Communications Officer for General Krajowski's group but he could not return to the Staff position owing to the pressure from Budyonny's offensive from the north. Eventually Maczek reported to General Iwaszkiewicz in Lwów requesting the chance of forming another motorized unit.

Captain Maczek's 'Storm Division', 1st Cavalry Division

Maczek went to Jarosław to receive the first orders for the organisation of an armed motorized unit from the Commander of the Central Reserve, Colonel Kamionski-Jarosz. Maczek learnt that plans for the reorganisation and training of such a unit in Jarosław would take several months but this was unrealistic as the situation at the front was dire and Budyonny was already advancing on Lwów. However, Maczek, with the support of the Chief of the General Staff, General Iwaszkiewicz, was allocated about 400 men from the reserve. Several days later Maczek received orders from the commander of 6th Army ordering him, with his men, to act as guard for the Lwów Infantry Division at Mosty Wielkie. At the beginning Maczek's outfit was not really a battalion but three companies with two heavy machine-guns. Nevertheless, it was still required to force a crossing over the River Bug and capture Hill 289, which dominated the town of Oserdów, ready for the regrouping of the Lwów Infantry Division.

Once again Maczek and his men enjoyed success, as he had done in the past at Chyrów with his 'Flying Column'. Maczek overran the outlying enemy pickets and captured two machine-guns, when from the north-east a fair sized column of Cossack cavalry, about a brigade, advanced towards the Polish position. The chance to engage closely-packed cavalry at 800 metres with heavy machine-guns gave Maczek a chance for revenge for the Cossack attack at Korce. This first battle was a victory for the 'Storm Battalion', as Maczek's unit was now dubbed. It was not a huge success but for the weak and virtually untrained recruits in their first engagement with cavalry, it was a huge fillip for their morale and so the 'Storm Battalion' was born.

During the night the 'Storm Battalion' was relieved by units from the Lwów Infantry Division and moved to the village of Dzibułki where orders were received for reorganisation from the commander of 6th Army. The changes were to be fundamental for the battalion's future as it was suggested that they should be merged into the 1st Motorized Division under the command of General Rómmel, as the 'Storm Battalion' of the division. The divisional commander had to ensure a necessary period of time for reorganisation, with Uhlan officers and NCOs who had lost their mounts to be drafted into the battalion. Furthermore, sufficient vehicles had to be made available for the battalion. However, Maczek had misgivings about this because, as he said, even though the 'Storm Battalion' had experienced only a few days of battle (or more honestly, skirmishes), already a certain form of tradition had set in. He was not happy that his units could be influenced in this manner of recruiting, especially the matter of mixing infantry recruits with cavalry. Maczek felt that this type of unit would cause it to lose some of the mobility that he and his men had enjoyed in their operations, as the cavalry seemed to be more staid in their tactics and not really open to alternative suggestions.

The reluctance of the cavalry to join the infantry became somewhat obvious in the form of a near mutiny. Maczek was suddenly confronted by a delegation of senior NCOs from the Wielkopolski Regiments, who declared that they accepted that they must fight as infantry owing to a lack of horses but they refused to live with the infantry. It was a critical moment for Maczek's career and he knew that he had to face down the mutiny. Maczek stood facing this circle of NCOs with only his faithful Cadet Officer Mrówka from the 'Flying Column' (only recently returned from hospital) in support.

Maczek nipped the mutiny neatly in the bud by having its ringleader arrested and put into the hands of a Field Court Martial. It would appear that the Court Martial was never

Polish defences near Milosna, August 1920. A posed photo, but good for showing details of the arms, uniforms and equipment of the burgeoning Polish Army. (Private collection)

held as Maczek later wrote positively about this mutinous sergeant-major who in a later battle was one of the first men in the battalion decorated for bravery. Maczek concludes this episode by relating that a similar situation arose 23 years later with the Polish 1st Armoured Division, the differences being between cavalry and tank units. This time men from tanks units did not want to fight alongside the cavalry, but this time he handled the mutiny somewhat differently, using psychology without using the threat of a Field Court Martial. Maczek, with maturity and experience, had realised by the mid 1940s that young people cannot be blamed for certain actions if senior officers had failed in their duty to discourage regimental exclusiveness.

The following day General Rómmel came to Maczek; Maczek's battalion was already divided up into training groups in preparation for weapon training. Rómmel understood that time was needed for training but owing to the present situation at the front no more than two or three weeks could be spared. Maczek considered that God would take care of everything but in the evening operational orders came from 6th Army which underlined the necessity of the 'Storm Battalion' participating in the next day's operations, with the battalion working with 6th Cavalry Brigade to smash the 24th Soviet Division's Front at Waręż. Maczek's battalion was to guide the Polish cavalry in dogging the very steps of Budyonny leading to the Battle of Warsaw.

Maczek had to bravely report that his battalion was not yet ready for such an undertaking or any such operation. When Maczek wrote his autobiography in the early

1960s he paused to reflect whether this was a correct response towards the Polish military situation in the first half of August 1920, as the Soviet Army penetrated deep into Poland and approached Warsaw itself. Despite his report, the battalion was pressed into action. It was dark when the column, which included the 8th Uhlans, with a group of officers who wore long Austrian overcoats against the chill of the night, reached the main route to Waręż. The battalion patrolled the flanks of the column and reconnoitred the way ahead.

Before dawn broke the column encountered the enemy for the first time, as the reconnaissance patrols came under heavy machine-gun fire from the northern side of the forest, from the hills that dominated both sides of Waręż. Before long, a Soviet artillery battery opened fire on the Poles. The Soviets appeared to have covered the Polish advance and were beginning to open fire, at first from infantry outposts and then some ragged heavy machine-gun fire from the forest which covered the open spaces. Maczek estimated the range to have been around 1,200 metres, observing it was concentrated fire from professional soldiers. The Poles counterattacked the Soviet units in the forest and Maczek was impressed by his young officers, whom he realised he had known for only a few weeks. As bullets whistled overhead, and despite their weariness, they launched themselves into the attack.

The battle was at its height but the Poles still lacked artillery support. It was known that locally there was a single Polish artillery piece that was being repaired, and furthermore, that it had no ammunition or orders. Maczek, however, noticed that the Soviets were not pressing home their advantage, in fact, their fire was getting weaker. Then artillery support from other Polish batteries opened fire. The artillery support was in co-ordination with concentrated heavy machine-gun fire and using every weapon available the Poles pushed their counter-offensive on, resulting in the breaching of the 24th Soviet Division. The fight for Waręż was fierce as it was important to both the Poles and the Soviets. Eventually the Poles captured the town and the route to the Soviet rear was open.

There were several Polish dead and scores of wounded but it was not a high price for such a victory. Several weeks later General Rómmel honoured the soldiers of the battalion by naming them the 'Racławski Battalion' after the April 1794 action at the Battle of Racławice in which Polish peasants armed with scythes charged and amazingly captured Russian cannon. It was only when night fell that Maczek, perhaps having simmered down after the day's fighting, realised the horror of war with the cries of the wounded against the background of the detritus and trivia of war such as field kitchens and battalion vehicles – the horrific against the mundane.

The fighting for Waręż was not completely over as the town. The Soviet 24th Infantry Division continually counter-attacked for the remainder of the day in an attempt to throw the Poles into the valley and close the route. Once again, Maczek, before evening fell, received orders from Brigade Staff Headquarters via Captain Morawski, to come down from the hilltops and follow 6th Cavalry Brigade, who had already moved from Waręż to Tyszowca. It was clear to Maczek that to move before dusk was impossible. This would make life difficult for Maczek and his men, as they obviously did not want to blunder into enemy patrols in the dark. Then, to make matters worse, the weather changed and it began to rain heavily. This meant that they had to march on foot, as in such heavy rain the vehicles would not move.

Maczek's group spent time weaving around Cossack patrols. They were able to march westwards in the steps of the cavalry, and then, from the rear, came a report that a column

A Polish poster c.1920, with the call 'To Arms' – 'We are saving the
Fatherland, We have to consider our futures'. (Private collection)

of the 9th Uhlans had come under attack from Cossacks immediately after Maczek's group
had left Waręż. Maczek sent part of his group back to the 9th Uhlans. By the time they had
got back the fighting was over and only the debris of the battlefield remained.

Caught in the storm Maczek's group was also in a mess, not only due to the mud but
also as they were bereft of communications, supplies and unable to move because of the
lack of vehicles. Later that morning Maczek made contact with Major Dembiński, the
commanding officer of the 9th Uhlans; he also had had no communications with the
division and could only tell Maczek in which direction the regiment was moving.

Maczek decided to requisition horse and wagons from local farmers. This was difficult
because the area was a war zone and there was not much that could be taken -most had
already been requisitioned. Eventually Maczek's group reached Zamość, where the
battalion was reorganised and underwent training. Maczek could not be certain, but he
felt sure that after a few weeks the soldiers and NCOs of the 'Flying Column' returned to
his battalion almost to a man after being discharged from hospital or leave. The battalion
reformed armed with machine-guns, mortars and following the example set by Budyonny,
armed wagons. Maczek's unit was known as 'Captain Maczek's Storm Battalion 1st
Cavalry Division' and was ready for battle. But already the war between the Poles and the
Soviets was over. Poland had been rescued at the Battle of Warsaw on 15 August 1920 and

the frontiers were established.[3] They were to be the bane of the Second Polish Republic throughout its entire existence and beyond.

---

3   Maczek, op. cit. 37-47. For a Soviet view of the war see, Isaac Babel, *Red Cavalry*, edited by Nathalie Babel, translated with notes by Peter Constantine, introduction by Michael Dirda, New York, W.W. Norton, 2003.

5

Maczek and Inter-War Poland, 1921-1939

The Polish victory at Warsaw in August 1920 prevented the spread of Communism into Europe for a generation. Poland took the credit for this, however this victory was to be the main problem for Polish military doctrine and eventually Polish domestic and foreign policy, ultimately leading to the destruction of the Polish 2nd Republic during the Second World War. Senior Polish figures, both military and political but especially Marshal Piłsudski, the founder of modern Poland, made foolish and sometimes bloody-minded decisions which doomed their country to dictatorship, illegal rule and loss of statehood between 1926 and 1989.

Zaloga makes some excellent points about the inter-war Polish Army, especially the lack of mechanization. The Polish-Soviet War was largely cavalry-based, which gave cavalry successes. However, given that both the Polish Army and the Red Army were heavily reliant on cavalry a bias was not in evidence. These successes heavily influenced military thinking in Poland, with the cavalry being highly honoured in the Army and a marked reluctance to change their tactics ensuing. Change did come in 1934 when the cavalry lance was dropped from front-line service, although it continued to be widely used in training. Even so, the cavalry regiments were considered to be the cream of the Polish Army and they attracted the best officers and men.[1] It should be noted that the German Army, the *Reichswehr*, only dropped the lance in October 1927 in the midst of great opposition.[2] Showalter also observed that in the 1920s the internal combustion engine was primitive, with early armoured cars being essentially road-bound. This meant that in Eastern Europe cavalry still had a role to perform. The Polish cavalry suggested that it took three years to turn men on horses into fighting troops.[3]

To look beyond the cavalry one looks at the Polish Army: it was Piłsudski's pride. Furthermore most Poles linked the army to Polish independence and spared nothing for its upkeep, giving it a larger percentage of the Polish national budget than other European armies received. The problem was that Poland was one of the poorest countries in Europe and the sums spent on its army were pathetically small when compared like-for-like with the military spending of the wealthier Soviet Union and Germany during the 1930s. The cost for equipping a modern armoured division, for example, exceeded the total budget for the Polish Army.[4]

The key to the inter-war Polish Army was Piłsudski himself – he was not a professional soldier and it showed. The Polish Army reflected him; both his frailties and strengths.

---

1   Steven J. Zaloga, *The Polish Army, 1939-1945*, London, Osprey, 1983, p. 5.
2   James S. Corum, *The Roots of Blitzkrieg: Hans Von Seeckt and German Military Reform*, Kansas, University of Kansas, 1992, pp. 71-2.
3   Dennis E. Showalter, *Tannenberg: Clash of Empires*, Connecticut, Archon, 1991, p. 119.
4   Zaloga, op. cit. pp. 4-5.

Higher staff training and command were rudimentary with an excessive reliance on 'improvisation'.[5] This may have been noteworthy in wartime but for providing a modern and reliable army it was nonsense. An army based on a single personality is a bad army. As Zaloga notes, most of the Polish military leaders had not fought on the Western Front during the First World War and were therefore immune to the demand for military mechanization as was seen in Western Europe. Quite simply, there was little understanding or enthusiasm for new technology such as motor vehicles, aircraft and tanks. This meant that by the outbreak of war in 1939 the Polish Army remained organised on a basis not dissimilar to that of 1914: 30 infantry divisions, 11 cavalry divisions (10% of the Polish Army) with little motorization and primitive signalling while much of the artillery remained horse-drawn. There was a nod to German rearming during the 1930s, as in 1936 a commission was formed which recommended that the Polish Army should begin to modernise. It was suggested that by 1942 there should be 4 mechanized cavalry brigades, but by 1939 only one was ready and another was being formed.[6] It was all too late by then, and Maczek's ideas for mobile armoured units had clearly been ignored by the Polish military leadership. We shall return to the theme of Polish defence immediately before the outbreak of war in September 1939, for now the story returns to our subject, General Stanisław Maczek.

Maczek finished the Polish-Soviet War as a captain. His memories are silent as what happened next. He only picks up the story once more in 1938 so we must go to other sources as well as looking at the situation in Poland to determine how Maczek, as a Polish officer, fitted into this Poland and its inter-war society.

On 20 May 1921, Maczek, still a captain, was sent to the 20th Infantry Division as a staff officer. It should be understood that from 20 January 1922 until 1930 he held the rank of major with effect from 1 June 1919.[7] This is curious but no doubt the fog of war and the peace settlement after the Polish-Soviet War took its toll on lesser matters of state.

On 26 July 1921 Maczek was the first staff officer in the HQ of 5th Infantry Division. A contemporary report of Maczek was extremely positive, remarking that Maczek was a conscientious officer with great ambitions and that his relationship with subordinates was model. Maczek was extremely fit and very interested in sports as well as being very intelligent. Furthermore he was extremely practical, quick to orientate himself in a confused situation and overall he was independent and did not have to rely on instructions: in modern parlance a 'self-starter'.[8] However well Maczek and his career may have been doing by 1921 Poland was not.

Stachura observes that the stabilization of Polish territorial integrity after the defeat of the Bolsheviks allowed for independence. However, this was never entirely secure as the twin invasions of Poland by Germany and the Soviet Union during September 1939 provides the evidence of the vulnerability of a nation between two hostile states.[9] Therefore there is a need to examine this insecurity and how it affected Maczek and the Polish Army during the inter-war period.

5   Ibid.
6   Ibid.
7   Piotr Potomski, *General Broni Stanisław Władysław Maczek (1892-1994)* Warsaw, Wydawnictwa Uniwersytetu Warszawa, 2008, p. 79.
8   Ibid.
9   Peter D. Stachura, *Poland, 1918-1945. An Interpretive and Documentary History of the Second Republic*, London, Routledge, 2004, p. 111.

The most obvious problem was Poland's immediate neighbours, Germany and the Soviet Union. As we have already seen Poland fought a war against the Soviet Union while Germany, shattered by the 1914-18 War, was quiet for over 10 years. Once Adolf Hitler and the Nazi Party took power in Germany in 1933 Poland had acquired hostile neighbours to the east and the west. Despite Germany's apparent weakness during the 1920s it should be recognised that Germans remained hostile to the reborn Poland and plotted with the Soviet Union against Poland to the extent that Germany was able to develop its forbidden air and armoured branches of its armed forces in Russia during the 1920s. Many Western statesmen were also not overjoyed at seeing Poland resurrected.[10]

McCauley claims that the Soviet Government at the Treaty of Riga (1921), which settled the Polish-Soviet War, tricked the Polish Government into accepting more territory than it was really intending to in the belief that the more non-Poles there were in Poland, the more unstable the country would become.[11]

By the 1930s Ukrainian resistance to Polish rule in Eastern Galicia led to a full-scale guerrilla war being waged by Ukrainian rebels (OUN) against the Polish Government and Polish landlords, similar to that of Sinn Fein against British rule in Ireland. This led to a so-called 'pacification' operation by the Polish Army which was badly handled and saw the Polish Army rampage in Eastern Galicia.[12] As we shall see, Maczek was not involved in this regrettable period of Polish military history.

Many people would be forgiven for thinking that the victory at Warsaw would have provided a sense of unity within the Polish Army but instead fierce rivalry between Piłsudski's Legionnaires and the professionally-trained veterans of the ex-Austrian Army continued to fester after 1920.[13] Furthermore, military development was hampered by the closed minds and military illiteracy of Piłsudski and his cohorts, despite the Polish-Soviet War being the largest European war fought between 1918 and 1936.[14] To the frustration of modern-minded officers, as Maczek was, including a number of officers who were published in the not inconsiderable Polish military press, all attempts towards the modernization of the Polish Army were ignored by Piłsudski, who *was* the Polish Army. Furthermore Piłsudski preferred the company of his Legionnaires not only politically but also strategically in post-1921 Poland.[15]

In ignoring the experience of Polish veterans who had fought on the various fronts of the 1914-18 War, including Maczek, who had fought in the Alps of the Italian Front between 1915 and 1918, Piłsudski set himself against the modern doctrine of the French Army.[16] The French military organised the modern Polish Army after 1921 following the

10   Norman Davies, *God's Playground: A History of Poland, Volume II, 1795 to the Present*, Oxford, Clarendon, 1981, p. 393.
11   Martin McCauley, *The Soviet Union 1917-1991*, London, Longman, 1994, 2nd Edition, p. 30. The 1931 Polish census revealed that only 69% of Polish citizens were actually of Polish nationality. 15% of Polish citizens were of Ukrainian nationality living predominately in Eastern Galicia.
12   Hans Roos, *A History of Modern Poland: From the Formation of the State in the First World War to the Present Day*, London, Knopf, 1966, p. 136.
13   Jerzy J. Wiatr, *The Soldier and the Nation. The Role of the Military in Polish Politics, 1918-1985*, Boulder, Colorado, Westview, 1985, p.26.
14   Lech Wyszczelski, *Polska Myśl Wojskowa 1914-1939*, Warsaw, MON, 1988, pp. 158, 190-91.
15   M.B. Biskupski, 'The Military Elite of the Polish Second Republic, 1918-1945: A Historiographical Review' *War & Society*, 1996, Vol. 14, pp. 49-86.
16   Wacław Jędrzejewicz, *Piłsudski: A Life for Poland*, New York, Hippocrene, 1982, p. 176.

conclusion of the Franco-Polish Alliance; conscription was introduced while Article 4 of the alliance obliged Poland to introduce two years of compulsory military service and maintain an army of 30 divisions modelled on the French Army.[17]

In fairness to Piłsudski it has to be mentioned that part of his problem with the French military doctrine was the concept of a lack of mobility, even if he was still thinking in the terms of horsed cavalry, the French still thought in terms of trench warfare as witnessed on the Western Front. Piłsudski accepted that Germany was a danger to Poland and that perhaps static warfare had its place for such an eventuality; he considered the Soviet Union to be the greater threat to Poland and that static warfare was not an option in the wide open spaces of the Steppe between Russia and Poland.[18]

A further problem was that civilian politicians were becoming wary of Piłsudski's personal power. This led to some of the thought behind the 1921 Polish Constitution, as there had been a general expectation that Piłsudski would be president; for that reason those drafting the 1921 Constitution provided for a weakened presidency. Piłsudski ruined this expectation by refusing to stand for a weakened presidency and withdrew from public life between 1923 and 1926.[19]

Despite Piłsudski's apparent withdrawal from politics, the Polish Army remained a political cockpit in both domestic and foreign policies, with Piłsudski's influence being critical in the selection of Gabriel Narutowicz as Poland's first president.[20] Piłsudski and the Army were able to do this because it was perceived by political parties of all hues that the Polish Army was directly responsible for the restoration of Polish independence.[21] Following Narutowicz's assassination in 1922 Piłsudski was furious as he considered that the Polish Government was morally responsible for his murder while Garlicki considers that there are arguments (undisclosed) that those morally responsible for Narutowicz's death were also working towards the death of Piłsudski.[22] Piłsudski's consideration that he was a target for assassination was one of his reasons for his seizure of power during May 1926 while the alleged attack on his children clarified the situation in his mind.[23]

Between November 1918 and November 1922 Piłsudski held the offices of Head of State and Supreme Commander; as noted previously, he did not contest the 1922 Presidential elections as he saw it as a weakened office. As a result the relationship between the *Sejm* (the Polish Parliament) and the Army altered. The reason for this was the nature of the next period of Polish history, 1921-26, which was largely characterized by the subjection of the military to civilian oversight.[24] This was conducted partly through the office of the President as described in the 1921 Constitution. The President was not responsible to the

17 Piotr Wandycz, *Soviet-Polish Relations, 1917-1921*, Cambridge, Mass., Harvard, 1969, pp. 78-9; Anna M. Cieciala & Tytus Komarnicki, *From Versailles to Locarno: Keys to Polish Foreign Policy, 1919-25*, Kansas, University of Kansas, 1984, pp. 28-9.

18 Jędrzejewicz, op. cit. p. 176.

19 Jon Elster (ed) *The Roundtable and the Breakdown of Communism*, Chicago, University of Chicago, 1996, p. 13.

20 Andrew A. Michta, *The Soldier-Citizen: The Politics of the Polish Army after Communism*, Basingstoke, Macmillan, 1997, p. 26.

21 Piotr Stawecki, *Polityka Wojskowa Polski, 1921-26*, Warsaw, MON, 1981, pp. 114-15.

22 Jędrzejewicz, op. cit. p. 235. Andrzej Garlicki, *Józef Piłsudski, 1867-1935*, Warsaw, Czytelnik, 1988, p.335.

23 Jędrzejewicz, op. cit. p. 235; Garlicki, op. cit. p. 387.

24 Andrzej Korbonski, 'Civil-Military Relations in Interwar Poland' in Timothy Wiles (ed) *Poland between the Wars, 1918-1939*, Bloomington, Indiana Polish Studies, Center, 1989, pp. 39-54.

Sejm but his power was exercised through ministers who were. He was the highest ranking military officer but in time of war, according to Article 46 of the 1921 Polish Constitution, could not be Supreme Commander. Instead during wartime, the President in collaboration with the Cabinet and the Minister of Defence would appoint a Commander-in-Chief.[25] Therefore nominally the President was Head of the Army but its parliamentary dealings were conducted by the Minister of War, an officer responsible to the *Sejm* for all acts of military officials, both in wartime and in times of peace.[26] This was what Piłsudski objected to: the principle of direct civilian rule over the military by government and parliament, arguing that the highest authority over the military should be the Commander-in-Chief.[27] Or, to put it another way, in reality – he, Józef Piłsudski, liberator of Poland – should be in charge of the Polish Army or indeed Poland itself.

Between 1921 and 1926 Piłsudski was thwarted in his ambitions as the various democratic Polish governments during that period removed Piłsudski-ites from power and replaced them with their political opponents, both military and political.[28] It was during this period of democracy that the future Polish wartime Prime Minister and sponsor of Maczek, General Władysław Sikorski, began his political career on a higher political plane as during April 1921 he was nominated as Chief of the General Staff. Sikorski served Piłsudski faithfully in this role but after the assassination of Narutowicz and the appointment of Sikorski as Prime Minister, Piłsudski became embittered with the political process in Poland.

During 1923 Sikorski was nominated to the post of Inspector-General of the Infantry and later accepted the post of Minister of Military Affairs. It was during this period that the program for bringing the Polish military under civilian control began to take shape. Piłsudski was furious and in response organised an anti-Sikorski propaganda campaign in a bid to gain public support as he sought to remove a political enemy as he perceived Sikorski. Piłsudski thought highly of Sikorski as a military commander but distrusted him politically.[29]

Piłsudski was furthered antagonised by successive Polish governments who, after 1921, ignored the concerns of the ex-Legionnaires, which caused them to nurse grudges against the professional officers, especially those from the former Imperial Austrian Army. This is important as Piłsudski did not look to the army for support but to his legionnaires, and so was willing to take up their cause.[30] With popular support, confronted by ineffective civilian administrations and with many officers remaining loyal to Piłsudski and the nation but not to the elected government, it was not surprising that it was relatively easy for Piłsudski to launch his coup in May 1926. Indeed many in Poland were relieved when he did seize power.[31]

Piłsudski justified his coup as necessary to forestall chaos in Poland. The Army,

---

25   *Constitution of the Republic of Poland (1921)* http://-personal-engin.edu~zbigniew/Constitutions/k1921.E.html Accessed 31 January 2003. Article 50 allowed the President to declare war but peace could only be concluded with the consent of the *Sejm*.
26   Antony Polonsky, *Politics in Independent Poland, 1921-1939*, Oxford, OUP, 1972, p. 48.
27   Michta, op. cit. p. 27.
28   Korbonski, op. cit. p. 43.
29   Andrzej Garlicki, 'Relations between Sikorski and Piłsudski 1907-28' in *Sikorski: Soldier and Statesman. A Collection of Essays*, (ed) Keith Sword, London, Orbis, 1990, pp. 29-42.
30   Wiatr, op. cit. p. 26.
31   Michta, op. cit. p. 26.

General Maczek, circa late 1931-33. (Narodowe Archiwum Cyfrowe)

because it was the only authority that most civilians accepted, became a political force in Polish civilian life.[32] Despite claiming that he was concerned that the Army might become a political tool; Piłsudski used the military for his own military-political agenda.[33] After his seizure of power, military professionals took a backseat. The large number of officers from the ex-Austrian Army now serving in the Polish Army and political enemies of Piłsudski became subject to a Piłsudski-ite purge. After the coup many junior officers complained that they had been passed over for promotion for being on the wrong side, coining a new adjective to describe their situation, 'Zmajowany' or 'May-ed'.[34]

More seriously, senior officers, including Sikorski, a quite capable tactician and modernizer, were placed into a 'professional limbo' that is neither purged nor involved in military life.[35] Rothschild noted that Piłsudski had to be grateful to Sikorski for not allowing his Lwów regiments to become involved in the fighting during the coup of May 1926 as Sikorski and his men remained aloof from Piłsudski's revolt.[36] Of course it would have been better for Piłsudski had they supported the coup as it might have given it a veneer

32   Andrew A. Michta, *Red Eagle: The Army in Polish Politics, 1944-1988*, Stanford, Hoover Press, 1990, p. 29. Poliakov made the point that Piłsudski considered that he knew what was best for Poland and was 'an educator rather than a dictator'. V. Poliakov, 'Pilsudski' *The Slavic Review*, Vol. 14, 1935-36, 44-52.

33   Joseph Rothschild, *East Central Europe Between the Two World Wars*, Seattle, University of Washington, 1990, p. 58.

34   Joseph Rothschild, *Piłsudski's Coup d'etat*, New York, Columbia, 1966, p.190.

35   Wiatr, op. cit. p. 63.

36   Rothschild, *Piłsudski's Coup*, pp. 107 & 185.

of respectability and perhaps would have preserved the inter-war Polish Army from the amateurs who would eventually destroy it.

Piłsudski's purges reversed the trend that had favoured the career prospects of the professional former Austrian officers in the Polish Army and saw the rise of political loyalists, predominately from the wartime legions. In 1920 only 10% of the Polish officer corps was former Legionnaires but by 1939 75% of all commanders of infantry (both active and reserve) and 54% of all commanders of cavalry and motorized brigades were ex-Legionnaires. In total 65% of the commanders of major formations were former Legionnaires as were the Inspector-General, the Chief of Staff and his deputies as well as the Minister and Deputy Minister of War.[37]

A further consequence of Piłsudski's personal rule was that by 1930 he decided on promotions and postings within the military following question and answer sessions which he personally held at war games; something that we have already seen in Maczek's story so far. This appears to be another example of the amateur nature of the Polish officer corps, as by 1939 only 4.84% of it, which averaged 18,000 to 19,000 officers during the Second Republic, were graduates of staff colleges.[38]

The lack of formal military education within the inter-war Polish officer corps was to be disastrous during the September 1939 Campaign while the politicization of the officer corps at the expense of professionalism was to lead to factionalism within the Polish armed services during the Second World War; a period when the Polish armed services, especially the army, should have focused on ways of defeating Germany, greater co-operation with the Allies and truly liberating Poland. As we shall see, the Polish armed forces continued in their weaknesses for politics during the war and thereafter. It was an arena that Maczek was proud to remain aloof from.

Piłsudski ruled Poland from 1926 until his death in 1935 as a virtual dictator, with his rule becoming harsher as each year passed, especially after the 1930 elections, which he and his followers stole using intimidation and fraud. In 1935 the Piłsudski junta overthrew the democratic 1921 Constitution and replaced it with the April 1935 Constitution which was tailor-made for Piłsudski, although he did not live long enough to enjoy it. The 1935 Constitution was to have grave consequences which could not have been foreseen, as after 1943 the Soviet Government questioned the legitimacy of the wartime Polish Government-in-Exile, which claimed its legitimacy from the 1935 Constitution. If the Soviet Government had been successful in proving its assertion that the 1935 Constitution was illegal (which it surely was) the legitimacy of the Polish Government-in-Exile would have been destroyed.

The death of Piłsudski was a profound shock for Poland. The nation mourned but his death left many problems at a time of increasing tensions in Europe. Within Poland there was political unease. After 1926 Piłsudski had allowed a praetorian type of civil-military relationship to become established. This meant that the army and the regime were based around him and not the government. This type of relationship is usually associated with weak and unstable regimes, as Poland was between 1918 and 1939, and based on a form of dictatorship. A characteristic of this type of rule is that little or no thought is given to a successor to the incumbent. Poland was no exception, as Piłsudski considered that there was

---

37   Rothschild, *East Central Europe*, p. 192.
38   Walter M. Drzewieniecki, 'The Polish Army on the eve of World War II, *The Polish Review*, vol. 26, 1981, 54-64. Michta, *The Soldier-Citizen*, p. 26.

Graduates of the Warsaw Military Academy from the class of 1923-24, shown in November 1934. Maczek can be seen third from the left at the rear. (Narodowe Archiwum Cyfrowe)

nobody who could replace him.[39] However, thought should have been given to a successor to Piłsudski, as after a serious illness during October 1931 he realised that he was dying.[40] Piłsudski was actually dying of cancer, whilst the British Foreign Secretary, Anthony Eden, after meeting Piłsudski on 2 April 1935, reported that he appeared to be senile.[41] Despite his being associated with the resurrection of Polish independence and its preservation, he failed to consolidate his rule. Indeed after his death the sham of his regime was exposed.[42]

After Piłsudski's death the activities of the Polish military became overtly political under the guidance of Marshal Edward Śmigły-Rydz and Colonel Józef Beck. As Polish Foreign Minister Beck was already well known, and he was a favourite of Piłsudski, but Śmigły-Rydz was unknown, and until he was touted as Piłsudski's successor he was considered to have been apolitical.[43] Śmigły-Rydz had been a member of the *Strzeleczy* and was born in the Austrian partition of Poland. In 1910 he was conscripted into the Imperial Austrian Army; in 1912 he completed officer training and left the military academy with

---

39 Jędrzjewicz, op. cit. p. 331.
40 Ibid, p. 363.
41 Stanisław Mackiewicz, *Colonel Beck and his Policy*, London, Eyre & Spottiswoode, 1944, p. 59. A.R. Peters, *Anthony Eden at the Foreign Office, 1931-1938*, Aldershot, Gower, 1986, p. 95.
42 Edward D. Wynot, *Polish Politics in Transition: The Camp for National Unity and the Struggle for Power, 1936-39*, Athens, Georgia, University of Georgia, 1974, Preface, p. ix; Rothschild, *Piłsudski's Coup*, p. 367.
43 Wynot, op. cit. pp. 41 & 48. In November 1918 Kazimierz Sosnkowski, destined to be one of the leading personalities of the Polish émigré community after 1939, observed that Śmigły-Rydz had no interest in politics. Ryszard Mirówicz, *Edward Śmigły-Rydz: Działalność Wojska i Polityczna*, Warsaw, Instytut Wydawniczy Związków Zawodowych, 1988, p. 47.

good marks, later joining the *Strzeleczy*.[44] Despite his Austrian Army background, Śmigły-Rydz's support of Piłsudski's coup ensured that his military career prospered. Many had assumed that General Kazimierz Sosnkowski, who had shared a German prison cell with Piłsudski between 1917 and 1918, would have succeeded Piłsudski, but he failed to support the May 1926 coup. In fact he tried to commit suicide during the coup.[45]

Śmigły-Rydz's relative obscurity meant that the Government's press agencies had to launch a campaign in an attempt to build him up as Piłsudski's successor.[46] Like Piłsudski, Śmigły-Rydz was neither head of state nor prime minister, but as head of the Polish Army, he, like his predecessor, ruled Poland and expected the president and prime minister to submit to his will. General Edmund Ironside, who led the British Military Mission in Warsaw during the later summer of 1939, noted that both the Polish prime minster and the president were dominated by Marshal Śmigły-Rydz and knew their place. He noted: ' ... The President is a figurehead and knows it. The Prime Minister never appeared. The two men who had all the power in their hands are the Foreign Minister, Colonel Beck and the Marshal Śmigly-Ridz' (sic).[47]

Not only was the political system dominated by Piłsudski-ites, even after his death, the military and the planning of it also remained under the thrall of Piłsudski. By the time of Piłsudski's death, in 1935, Germany was rearming while Polish military doctrine remained neglected and backward-looking, remaining reliant on horsed cavalry. Nothing had changed in the 15 years that had followed the Polish victory at Warsaw and it was not until October 1938 that the Polish High Command ordered exercises based on the real material status of the Polish Army and not its theoretical status. At that time it should be noted that politically Poland was very close to Nazi Germany.

The main exercise was based on the premise of war with the Soviet Union – Plan 'W' (*Wschód* [East]). This exercise revealed a lack of ammunition available to Polish forces.[48] Plan 'W' was finally completed on 20 March 1939 while the plan for war with Germany, Plan 'Z' (*Zachód* [West]) was not started until 4 March 1939, once Poland had fallen out with Germany. Plan 'Z' was defensive in nature with the time, place and method of attack being chosen by the enemy. By March 1939 Poland was surrounded from three sides by Germany.[49]

Karski observes that in 1939 Poland had fewer military plans than it had in 1925, the year before Piłsudski's *coup d'etat*, and despite 50% of the Polish national budget being spent on defence between 1933 and 1939, a huge expense for an underdeveloped country, it was

---

44   Ibid. pp. 16-17.
45   Ibid, pp. 83 & 99. Śmigły-Rydz in 1920 was already a general when he led the Polish Army to Kiev during the Polish-Soviet War. Ascherson observes that Piłsudski had intended his favourite, Walery Sławek, to replace him but Sławek's colleagues considered that he lacked the necessary authority for such an office. Eventually the office of Inspector-General of the Armed Forces fell to Śmigły-Rydz, 'a stiff and unimaginative officer' and he assumed Piłsudski's 'mantle'. Ascherson further observes that the 'mantle always seemed too big for him [Śmigły-Rydz]'. Ascherson, op. cit. p. 75. Marian Romeyko, *przed i po maju*, vol. 1, Warsaw, MON, 1976, pp. 334-5.
46   Mirówicz, op. cit. p. 111. Śmigły-Rydz was quoted as being the 'First Soldier of the Republic'. Ibid. p. 7.
47   NA (National Archives, Kew, London) Prime Ministers' Office, PREM 1/331A, Roseway to Rucker, August 1939.
48   Andrzej Suchcitz, *A Brief of the Military Planning and Preparation for the Defence of Poland, October 1938-August 1939* (MA dissertation, University of London, 1981) Suchcitz also observes that the dispersal of Polish war industries was more suited for war with the Soviet Union. Ibid. p. 7.
49   Ibid. pp. 3-4.

not enough. According to German data for the same period, Germany spent 30 times more on the *Wehrmacht* alone.[50] Ironically between 1921 and 1926, the period of democracy in Poland and prior to military rule, two plans had been provided for in readiness for war with either Germany or Russia.[51] As Polonsky remarks, by 1939 it was all rather late.[52]

The reason for it being 'rather too late' was that despite beginning to build an arms industry complex after 1936, Poland compounded its neglect of the military by becoming too close to Germany and preparing initially for war with the Soviet Union. This went as far as strategically positioning its war industries in a position that suggested a war with the Soviet Union rather than Germany, but not both, as had been the case in the preparations for war between 1921 and 1926. The concept of such a war was a failing of Piłsudski and the Polish military regimes in understanding the nature of Nazi Germany. Piłsudski's policy had always been 'Eyes East!' – Russia was the enemy. This policy had served him well and his successors saw no reason to change it.[53]

Poland's final act of co-operation with Germany was the annexation of the disputed region of Teschen, in Czechoslovakia, during October 1938. This was the nadir of the Polish military regime and caused Poland to lose support in the West. Indeed, Sir Alexander Cadogan, the Permanent Under-Secretary at the Foreign Office (FO) referred to Beck in his diary as a 'brute', in reference to the Polish ultimatum to the Czechoslovak Government.[54]

The Polish annexation of Teschen was the first time since 1920 that Maczek went on what should be considered as active service overseas.

Since 1921 Maczek's career had been quite, very quiet. On a personal level he married Zofia on 22 June 1928; they had 2 children in Poland, Renata who was born in 1929 (4 October 1931 according to Potomski) and Andrzej, born during 1934.[55] This little family were destined to follow Maczek into exile after the defeat of Poland in 1939. A third child, Magdalena, was born in exile, sadly handicapped, but the Maczeks were as stoic as ever,

50   Jan Karski, *The Great Powers & Poland, 1919-1945. From Versailles to Yalta*, Lanham, University Press of America, 1985, p. 234.

51   Tomasz Kośminder, *Planowanie Wojenne w Polsce w Latach 1921-1926*, Toruń, Adam Marszałek, 2001, pp. 112-14. David G. Williamson, *Poland Betrayed: The Nazi-Soviet Invasion 1939*, Barnsley, Pen & Sword, 2009, p. 48.

52   Polonsky, op. cit. p. 492.

53   Ascherson, op. cit. pp. 75-6. Ascherson recounts the suggestion that Piłsudski made to the French Government for a preventative war against Germany in 1933. Gasiorowski asserts that the Polish Government, despite its lack of wisdom in its foreign policy between 1919 and 1933, was the first government to recognise the danger of Germany under Nazi rule. Piłsudski, as early as March 1933, warned the French Government that German rearming was progressing too fast and that a preventative war was necessary to prevent the German threat growing any further. Once Piłsudski was certain that the British, French, Italian and German governments were working together at the expense of Poland, he threw himself into the 'vanguard of the race for appeasement'. Zygmunt J. Gasiorowski, 'Did Piłsudski Attempt to Initiate a Preventative War in 1933?' *The Journal of Modern History* Vol. XXVII, 1955, 135-51.

54   David Dilks (ed) *The Diaries of Sir Alexander Cadogan, 1938-1945*, London, Cassell, 1971, p. 111. Diary entry, 1 October 1938. Davies claims that Beck secured the area to deny Germany strategic control of the Moravian Gate. Davies, op. cit. p. 497. Mackiewicz, a critic of the Piłsudski-ite camp, claimed that Beck had been attacking Czechoslovakia diplomatically since 1935. Interestingly Mackiewicz made two observations regarding Beck: he noted that Śmigły-Rydz and his staff disliked and distrusted Beck and that it was unfair to claim that Beck was pro-German in his foreign policy. Beck basically tried to maintain correct relations, as he saw it, under the most difficult of conditions with Germany. Mackiewicz, op. cit. pp. 79, 105, 119.

55   Potomski, op. cit. p. 79. Jerzy Majka, *Generał Stanisław Maczek*, Rzeszów, Libra, 2005, p. 31.

looked after her and she outlived her parents. Maczek's career in the inter-war peacetime Polish Army was slow but sure. On 22 January 1922 he was promoted to major, with the appointment being backdated to 1 June 1919. He was involved in General Staff work as well as heading the intelligence division of the General Staff. On 30 October 1927 Maczek was promoted once more; he was now Lieutenant-Colonel and Commander of the 76th Infantry Regiment. This was followed by another command, when he was made commander of the 81st King Stefan Bathory Rifles, stationed in Grodno.[56]

The Polish invasion and occupation of Teschen in 1938 was a mistake, as during World War Two it was to rebound against the exiled wartime Polish Government in London when the British Prime Minister, Winston Churchill, recalled it and condemned it; the surrendering Czechoslovak general predicted that the Poles would soon be surrendering their territory to Hitler.[57]

This proved to be the case and the whole incident of the Polish invasion of Teschen was an extremely foolish mistake; the sadness is that Maczek was involved in it.

As a professional soldier Maczek had no choice but to obey orders to move into Czechoslovakia. The Czechoslovak expedition was a disaster for Poland, even if they claimed that the Czechoslovaks had annexed the lands in question during 1919 while Poland was distracted by war on its eastern frontiers; their Foreign Ministry lacked the wit to realise that attacking Czechoslovakia during October 1938 was a gross blunder. It made the Poles look like sycophants of Hitler while losing sympathy in the West at the same time and later during the war.

It is not clear why the Polish regime decided to invade Czechoslovakia during the autumn of 1938, especially at a time of international crisis concerning the fate of that unhappy country, but one suspects it was done in the name of popularism as the Polish junta became more and more disconnected with the Polish populace while the country began to drift politically and economically. Indeed Deszczyński writes that the Polish

---

56   Ibid. pp. 100-101.
57   Richard Hargreaves, *Blitzkrieg Unleashed: The German Invasion of Poland, 1939*, Barnsley, Pen & Sword, 2008, p. 34. In a meeting with Stanisław Mikołajczyk, Sikorski's successor, Churchill informed Mikołajczyk that it would be impossible for the Poles to retain Vilna (Vilnius) as the Soviet Government had already incorporated Lithuania into the Soviet Union, furthermore Churchill also mentioned that he had heard Poles speak of a 'Second Munich' but countered this with the retort 'no Pole should say this because the Poles had participated in the pillage of Czechoslovakia': a reference to the Polish annexation of Teschen in 1938. NA, PREM 3, Prime Ministers' Papers, PREM 3/335/8, Record of a Meeting held at No. 10 Downing Street, 16 February 1944. In another incident, when Churchill noticed that the British Ambassador to the Polish Government-in-Exile, Sir Owen O'Malley, quoted that the Poles spoke of 'another Munich', Churchill replied that the taunt might be justified (he failed to say to whom) but not the Poles who ' ... jumped on the back of Czechoslovakia in that moment of agony and helped rend her to pieces ... ' NA, PREM 3/355/8, Churchill to Eden, 15 February 1944.
The British secretary of State for War, Leslie Hore-Belisha, after the Polish annexation of Teschen, showed a rather astute understanding of Polish problems when he remarked to Lieutenant-Colonel Edward Sword, the British Military Attaché in Warsaw, that regarding Teschen he thought that an additional minority might be a source of weakness for Poland. Elizabeth Turnbull & Andrzej Suchcitz, (eds), *Edward Roland Sword: The Diary and Despatches of a Military Attaché in Warsaw, 1938-1939*, London, Polish Cultural Foundation, 2001, pp. 31-2. This should be compared with the Treaty of Riga, where some critics have considered that Lenin fooled the Poles into accepting more territory than was good for them, and the resulting acceptance of a large Ukrainian population which caused an imbalance in the demographic makeup of the Polish state, whereby the Poles were in danger of becoming a minority in their own country. See also Sword's remarks, ibid, pp. 68-9.

Maczek addressing men from the 10th Motorized Brigade,
November 1938. (Narodowe Archiwum Cyfrowe)

annexation was an attempt to boost Śmigły-Rydz's popularity in Poland.[58]

The decision to attack Czechoslovakia was taken because as Poland was a dictatorship there was no real discussion about such a move and as the British general, Edmund Ironside, noted during July 1939 Polish civilian politicians had no say in the running of the country: the Polish Army was firmly in charge.[59]

Maczek was made commander of the 10th Motorized Cavalry Brigade as the end of October 1938. It was quite a surprise to him when he arrived in Warsaw from Częstochowa to receive this appointment after 18 years of faithful peacetime service in various regiments within Poland as well as time spent at the Staff College. For the previous four years he had been second-in-command of the 7th Infantry Division in Częstochowa.

Maczek swiftly began to orientate himself with the latest military literature as well as acquaint himself with the current international situation regarding Italy, Germany and the Soviet Union. It seemed to him that the international situation was grim and deteriorating still further. Poland had already occupied Teschen at the beginning of October 1938; Maczek was to be sent with his brigade to participate in its occupation. The 10th Motorized Cavalry Brigade was the first completely motorized organisation in the Polish Army and Maczek and his 'Flying Column' and 'Storm Battalions' of 1920 had been suddenly remembered in Warsaw after years of neglect; now he was recalled as war beckoned.[60]

After March 1939, with the German absorption of the remainder of the Czech

---

58   Marek Piotr Deszczyński, *Ostantnio Egzamin Wojsko Polskie Wobec Czechosłowachiego, 1938-1939*, Warsaw, Neriton, 2003, p. 424.

59   See above p. 79.

60   Stanisław Maczek, *Od Podwody do Czołga*, Edinburgh, Tomar, 1961, pp. 51-2.

lands, Hitler turned his ire on Poland. Britain made promises to stand by Poland if she was invaded by Germany; a rash act, according to Ironside, as there was little that Britain could immediately do in a ground war, as the British strength lay with its navy.[61] The stage was being set for war as both Britain and France were outflanked by the more aggressive foreign policy of Nazi Germany. The British and French governments were not prepared for treachery as practised by Hitler, who however was quite clear in his policies regarding Eastern Europe. Western statesmen ignored his rhetoric and continued in their French-speaking twilight of gentlemen's diplomacy. Finally the dogs of war burst forth on 1 September 1939, changing Europe and Maczek's life forever.

---

61   Colonel Roderick Macleod & Denis Kelly (eds) *The Ironside Diaries, 1937-1940*, London, Constable, 1962, p. 216, diary entry, 12 February 1940.

6
The Polish Campaign,
September-October 1939

War came to Poland brutally out of the sky, from the sea and over land on 1 September 1939. It had long been expected and finally came like a proverbial bat out of hell. A report from the British Military Attaché, however, soon revealed that the Germans were not having it all their own way. He reported that initial unexpected Polish resistance had already upset the German timetable, whilst the German General Staff hoped to get their timetable back on track, with the entire Polish operation being based on three weeks of operations. Losses on both sides were severe while the Germans expressed disappointment at the results of their bombing raids over Poland. There was also a report that German civilian and military morale was low, and this concerned the German General Staff.[1] At a stroke it is obvious that German planning was not as seamless as so many have considered ever since the invasion of Poland in September 1939.

Despite the valiant defence which the Poles put up against the German invasion of their country, the British Government, following Anglo-Polish staff conversations during the summer of 1939, was aware that it was unlikely that the Poles could defend Poland for more than 6 months without outside assistance, and that this was an optimistic estimate.[2] It had already been lamented by Sir Bernard Pares to Lord Halifax that it would be better if Russian (Soviet) aid had been secured before Britain gave its pledge to guarantee Polish independence during March 1939.[3] Of course, this would have been anathema to the Poles; Russian aid always seemed to come with strings attached, according to the collective Polish experience. Even before the German attack on Poland it had already been noted by the British Cabinet as a result of Anglo-Polish staff conversations that the Poles were less hostile towards the Soviet Union than they had been previously but there was still a real need to impress on them that the Soviet Union was the only real source of military aid of a war against Germany.[4] Once the fighting got going the British began to write the Poles off, as Hankey minuted to Halifax that it was obvious that the Poles had no chance against Germany; marginalia notes 'defeatist'.[5]

The second meeting of the British War Cabinet noted that Poland was bearing the

---

1   NA, (National Archives, Kew, London) PREM 1, Prime Ministers' Papers, PREM 1/331a, Sir N. Henderson (Berlin) 2 September 1939.

2   NA, FO 371, Foreign Office Correspondence, FO 371/23129 C9510/27/55 COS 927, 15 June 1939. These talks had initially made an unfavourably impression on Poland as the original British delegation was relatively junior. See NA, FO 371/23129 C7962/27/55, Sir H. Kennard to Sir O. Sargent, 30 May 1939; FO 371/23129 C8327/G, Lieutenant-General Ismay to Sir Orme Sargent, 9 June 1939. By July 1939, the British Military Mission was beefed up with the presence of General Edmund Ironside.

3   NA, FO 800, Halifax Papers, FO 800/309 H/1/5, Sir Bernard Pares to Halifax, 24 August 1939.

4   NA, CAB 66, War Cabinet Memoranda, CAB 66/1 DCOS Enclosure no. 1, Anglo-Polish Staff Conversations, 14 July 1939, Report by United Kingdom Delegation, Paragraph 3.

5   NA, FO 800/317 H/XV/280, Hankey to Halifax, 12 September 1939.

main brunt of the German attack and that every effort should be made to relieve Poland. Already the shortcomings of the British guarantee were being exposed as it was only considered that the Royal Air Force could do anything to aid the Poles, whilst the French could attack Germany overland.[6] The problem was that the British lacked a suitable army to immediately launch a European campaign; Leslie Hore-Belisha, the Minister for War told the British Prime Minister, Neville Chamberlain during April 1939 that the British Army was dangerously short of men at a time when nearly every European country was in some stage of mobilization.[7] The British War Cabinet, within days of the outbreak of war, noted that Polish resistance might be broken and considered that there would then be a long period of stalemate on the Western Front, as had been the case between 1914 and 1918.[8] However General Ironside, the newly appointed Chief of the Imperial Staff (CIGS) reported that the concentration of 32 German divisions coming out of Slovakia had come as a surprise and that his personal view was that Poland would be defeated within a few weeks.[9] The Poles were equally surprised, because as Corporal Adam Rubaszewski recalled in 1946, Slovakia was considered neutral, yet a strong German attack came from the south out of so-called neutral Slovakia.[10]

Ironside had already entertained doubts about Poland's ability to defend itself, as in July 1939 he felt that even though he was impressed by the Polish soldier he was less than impressed with Polish defence plans.[11] The lack of military professionalism in the Polish Army was quite clear to a properly trained soldier and the British Military Mission considered that the Poles were overconfident and their opinion of Germany too low; they underestimated the ability of their future opponents. An equipment shortage in the Polish Army was also identified by the British, a direct result of the Polish neglect of domestic war industries as had been practised during the Piłsudski years. Therefore even if Poland had plenty of troops available, they only had enough equipment for a three-month war.[12] Eventually, the Polish collapse was foreseen by the British Military Mission (except for the unforeseen attack on Poland by the Soviet Union). As was reported to the British War Cabinet, the Poles had not only overestimated their own capabilities while underestimating the German strengths, but they had also made an incredibly stupid assumption that the lack of roads would impede German motorized forces and give the advantage in a war of movement to their own horsed cavalry. Consequently the Poles had made few defensive preparations. As one wag put it 'the Polish Army of 1939 was admirably prepared for the war of 1918'.[13]

The Piłsudski-ite chickens had come home to roost, and were to haunt Poland for another 50 years. It must be admitted that unlike the Allies, the Germans also continued to depend on horse-drawn artillery and transport as well as infantry marching on foot, even if

---

6   NA, CAB 65, War Cabinet Minutes, CAB 65/1 War Cabinet 2 (39) Minute 5, 4 September 1939.
7   NA, PREM 1/296, Hore-Belisha to N. Chamberlain, 15 April 1939.
8   NA, CAB 65/1 War Cabinet 2 (39) Minute 1, 4 September 1939.
9   Ibid, Minute 7.
10 PISM, (Polish Institute and Sikorski Museum, Kensington, London) B.I. 58 – Depositions 10 Motorized Cavalry Brigade, B.I.58/F, Corporal Adam Rubaszewski, Maczkow, 21 January 1946.
11 Colonel Roderick Macleod, Denis Kelly (eds) The Ironside Diaries 1937-1940, London, Constable, 1962, p. 82.
12 NA, CAB 66/1 Enclosure II Anglo-Polish Staff Conversations, 1939, 12 June 1939.
13 NA, CAB 66/1 C.O.S. (39) 44 21 September 1939.

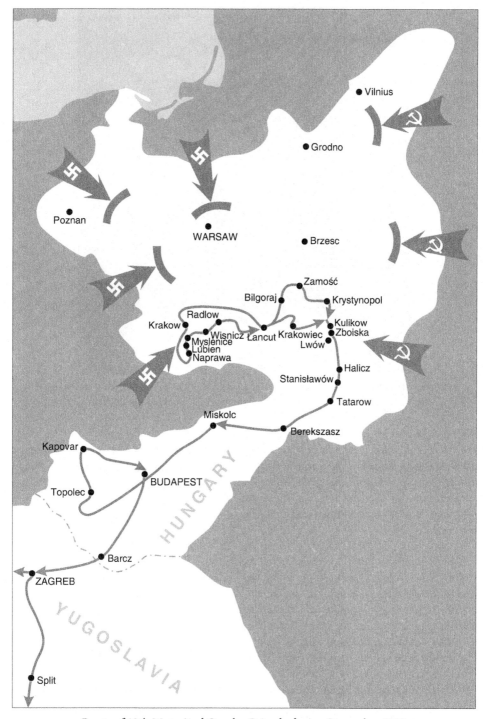

Route of 10th Motorized Cavalry Brigade during September 1939.

Maczek with officers of the 10th Motorized Brigade, 1939. Note the black leather coats,
hence the name 'Black Devils', and the German-pattern steel helmets. (Private collection)

they did have an initial superiority in armour.[14]

Where did this leave Maczek at the outbreak of war? During the middle of August
1939 Maczek's brigade moved to the Kraków military district, as part of 'Army Krakow'
under the command of General Szylling. Maczek's area of operations was in the direction
of Pszczyna, Bielsko, Zawiercie and Katowice with the objective of reconnaissance and
linking up with the divisional commanders in the area – Generals Boruta, Mond and
Sadowski.

On 29 August 1939 Maczek received another destination for his brigade, Nowy Targ,
where they were to link up with other regiments in the border regions and prepare for the
coming invasion. The invasion came at dawn on 1 September; Maczek and his men bore
the brunt of the invasion from the south. They were not alone, as Poland was attacked from
every frontier that it shared with Germany, across land and from the air, while there were
further attacks from the sea. Poland was shocked at the ferocity of the German attacks.

The German attacks on Army Krakow had the intention of outflanking the Poles
defending Silesia and its environs. The Germans crossed the passes in the Tatra Mountains
and attacked the towns of Chabówka and Nowy Targ with orders to seize Myślenice no
later than 3 September. The intention was to encircle the entire Polish army in that area.

---

14   Geoffrey Megargee, *Barbarossa, 1941: Hitler's War of Annihilation*, Stroud, Tempus, 2008. The caption
        accompanying photograph 21 notes that Operation Barbarossa, the German invasion of the Soviet Union
        in June 1941, called for 300,000 horses.

Polish TKS tankettes of the 10th Motorized Brigade, Poland 1939. (Private collection)

Maczek received orders that were quite simple – hold the German advance and make their lives as difficult as possible. Easier said than done! Maczek and his soldiers, as had been the case when soldiers had fought for Polish independence 20 years earlier, put up the most stubborn defence despite the overwhelming numbers and technical superiority of the German onslaught and brought the German advance into southern Poland to a bloody and fiercely contested crawl through the Polish mountains. The Poles knew that they were fighting for their very survival.

Maczek was aware of who was opposite him owing to information gleaned from prisoners and captured documents. He was already aware of the strength and numbers of the German motorized armoured units pitted against him, not just from the fighting alone but from captured information – 2nd Panzer Division, then in turn 4th Light Division and finally 1st Mountain Division, who were trying to trap the Poles in a pincer movement and thus trap them in southern Poland.

Maczek's brigade was supported by a Border Defence infantry battalion, an artillery battery and local volunteers of the National Defence. Maczek also mentions aerial attacks. Overall the Poles were outnumbered 10:1. And so began a running battle in which the Poles acquitted themselves well. They did all that they could in fighting the Germans in the mountain passes in an attempt to prevent them from reaching Myślenice and Dobczyce, and a desperate struggle developed.

The Poles were undermanned and under-armed but Maczek made the best of a bad, chaotic and frequently changing situation. In the early battles for Poland Maczek has been depicted favourably. At the outbreak of war he was a Colonel, and was described as being a 'tough uncompromising leader' similar to the German Panzer commander, Guderian. Maczek's 10th Cavalry Brigade, dubbed the 'Black Brigade', fought a series of delaying battles as part of Army 'Krakow' and never allowed the numerically superior panzer forces to gain the advantage. As their history records, 'the soldiers proved splendid fighters, without a trace of any 'armour panic', especially the tank units [whose] 37mm anti-tank guns confirmed the hopes that we had placed in them. In the course of the day the enemy lost about 30 tanks. The 2nd of September had an excellent influence in the morale of the Brigade'.[15] It was Guderian who defined the requirements for a decisive tank attack as being suitable terrain, surprise and mass attack in the necessary breadth and depth.[16] Mountain passes proved not to be the most suitable terrain, even if there was an element of surprise with German armoured columns coming our of what had been considered, somewhat naively, neutral Slovakia. Heavy armour was not used in Poland; there were no great tank battles; no sizeable tank concentrations and no tank armies. Indeed when the Germans looked at the lessons of Poland 1939, they were more concerned about the quality of the horses used rather than the problems with the MG34 machine-gun, which frequently jammed in the mud and dust.[17]

Lieutenant-Colonel Skibiński made a full report on the fighting in the area. Maczek had already discussed with Colonel Wójcik the news that strong enemy motorized armoured columns had crossed in two columns at Jabłonka and Nowy Targ. 1st Border Defence Regiment (1st KOP) had been fighting since dawn 1 September 1939. Its outposts had engaged enemy tanks and during the course of the day had destroyed several of them.

At about 16:00 hours 1st KOP, holding the hills to the south from Jordanow, came into contact with then enemy which was advancing northwards into Poland. The enemy attacks from the Jabłonka-Jordanow direction were strong and the Germans began to shell Polish positions with heavy artillery. Skibiński was critical of the lack of a solid line in the Polish defences because if one moved to the east, there was nothing there while to the west 12th Infantry Regiment, part of the KOP Brigade, could be found.

Maczek quickly decide that there was a definite need to defend the region between Jordanow and Rabka, a line of about 20 kilometres. This immediately placed a barricade across the German northward advance. He concentrated his units on the hilltops with the twin purposes of pushing back any German offensives during the night as well as trying to assess the numbers and presence of the numerous motorized German units.

The battle for the Jordanow-Rabka position was next. The enemy headed towards Wysoka and Ludwik Hills in the general direction of the town of Skomielna Biała. The offensive was weak and easily held. The Germans attacked *en masse* using 200 tanks preceded by an artillery barrage, but the Poles destroyed 30 of these and the enemy withdrew.

The next offensive began at 15:00 hours (2 September 1939) with another artillery bombardment and with machine-guns and anti-tank guns attacking the Polish positions. After a stubborn fight two artillery observation points were broken up and taken by the enemy.

There was a counterattack from two squadrons of the 24th Uhlans and for a short while they were able to check the enemy advance and cause them casualties before being

---

15   George Forty, *Tank Commanders: Knights of the Modern Age*, Poole, Firebird, 1993, p. 58.

16   Heinz Guderian (Major-General), *Achtung – Panzer! The Development of Armoured Forces, Their Tactics and Operational Potential*, London, Arms and Armour, 1995, Translated by Christopher Duffy, Introduction and Notes by Paul Harris, p. 181.

17   Len Deighton, *Blitzkrieg: From the Rise of Hitler to the Fall of Dunkirk*, London, Pimlico, 1996, pp. 99-100, 102, 199.

pushed back. The Polish tank crews moved from the safety of the hills, owing to the arrival of German armour, and took to the countryside around Jordanow. The enemy, after capturing the hills, did not attack in the direction of Jordanow, as a single reconnaissance patrol supported by artillery was able to hold them up.

The Poles then regrouped in the Skomielna Biała area as well as sending out a reconnaissance mission to explore a gap which had been created in the hills around Dolna Skawa; it was realised that this position could be reasonably easily held and this concluded the reconnaissance offensive.

September 2 1939 finished at dusk with the Polish artillery batteries taking the opportunity to shell enemy tanks assembled in the Wysocki area.

Skibiński made the following observations of the fighting on 2 September 1939. It was asserted from captured documents and prisoners that the Poles were facing the 2nd Panzer Division of General List's 14th Army. It was clear to the Poles by the end of the second day of fighting that they were faced with gigantic odds against them particularly in the air, in armour and artillery, but the Poles had also realised that they were quite capable of putting up a very stiff resistance which would have serious consequences for the German invasion timetable.

The Polish troops had fought splendidly without any sense of inferiority and certainly did not panic in the face of superior numbers of enemy armour. The Polish anti-tank defences had fought well and had given an excellent account of themselves. Now and then, Skibiński reported, crews of the Polish 37mm tankettes had fought to the death, destroyed their guns with grenades to prevent them being captured and used by the enemy or fought to destruction while fighting off armoured attacks. These bloody engagements between the Poles and the enemy served not to dismay the Poles but instead had the effect of increasing morale and stiffening the resolve to defend their country to the death.

Skibiński observed that 2 September 1939 played a prominent role in the history of the Brigade. On its first day of combat, despite the German reputation of terror in how it deployed its Panzer units; the Poles had been unafraid, if outnumbered and out-gunned. The Poles fought well but continued to lose ground.[18]

Maczek also recalls 2 September 1939 as being a very painful day. The Polish casualties had been painful, very painful. Not only had there been terrible human casualties, equipment, which was not in plentiful supply, was also destroyed in large quantities. Maczek wrote that the German casualty rate was some compensation for the injury that the Poles and Poland were suffering owing to the German invasion. Maczek, like most of the Polish commanders, was aware of the huge differences between the German armed forces and the Poles in modern equipment as he mentions that several Polish modern fighter-bombers, (Łos [PZL.37]), were able to bomb the German army at Spytkowice; he regretted that the Poles did not have more of these aircraft at their disposal.

At the same time sections from Colonel Dworak's troops were involved in a stiff battle with German tanks from the 2nd Panzer Division. However, in the southern sector, commanded by Lieutenant-Colonel Wojcik, closing the direction to Chabówka, the situation was easier. Against the Poles was a large new unit which was soon indentified as the 4th Light Division moving strenuously and with great difficulty across the terrain, not helped perhaps by the destruction of bridges by Polish sappers; by the evening 2 September

---

18   PISM, B.I. 58/B, Lieutenant-Colonel Franciszek Skibiński, 10th Motorized Cavalry Brigade in the September Campaign.

1939 the area was guarded by the Border Defence Regiment.[19]

In the meanwhile changes had to be made regarding communications with the commander of the operational group, which had been disrupted by the fighting. It was decided that Maczek should co-ordinate the action. During the night of 4/5 September 1939 Maczek was given an infantry division that had been moved to the Bochnia region to act as a shield for the south and its flanks. This trust was furthered when the KOP Brigade commanded by Colonel Gaładyka and a division of heavy artillery was also placed under Maczek's command. This was excellent growth in the strength and breadth of the Brigade (already known as Colonel Maczek's group). By midday 4 September 1939 the actions for the next day had been decided upon.

There were three strings to the offensive for 5 September 1939: a) there were to be strikes against the enemy using the 24th Uhlans and three or four battalions of infantry strengthened by two companies of tanks; b) security was to be provided in the direction of Myś; c) during the night 'flying units' fought the enemy who were attacking 10th Mounted Rifles.

Maczek, when he was later a Brigadier-General, discussed this period, comparing it with the tactics of the 1914-18 War and pronounced on the idea of the deployment of large organised armoured formations:

> At the battle of Jarosł in 1914 the following episode occurred – two battalions of infantry were providing protection for a cavalry division commanded by General Zaremba when from hidden positions a Cossack artillery battery began to shell the infantry, which caused panic amongst the infantry who ran to a nearby bridge crossing the River Gnila Lipa. Amongst those fleeing was a young Second Lieutenant who raced across the bridge screaming that the military regulations were wrong and that it was not infantry which was the main weapon but artillery.

Four years later, on the Western Front, this assertion was largely accepted but even if artillery could win territory, it was the infantry which held it. Maczek remarked that on 8 August 1918, at the Battle of Amiens, 400 tanks had been deployed by the Allies. Tactics had changed dramatically during the four years of the First World War; mechanization had already made that difference.

The experience of the fighting on 2 September 1939 revealed that in the Wysoka area on a two kilometre front seven anti-tank guns had held up the German offensive, destroying or damaging 35-50 tanks. Meanwhile, using three to four divisions of artillery firing directly at the enemy, 50% of the enemy's guns were destroyed while the German tanks were pushed away, which had the effect of paralyzing the momentum of the German offensive.

The deployment of every tank from the German 2nd Panzer Division was held up by the resolute action of 2nd Motorized Battery and other anti-tank units. This perhaps causes a paradox because while Maczek advocated the use of mass armoured units, the experience of the fighting of 2 September 1939 illustrated that well-positioned and well-prepared anti-gun guns could cause havoc with the deployment of massed ranks of armour units, which suggested that armour needs artillery support and air support.[20]

Lieutenant Henryk Greiner also witnessed the fighting of the opening days of the

19   Stanisław Maczek, *Od Podwody do Czołga*, Edinburgh, Tomar, 1961, pp. 59-61.
20   PISM, B.I. 58/B, Skibiński.

German invasion of Poland and recorded that on 2 September 1939, with an anti-tank gun, he was able to destroy two German Mk III tanks and was involved in further heavy fighting which cost the lives of Second Lieutenant Hawrysz and Corporal Babski, while Gunners Janasiewicz and Schwarc were wounded, as was Major Zmudzinski, who was badly wounded and later died in a German hospital. The next day, 3 September 1939, the Germans regrouped and attacked in force using combined tank and aerial attacks and the Poles began a fighting retreat.[21] The Polish retreat was not a disorderly rout but a disciplined fighting action; this is in total contrast with the Polish military government, which fled Poland while its own army was still in the field. The diary of Captain Ludwik Stankiewicz, staff officer 10th Cavalry Brigade, illustrates the fate that befell Polish troops during September 1939.

On 1-2 September 1939 Stankiewicz was in Krzeczow and then between 2-3 September was in Lubien followed by a march to Dobczyce, 3-4 September. There was a short stay there and then another march, this time to Wisnicz during the night of 5-6 September, then another march to Radomyśl via Dunajec and then yet another march to Rzeszów, 7-8 September, before moving on to Łancut, 8-9 September, and yet another march via Jarosław to Wolo Ryszk, 9-10 September 1939. Then followed a march to Lipnice and an overnight stay there 10-11 September, overnight then another march in Jaworow 11-12 September, followed by another march, this time to Żółkiew. Between 13 and 16 September 1939 Stankiewicz and his comrades stayed in Soposzyn before moving to Dublany, 16-17 September. On 17 September 1939, the Soviet Union, aiding Germany, completed the long planned destruction of Poland by invading from the east. The Poles realised that further resistance was futile and began to move towards Hungary, which was neutral but sympathetic towards the Poles. By 23 September 1939 Stankiewicz was in the Hungarian capital, Budapest and almost immediately, 25 September 1939, he was already in France, ready to fight once more.[22] Stankiewicz's odyssey is confirmed by the testimony of Tadeusz Walewicz, who joined Maczek's brigade during the middle of August 1939 in Rzeszów and was assigned to a reconnaissance unit. Once fighting between the Poles and Germans began Walewicz recounts the Polish retreat, mostly at night, as they tried to establish new defensive lines for the next day against further German attacks while the Poles did their best to slow the German advance. Walewicz gives an account of how he and his comrades passed through Myslenice, Wisnicz, Rzeszów, Łancut and Jarosław heading towards Lwów. Walewicz claims that he saw soldiers sleeping and walking.[23] What else could these valiant men do?

Not withstanding the cowardly Soviet attack from the east the Poles were not only defeated by overwhelming German numbers and tactics but were also undone by the neglect of Polish military doctrine during the Piłsudski era and the incompetence of the military amateurs that he and his legionnaires undoubtedly were.

From internment in Győr, Hungary, officers, including Maczek and Colonel Kazimierz Dworak, commander of the 24th Uhlans, noted the main mistakes of the organisation of the Polish armoured brigade during the September Campaign of 1939. Principal concerns

---

21   PISM, B.I. 58/F, 16 DAL. MOT, 'Wspomnienie z Walk wrzesniowych 1939 (Memories of the September Campaign) – Lieutenant Henryk Greiner.

22   PISM, B.I. 58/B, Diary of Captain Ludwik Stankiewicz, Staff Officer 10th Cavalry Brigade.

23   Evan McGilvray, The Black Devils' March – A Doomed Odyssey – The 1st Polish Armoured Division, 1939-45, Solihull, Helion, 2005, p. 3.

were the small amounts of armour deployed in the fighting against the Germans as well as the poor quality of Polish reconnaissance. Furthermore there were failings in the use of artillery, which was not only out of date, with only small numbers available compared with that available to the Germans. This was compounded by an unreliable communications system and a lack of air cover. There were also concerns about the lack of trained technicians as well as no organised medical care or procedure for the evacuation of the wounded and sick in the Polish ranks. Part of the problem was the lack of suitable vehicles available to the Polish Army in 1939.[24] Regarding vehicles it should be noted that Liddell Hart, an eminent proponent of mobile warfare considered the arrival of the 6-wheel truck as a landmark in military history; its role by the 1930s had been recognised as vital by military experts.[25] But the Polish military maintained its preference for the horse and of course how many peasant conscripts would have been familiar with vehicles? It would have been outside of their world remit and the army would have had to teach them to drive – a further expense!

General Kazimierz Sosnkowski also bewailed the state of the Polish Army in September 1939 as he said the Polish Army was backward: it lacked mobile units and artillery but was beset with thousands of peasant carts. As Sosnkowski put it, the Polish Army of 1939 had more to do with the 17th Century rather than one obliged to face up to the rigors of the epoch of blitzkrieg.[26] Sosnkowski related his experiences of the September Campaign later. He recalled that the 10th Motorized Brigade took to the field with a single company of Vickers tanks but that all were lost over several days in the Mielec area. Sosnkowski posed the question how to get to Przemyśl. At the beginning the intention was to execute this, using special units from the 10th Motorized Brigade. Sosnkowski ordered Maczek to report to nearby Janow at around midnight. Sosnkowski had already calculated that the Brigade's casualties were 70% in equipment and 60% in personnel. Maczek and Sosnkowski conversed quickly about these casualty rates, with Sosnkowski asserting that he was conscious that on the night of 10-11 September 1939 German motorized units consciously avoided Maczek's brigade when they crossed the River San to the north of Jarosław.

Sosnkowski considered that it might be best if Maczek's unit moved out at dawn via the south, as there was already fighting in Przemyśl. Maczek suggested an alternative route: his suggestion was to force a route from the west running from the south from Grodka Jagiełłski. Intelligence suggested that it was more than likely that the Poles would meet German units in the hills and that Maczek's plan was probably safer. It was considered that to arrange the entire enterprise properly and not to go off half-cocked Maczek would need twenty-four hours to prepare everything.[27]

Maczek and his brigade fought their way across Poland heading towards Lwów, making the German advance difficult by making them fight for every bridge and ford on the way. Maczek's brigade, despite facing superior odds, carried out every order they were given and outside of Lwów actually counterattacked a German Mountain Division and regained territory off it. This was the celebrated retaking of the Zboiska Heights, where the Brigade had fought the Germans, as part of the defence of Lwów, between 14 and 17 September 1939. Nevertheless, all of this was in vain as during the night of 16/17 September the Soviet

---

24   PISM, B.I. 58/C, 24th Ulans. Evidence of Colonel Maczek, Györ, 23 September 1939; Colonel Kazimierz Dworak, Paris, 12 January 1940.
25   Deighton, op. cit. p. 26.
26   PISM, B.I. 86/A, General Sosnkowski: Memories of September 1939.
27   Ibid.

Union invaded Poland from the east.[28] Poland was fatally wounded. It should be noted that Maczek was the only Polish commander to retake territory during the September Campaign from the attacking Germans.[29] When the news of the Soviet invasion of Poland arrived in Lwów Maczek was attending a meeting there. He immediately returned to his Brigade to give orders to cease fighting and move south towards the Polish-Hungarian frontier.[30]

The Soviet stab in the back of Poland was precisely what Piłsudski had long warned against right up to his death in 1935. The question of how the Poles would have managed in the September fighting is one that should be asked, as it was obvious that the Poles were fighting much harder than anybody could have anticipated. Perhaps it might have been possible that once the Germans had to fight for rivers and marshes it might have been just possible that the Poles could have pulled off some form of stalemate in the fighting – unlikely but not impossible. Just as the Soviet Union invaded Poland the weather broke and heavy rain, the first for nearly two years, began to fall. Poland had suffered near drought conditions since 1937.[31]

The extremely dry and flat Polish terrain made it very easy for the German armour to move across the land; the hills and mountains in which Maczek repulsed the Germans was quite a different matter but even so, as the author can vouch, Poland until the late 1990s had a very poor road infrastructure, therefore the unmetalled roads in Poland in 1939 would have posed many difficulties for the German Army because once the rain turned the dust into a thick mess of mud with a porridge-like consistency German vehicles would have found the going extremely tough, especially when they were reaching the first Polish geographic barriers outside of the mountains, rivers.[32] It is true that the Germans easily forded the River Vistula at Warsaw but the dry season was coming to an end when the Soviet Union attacked Poland from the rear.[33]

The Soviet Government attempted to justify its invasion of eastern Poland by claiming that as a result of the German invasion of Poland ' ... there was no proper government in Poland with whom they could get in touch, and that, without abandoning their neutral attitude; they felt compelled to protect the interests of White Russian and Ukrainian minorities in Poland.'[34] By the end of the war this would be exposed as rank hypocrisy but nobody took any notice: the Soviet Union by 1945 was a superpower and too powerful to be attacked.

It is ironic that during July 1939 the British Government tried to convince the Polish

---

28 McGilvray, op. cit. pp. 3-4.
29 Evan McGilvray 'General Stanisław Maczek and Post-War Britain' in Peter D. Stachura (ed), *The Poles in Britain, 1940-2000. From Betrayal to Assimilation*, London, Frank Cass, 2004, Foreword by Stanisław Komorowski, pp.59-68.
30 McGilvray, *The Black Devils' March*, p. 4.
31 PISM, B.I. 58/A, M.W. Zebrowski, 25 April 1968, recollections of the September 1939 Campaign.
32 See Sword, op. cit. p. 88. The British War Cabinet had hoped for such a situation, as on 4 September 1939 it was considered that perhaps the Poles might hold out for a few months and that a First World War situation might emerge on this front in the form of a stalemate; General Edmund Ironside (CIGS) spoiled this hope as he reported that the concentration of as many as 32 German divisions in Slovakia had come as a surprise (Maczek was involved in fighting these) and gave his personal view that Poland would be defeated within a few weeks. NA, CAB 65/2 (39) Minutes 1 & 7, 4 September 1939.
33 NA, CAB 65/9 (39) Minute 4, 9 September 1939. The Poles had destroyed the bridges over the Vistula at Warsaw but the 'abnormal drought' had allowed German troops to wade across the river.
34 NA, CAB 65/18 (39) Soviet Invasion of Poland, Minute 3, 17 September 1939.

Government that the Soviet Union was their only real source of aid in the case of a war against Germany.[35] But that was before the signing of the Molotov-Ribbentrop Treaty during August 1939, which was a commitment to destroying Poland. In any case, the British Government was well aware of the real Soviet intent: the spread of world revolution; the extension of Soviet influence and regaining former imperial Russian territories.[36]

A particularly significant weakness of the Polish Army was their own lack of reality in 1939, as was noted by the British Military Attaché in Warsaw, Lieutenant-Colonel Edward Sword, who in January 1939 reported that 'the chief weakness in Polish field training appear to be undue optimism as regards the effect of enemy fire in the attack, and a lack of attention to administration during exercises. The morale of the Army seems to be very high, and bloodless successes over Lithuania and Teschen have probably raised it further'.[37]

It was left to Maczek and other gallant and brave Polish officers and men to deal with the consequences of twenty years of Polish military neglect. They acquitted themselves well and fought against overwhelming odds but the treachery of the Soviet Union was too much and so many Poles headed for exile, including Maczek. The Polish military government had already fled, whilst their gallant army was still fighting. Treachery was abundant as Maczek and his men headed for the Hungarian frontier and an uncertain future.

---

35   NA, CAB 66/1, Anglo-Polish Staff Conversations, 14 July 1939.
36   NA, CAB 80 Chiefs of Staff Memoranda, CAB 80/3 (39) Annex I Russian Policy, 6 October 1939.
37   Sword, op. cit. pp. 75-6.

7

1939-40: Into Hungary and France

After the defeat of Poland following the joint Nazi-Soviet invasion during September 1939, Maczek and his men withdrew to Hungary. The defeat of the Polish Army and of Poland was a disgrace at three levels:

1. The naked aggression of German policy. The reality was that Germany had not accepted its defeat in 1918 and the loss of lands, especially to Poland, notably the partition of Germany, with East Prussia being detached from the remainder of Germany by the Polish corridor. This caused Germany to seek the reunification of its lands using a pseudo pro-German policy at the expense of the Slavic lands.
2. The cowardly attack by the Soviet Union on Poland.
3. The craven attitude of the Polish military government, which fled to Romania while the Polish Army was still in the field, fighting both the Red Army and the German Army.

This action was to have ramifications for this government as exiled Poles, especially the Polish Government-in-Exile, sought to put distance both geographically and politically between themselves and the former military government. It should be recognised that Maczek and his men had fought well and with honour and it was with pride that they headed towards exile.

After seventeen days of fighting the brigade was given orders from Poland's military leader, the amateur soldier and failed politician, Edward Śmigły-Rydz, to leave the country via Romania or Hungary. As became apparent later it was lucky that Maczek and his men left for Hungary, as the Romanian Government, under pressure from the German Government, took a more robust approach towards Poles entering their country seeking sympathy and a route out to France. Indeed, the Romanian authorities interned the Polish leadership once they entered Romanian territory. The Romanians furthermore claimed that the Poles compromised themselves by sending an (unspecified signal) from Romania to London and Paris. The Polish Government disputed this, but to no avail.[1] The British and the French Governments were well aware that the Romanians were being pressured into interning Poles who might retreat from Poland into Romania seeking passage to France.[2] Count Edward Raczyński, the Polish Ambassador to the United Kingdom, asked the British and French governments to intercede on behalf of Poland and try to persuade the Romanians to release the Polish President and the Polish Government or at least allowed President Mościcki to leave Romania. However the British Ambassador in Bucharest pointed out that it would be folly if he tried to persuade the Romanian Government to

---

1 George V. Kacewicz, *Great Britain, the Soviet Union and the Polish Government in Exile (1939-1945)* The Hague, Nijhoff, 1979, pp.30-1.
2 NA (National Archives, Kew, London) CAB 85 Allied Forces (Official) Committee, CAB 85/1 MR (39) 11 Meeting (Mtg) Anglo-French Liaison, 16 September 1939.

Men from the 10th Motorized Brigade shortly before crossing the border
into Hungary, 1939. Maczek stands in the centre, next to Lieutenant-
Colonel Franciszek Skibiński. (Narodowe Archiwum Cyfrowe)

defy the Germans in this matter as it would help neither the Romanians nor the Poles.[3] This
was a very early indication of how unimportant the Poles were to the Allies, especially an
undemocratic government, which the Polish government was.

The orders to leave Poland troubled Maczek because, as with thousands of other Poles,
he wondered where his family was and what was to become of them. As it turned out,
they were close at hand, in Stanisławów, at his mother-in-law's home. On receiving this
incredible news Maczek took a car to collect them and brought them to his position.

The question arises as to how Madame Maczek appeared at Stanisławów? It seems that
she was just as resourceful and thoughtful as her husband. On the second day of the war
Madame Maczek, with her two small children, was travelling from Rzeszów to Wołyn,
away from the fighting and to the east and north; this is prior to the Soviet invasion of
Poland, a move agreed between Maczek and his wife. En route the Maczek family, with
others, were bombed and got stuck at Tarnopol in traffic and chaos. No doubt this chaos
was the result of refugees fleeing the German invasion and heading towards the perceived
safety of eastern Poland. Madame Maczek discovered that travelling conditions to the
north were very difficult and getting worse, and after taking advice from one of Maczek's
officers, Lieutenant Kazia Chojowski of the 81st Regiment, she decided to move to her
mother's home at Stanisławów. There she decided to stay, having no news of her husband
and his brigade beyond rumours that they were still fighting.

Maczek considered that it was God who decided the fate of his family because his wife's
sisters were shot later in the war by Ukrainians in the service of the Germans. The brigade

---

3   NA, FO 371 Foreign Office Correspondence, FO 371/23151/C14339/8526/55, telegram from Sir R.
Hoare, Bucharest, 19 September 1939.

overnighted for the last time in Poland on 18-19 September 1939 in the Tatra Mountains which Maczek knew well as a holiday venue in happier and peaceful times.

On the afternoon of 19 September 1939, 1,500 men out of the original 3,000 men of the brigade who first took to the field on 1 September 1939, crossed from Poland into Hungary in a column as if on parade, carrying all of their arms, including heavy weapons and banners.

Years later, in his autobiography, Maczek remarked on just how quiet the Hungarian side of the border was: there were no sounds or clamour of war, no artillery explosions, no bombs screaming, no telephone or the monotony of the telephonist (an interesting little detail). He did not even have to lie awake worrying about his family as they were with him, only a few steps away and in good health.

The first eighteen days of the war had not allowed the Polish troops to sleep properly, which left them, Maczek included, exhausted. All that they really wanted as they headed towards exile in Hungary was sleep. Of course they were extremely unhappy to leave their homeland but many considered that this defeat was merely a temporary setback and that they would soon be able to return to Poland. Maczek wondered, what now – what was the future for him, his family and Poland? He wondered about the reception that the Poles might receive once on Hungarian soil and whether they would be allowed to regroup their forces on Allied territory. Hungary was not an ally but Maczek considered the Hungarians and Poles to be brothers – two close brothers. There was certainly, between the two countries, a history of opposition to Russian hegemony.

A brigadier from the Hungarian General Staff arrived from Budapest and proceeded to deal with the Poles, delicately, as one might with children. His purpose swiftly became clear; the Hungarian Army lacked anti-tank guns and wanted the Poles to help them in this matter. At first this appeared to be a request but after two days orders came from Budapest – the Poles were to hand over their weapons to the Hungarian Army, as simple as that.

The Poles were increasingly frustrated with their inability to leave Hungary, especially as they had had their weapons confiscated. All the Poles wanted to do was leave Hungary and continue their war against Germany and now the Soviet Union from French territory. There were several long conferences between the Hungarians and the Poles in an attempt to try to decide what to do about their situation; the Hungarians were extremely nervous about offending the Germans in their dealings with the Poles. The result was that the entire brigade was to be interned in Hungary. It would seem that the Hungarians were somewhat lackadaisical in guarding the interned Poles and so, in small groups, most of the Poles were able to escape from their Hungarian captors. It could be considered that the Hungarians were possibly acting out of sympathy for the Poles or more practically glad to be shot of this large number of well disciplined and motivated men who were hell bent on setting out for France in order to continue their war. Quite simply, once the brigade was off Hungarian soil it was no longer a Hungarian problem or responsibility.

For the Poles a good piece of good fortune was that the Polish Consulate was still functioning in Budapest and from there false documentation was provided for escaping Polish servicemen. The necessary paraphernalia for escaping was sent to Maczek's internment camp disguised as a gift from a Hungarian aristocrat for the 'poor internees'. This is further evidence of the good intentions of the Hungarians, as Polish soldiers were allowed to escape under a veneer of security. Maczek and his party were able to escape from Hungary dressed in civilian clothes and posing as part of a Polish diplomatic party. They travelled via Yugoslavia and Italy, at that time still uninvolved in the war between Germany and the Western Allies, and were able to arrive in France on the evening of 21 October 1939.

The ability to escape from internment was common amongst the Poles, as many were not only able to get away but also received hospitality whilst on the run, notably from Yugoslavs and Polish diplomatic staff along the way. What is incredible is that Maczek, in his civilian clothing, was able to travel with his wife and two children out of Hungary to France. It was most unlikely that an escaped foreign military officer would have been travelling with his wife and two small children. This was part of Maczek's good fortune; he did not look like somebody escaping but instead the little party looked like a diplomat and his family travelling across Europe.

During the night of 21/23 October 1939 Maczek travelled with his family to Paris. At 10 o'clock in the morning he reported to the Polish military commander, General Władysław Sikorski, at the Regina Hotel, Paris. Maczek was warmly welcomed by Sikorski; they had known each other since the 1920s and Sikorski was also aware of the bravery of 10th Armoured Brigade during the September Campaign and the invaluable leadership of Maczek during the fighting. He promoted Maczek to Brigadier-General with the responsibility for training Polish troops in France, as the Polish Army tried to resurrect itself after its defeat.[4]

The problems for the Poles once they arrived in France were numerous, but they can be reduced down to diplomatic recognition of a Polish government to be formed in exile and how best to continue the Polish military contribution to the war, even if it might amount to no more than symbolism.

Sikorski may also have been grateful to see Maczek emerge from the wreck of what had been Poland as there was a problem with the type of Polish officer arriving in France after September 1939. Before the outbreak of war a majority of commanders of large Polish units had belonged to the amateur Piłsudski-ite Legions.[5] The lower ranks were understandably bitter towards those senior officers, some of whom had clearly failed in their duty during the September Campaign and had fled Poland, leaving many ordinary soldiers to face their fates as the Germans and Soviets overran and divided up Poland. At his first officers' briefing on 28 September 1939 Sikorski reminded his officers that there was 'no place, nor could there be any place, for party politics or the politics of a clique in the Polish Army'.[6] Therefore it must have been with great joy that Sikorski received Maczek, a popular, successful, brave and apolitical officer, when Maczek reported for duty in Paris.

The Poles were most anxious to establish a recognised government-in-exile in order to forestall any attempt by the Soviet or German governments to establish puppet Polish governments which may be recognised in the world as the official mouthpiece for the Poles and Poland. The Soviet Government did this after 1943 with the establishment of the so-called 'Lublin Committee', a group of renegade Polish communists who participated in the Sovietisation of Poland. The question was, who should head such an organisation? It became apparent that the old regime in Poland was dishonoured and had been interned in Romania. It was also very obvious that the Allies, especially the French Government,

---

4   Stanisław Maczek, *Od Podwody do Czołga*, Edinburgh, Tomar, 1961, pp.95-100.

5   Joseph Rothschild, *East Central Europe Between the Two World Wars*, Seattle, University of Washington, 1974, pp. 190-2.

6   PISM, (Polish Institute and Sikorski Museum, Kensington, London) KOL 1, Journal of the Activities of the Supreme Commander, KOL 1/2, 28 September 1939.

Maczek with Skibiński, France 1939-40. (Narodowe Archiwum Cyfrowe)

were determined that they wanted their own views represented in the Polish political arena. They saw this as being with General Sikorski, who had been in virtual internal political exile in Poland between 1926 and 1939. He had been an opponent of the inter-war Polish dictator, Marshal Józef Piłsudski, and despite being one of the most able Polish officers, according to British reckoning after the Polish victory against the Soviet Union in 1920, Sikorski was doomed to be cast aside as a military reject in the outdated and outmoded inter-war Polish Army.

Between 1926 and 1939 Sikorski had written a treatise on modern warfare as well as other military works, very much in the mode of western modernisers, Liddell Hart and Charles de Gaulle. His ideas were ignored in Poland but the French recognised his talents and were eager to promote him over what might have been a typically mediocre Polish political appointment. It must nevertheless be noted that the French Government were self-serving in their support for Sikorski, as it would not have made any sense to influence the appointment of somebody who might oppose them.

The French Government really had no plans for Sikorski apart from his being a figurehead and a focal point to whom Poles in exile could gather around, and someone that the French Government could work with.[7] A further problem within Polish politics was that after thirteen years of military dictatorship, which after 1935 saw the Polish Government become quite close to Hitler's Germany, the Polish political opposition which

7   Anita Prazmowska, *Britain and Poland, 1939-1943: The Betrayed Ally*, Cambridge, CUP, 1995, p. 11. Yves Beauvois, *Les Relations Franco-Polonaises Pendant Le 'Drole de Guerre'*, Paris, L'Harmattan, 1989, p. 73.

was considered to be uncompromised politically both at home and abroad were waiting in the wings to take power. Indeed they seemed to represent the majority of politicians who had successfully escaped from Poland to France. The anger against the inter-war regime should not be ignored, because a certain Lieutenant-Colonel Jan Kornaus, having just arrived from Romania, reported to Sikorski that he considered the Polish inter-war Foreign Minister, Colonel Józef Beck, to be a menace to Polish interests and suggested that he should remain interned in Romania.[8] Furthermore the British ambassador to Warsaw, Sir Howard Kennard, reported to the British Foreign Minister, Lord Halifax:

'The Polish collapse and hasty retreat into Rumania have caused great resentment amongst representative Poles. The Marshal (Śmigły-Rydz) and Colonel Beck are especially criticized and it is freely stated that Polish people will not trust their future destiny to their former leaders.'[9]

Sikorski found his political platform owing to his association with the inter-war Polish political opposition while as the most senior Polish soldier to emerge from the wreckage of the Polish defeat he could demand loyalty and obedience from the Polish Army. He also sought to distance himself from the inter-war regime, as in a broadcast to Poland he asserted 'in future we rule out the cult of personality mode of government, irresponsibility and uncontrolled government ... '[10]

From a military point of view all of the above was a great advantage to the Poles as they wanted to be seen as 'Fighting Poland', but it should also be realised that they always overplayed their hand, never really understanding that they were a minor ally even if they considered themselves to be 'First Ally'. Eventually Poland was left behind to be occupied by the Soviet Union while the British and American Governments and peoples considered Poland to be an irritant and irrelevant to the war. However, in October 1939 it was extremely unclear just how the war was going to develop. Poland had been overrun, as predicted, and it seemed that there might be a period of trench warfare in the West, as had been case on the Western Front between 1914 and 1918. This was to prove to be wishful thinking.

Sikorski's immediate task was to reform a Polish fighting force. He must have been overjoyed to have Maczek who, unusually for a Polish military officer, was apolitical and was someone around whom Sikorski could rebuild a military force. There was a problem due to the legacy of political interference in the Polish military and many officers were compromised. A scandal arose in France and later in the United Kingdom when Sikorski interned those officers whom he deemed to be politically unreliable, thus giving rise to accusations that he was imprisoning his political enemies. This was a problem of civil-military relations which the Allies, on the whole, were able to avoid, the French to a lesser extent, nevertheless, many normal relations were suspended during the war.

Sikorski's position at the time was not secure because General Kazimierz Sosnkowski was still missing. He was senior to Sikorski and had fought an admirable campaign in the defence of Poland during September 1939, his leadership credentials thus remaining intact. It should be considered that some Polish commanders who had not fought well were no longer trusted and some who had withdrawn prematurely from Poland were liable to face court martial for desertion. This was the complicated situation that the Poles faced in

8   PISM, PRM, Prime Ministers' Office (Polish), PRM 14B/40, 'Notatka Słuzbowa ppłk. J. Kornaus, Bucharest, 9 March 1940.
9   NA, FO 371/23151C/14615/456, Kennard to Halifax, 22 September 1939.
10   PISM, KOL 1/5, Part 1, 'Do Społeczenstwa do Polsce' 18 December 1939.

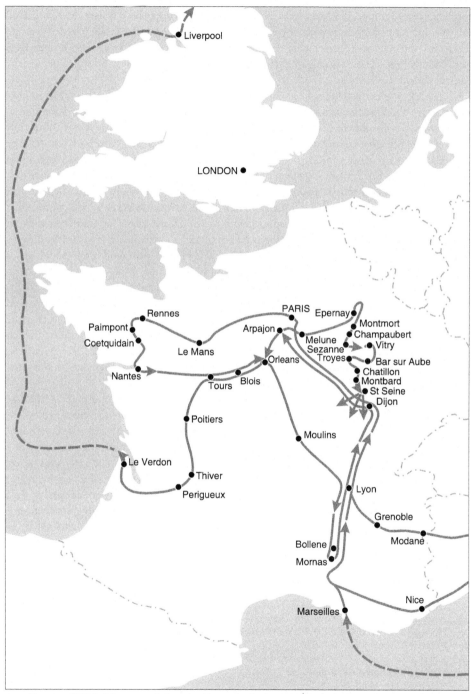

Route of 10th Motorized Cavalry Brigade during the French Campaign, 1940.

October 1939. Furthermore the Allies were not certain how the war would develop. The period from October 1939 to April 1940 became known as the 'Phoney War', a period of very little military action on the front in Western Europe. In other parts of Europe the war continued in earnest, with the Soviet defeat of Finland between November 1939 and March 1940. There was also fighting on the high seas, whilst Poland was raped by the Germans and the Soviets.

Szudek asserts that throughout the winter of 1939 and spring 1940 Sikorski attempted to acquaint the French authorities with the lessons that he had learnt from the September Campaign, but found that the French were not really interested.[11] This is not completely true, as the French commander, General Gamelin, paid attention to reports concerning the combined air-armour methods used to destroy the Polish Army.[12] General Sosnkowski wrote in 1940 of the devastating effect of German airpower between 10 and 25 May 1940.[13] It should be realised that the inter-war Polish military regimes had relegated the Polish Air Force to that of an auxiliary force supporting the Army. However what is not clear is whether the French High Command understood the 'shock effect' of these methods on soldiers who were experiencing war for the first time.[14] Consequently, it is misleading to imply that no improvements came from the French High Command after studying the September Campaign. There was certainly ambiguity, as on 7 June 1940 the American Ambassador to Paris wrote to the American State Department that Gamelin and his 'aristocratic' High Command had drawn no lessons from the German invasion of Poland and that the French treated the Poles with contempt. The French had concluded that the German tactics would not have the same effect on the French Army and therefore French troops received no training regarding the German method of attack. The American ambassador noted that the same methods were employed against the French with the same result. Alexander dismisses this argument.[15]

It should be considered that the French Army *had* studied the German method of attack but had failed to understand its ferocity and speed, with disastrous consequences for both the French and British armies. Furthermore, the arguments regarding the conduct of the French Army in 1940 are still being debated. Martin Alexander asserts that after the evacuation of the British Army and French forces from Dunkirk in the early summer of 1940, the period which many people associate with the surrender of the French Army, for three weeks thereafter the French Army fought harder and endured higher casualty rates, both wounded and dead, than had been the case before Dunkirk. This suggests that once civilian politicians removed themselves from France, the French soldiers fought harder as they approached defeat. Before Dunkirk they were more likely to have surrendered.[16]

Prazmowska raises the point that reality was not a strong feature of the Polish camp

11   P.A. Szudek, 'Sikorski as a Strategist and Military Writer' in Keith Sword (ed) *Sikorski: Soldier and Statesman. A Collection of Essays*, London, Orbis Books, 1990, pp. 75-97.

12   Martin S. Alexander, *The Republic in Danger. General Maurice Gamelin and the Politics of French Defence, 1933-1940*, Cambridge, CUP, 1992, p. 315.

13   PISM, B.7. Sosnkowski, May 1940.

14   Jeffery A. Gunsburg, *Divided and Conquered. The French High Command and the Defeat of the West, 1940*, London, Greenwood, 1979, pp. 92-3.

15   Alexander, op. cit. pp. 344-48.

16   Professor Martin S. Alexander, University of Wales at Aberystwyth, 'The Surrender of France in 1940: Men and Command' Paper given at *Why Fighting Ends: A History of Surrender*, International Conference, Weetwood Hall, University of Leeds, June 25-28 2009.

in France. This assertion is based on the attitude of the Poles in France, who considered that they alone had been chosen to return freedom to Poland and had been entrusted with the spiritual and political leadership of the country.[17] This is reminiscent of the attitude of Piłsudski's Legionnaires and the inter-war Polish Army, who considered that they and nobody else was responsible for Polish independence and the re-establishment of the Polish state. By adopting this stance they were ignoring the reason why they were in France between 1939 and 1940: they were a defeated force and lacked any semblance of military prestige. They were not embarking on a divine mission but were merely engaged in a struggle for the survival of the Polish state.

During that winter the British, located on the French frontier with Belgium, spent their time digging an extension to the French defensive line of fortified forts, the Maginot Line. The British line was known as the 'Gort Line' after the British commander in France, Lord Gort. Like the Maginot Line, the Gort Line played no part in the defence of France in 1940; it was easily bypassed by the invading Germans.[18] Maczek recorded that the French general, Faurey, told him that the Polish armoured brigade at that time (October 1939) was not needed as they, the French, had the Maginot Line.[19] This revealed the defensive nature of French military doctrine at the outbreak of war in 1939. The British were no better; while British soldiers dug defensive trenches, their Secretary of State, Sir Kingsley Wood, expressed outrage over plans for the RAF to bomb private property in Germany.[20] There was very little co-ordinated policy between the French and British governments, something that was not apparent until the German attack on Norway in April 1940.[21] This would go some way to explain why there was no joint attack on Germany. It was as if the two governments wanted to wish away the war until reality caught up with them during the late spring and early summer of 1940, and the attack on the Low Countries and France itself.

The establishment of a Polish fighting force in France was difficult from the very beginning. In January 1940 it was a question of basics, as the Poles complained of the lack of uniforms. However, in April 1940 a far more serious hindrance occurred at a time when the Poles were trying to recruit for their new armed forces – the French Government told the Polish Government that a certain percentage of Poles recruited would be retained by the French to work in French coalmines. Furthermore, Poles living in the coalfields of northern France could not be conscripted, as they were essential for mining coal.[22] Despite this, Sikorski and Maczek had to set to and form a Polish fighting force.

Maczek had been promoted to Brigadier-General on 15 October 1939 and until February 1940 he commanded the Polish garrison at Coëtquidan. After this Maczek was made commander of the (Polish) Light Armoured Brigade at St. Cécile and remained in this post until June 1940 when France fell.

When Maczek arrived at the original Polish military bases in France at Coëtquidan he must have been quite depressed – the men lacked everything, including essentials such as uniforms. Maczek recalled that Poles from all over the world were converging on this

17   Prazmowska, op. cit. p. 11.
18   Charles Whiting, *The Poor Bloody Infantry, 1939-1945*, London, Guild Publishing, 1987, p. 18.
19   Maczek, op. cit. p. 102.
20   Whiting, op. cit. p. 25.
21   *British Foreign Policy in the Second World War* (Volume 1) Sir Llewellyn Woodward (ed) London, HMSO, 1970, p. xxxi. Hereafter referred to as *BFP1*.
22   PISM, PRM 13/2, 20 January 1940; PRM 13/17, 24 April 1940.

Officers of the 10th Motorized Brigade in France 1940. Maczek stands
at centre. At front right is Colonel Kazimierz Dworak, commander
of the 24th Uhlans. (Narodowe Archiwum Cyfrowe)

military base, not only those Poles living in France but also, like Maczek, from Hungary
and Romania as well as other parts of the world.[23] With the agreement of the French
Government Sikorski was permitted to recruit for his ranks but as we have already seen
it soon became clear that there were limits to this recruiting. The under-equipping of the
Poles in France remained throughout this period. Tadeusz Walewicz, a Polish veteran,
made certain observations of the French at the time. After escaping to France via Hungary,
Yugoslavia and Italy, Walewicz was at first sent to the camp at Coëtquidan and then to St.
Cécile, near Avignion, to rejoin his original unit, the 10th Armoured Brigade. He claims
that the French provided them with a few very old tanks for training but when Germany
attacked the Netherlands and Belgium on 10 May 1940, the situation changed dramatically.
Suddenly the French military wanted the 10th Armoured Brigade to join the French forces
that were already fighting. The brigade was not up to strength but still it was moved to
a huge military depot near Paris. The depot contained tanks, guns and ammunition, all
of the material necessary for fighting a campaign. The Poles were given a brief period to
study the equipment and, despite not being familiar with the new French equipment, they
entrained for the front.[24]

Once the German invasion of France was underway, Polish armour was mobilised and
all eyes were focused on Maczek, looking for a lead as to how to deploy the Polish armour
in the face of the German invasion.[25] The Poles were to cover the French withdrawal, which
was fighting along the route from Avise to Moloy near Divon. At Montbard, the final battle

---

23   Maczek, op. cit. p. 101.
24   McGilvray, *Black Devils'*, p. 4.
25   PISM, B. 817, *Historyczny Polskiej Broni Pancernej we Francji, 1939-40 r.*

Maczek and officers of the 10th Motorized Brigade in France, April 1940,
shortly before the German invasion. (Narodowe Archiwum Cyfrowe)

took place. On 17 June 1940 the Brigade, lacking fuel and surrounded by Germans, was ordered to destroy the remainder of its equipment and try to escape in small groups to the unoccupied section of France (Vichy).[26] Maczek adds strength to Walewicz's words, as he also recalled that suddenly in May 1940 the French wanted the Poles to help defend France whilst totally ignoring the Polish situation regarding training and equipment.[27] On 6 June 1940 Maczek estimated that his 10th Armoured Brigade would be ready within the following 7-10 days. The Germans attacked on 9 June 1940 and the Poles were pitched into battle.[28]

It was not only military action and French indifference that caused the Poles fighting in France problems; the chaos of civilian refugees also added to the confusion that was France during the summer of 1940. A Minute in a Cabinet meeting of the Polish Government-in-Exile discussed the fact that there had been plans to unify Polish armour and anti-tank units around the Paris area but enemy propaganda was panicking the civilian populace, spilling them onto the roads as they clamoured to flee the advancing enemy and clogging up any routes that the military might try to use as they manoeuvred against the enemy.[29]

Even if the French Government and Military did not take the lessons of the September Campaign too seriously, the Poles did, and looked at other aspects of the fighting, such as the diversions created by the Germans and ethnic Germans living in Poland which caused

26   McGilvray, *Black Devils'*, p. 4. See also Witold Bieganski, *Wojsko Polskie we Francji 1939-1940*, Warsaw, MON, 1967, pp. 213, 302.
27   Maczek, op. cit. p. 103.
28   PISM, B, Individual Accounts of the French Campaign, 1940, B.3103, General Maczek, 6 June 1940.
29   *Protokoły z Posiedzeń Rady Ministrów Polskiej*, Vol. 1. October 1939-June 1940, IPMS, PRM-K.102/25, K.1.9, 28 May 1940, Kraków, Secesja, 1994, p. 309.

General Maczek talking to Poles and French guests at a
dinner, April 1940. (Narodowe Archiwum Cyfrowe)

chaos behind Polish lines in 1939.[30] This was a lesson that was not learnt, as the Germans
easily infiltrated Allied lines in 1940 while during the winter of 1944-45 German special
forces infiltrated American lines in the Ardennes and for nearly two weeks caused chaos
and dismay while nearly breaking the Allied advantages gained since June 1944. It should
be noted that this Polish document was distributed within the Polish-French Military
Mission – whether the French High Command actually read it is quite another matter!

The question of a large German minority co-operating with the advancing German
Army was one that the British and French missions during the summer of 1939 had missed
and probably one that the Poles had not considered, but their treachery was significant. It
was the beginning of the so-called 'fifth columns' which did cause panic during 1940 but
had been widely ignored, except in Poland during 1939. It would seem that apart from the
Poles only the Germans learnt any lessons from the September Campaign. This campaign
had taken longer than anticipated and had caused the Germans more casualties than they
had expected, therefore they hit France faster and harder than when they had invaded
Poland.[31]

A further problem for the Poles was the French attitude towards them. Even if the
Polish Army was under French command it was a step too far when the French military
tried to surrender the Poles alongside themselves. Sikorski was furious and refused to agree

---

30   PISM, A. XII.24/98, *Biuletyn Nr. 3 'O Sposobach Działania Wojsk Niemieckich w Wojnie Polsko-
Niemickiej. Dywersja i Desanty'* Colonel Kędzior, Paris 29 January 1940.

31   Tim Ripley, *The Wehrmacht. The German Army in World War II, 1939-1945*, London, Fitzroy Dearborn,
2003, p. 99.

with the French plan. In a bitter row with French commanders he decried the 'paralyzed defeatism at the top of France's military and political commands'.[32] An added problem was that Sikorski had put too much faith into the French Government and military leadership, who he had considered to be his friends, and so it was a great shock to discover that he was nothing to them but a minor ally; possibly an asset, but mostly a bargaining chip when the French authorities were trying to save their own skins.

Maczek records that some training and courses were provided for the Poles by the French, but nothing serious. All of the equipment was obsolete, and only enough to equip four tank battalions.[33] It was quite clear that the French military had reservations about the Poles and refused to take them seriously. Equally the French may have been suspicious of a ragbag army that had previously been quite close to Germany and then had been defeated by Germany (and the Soviet Union). This criticism would have been unfair, but so is life, and the Poles were a remnant of a defeated army and not the saviours of Western Europe.

In May 1940 the German offensive in the West attacked the French front simultaneously from the north while German Panzer divisions led from the Somme and smashed their way up from the south via Avignon. The speed of the German advance created chaos as it was obvious that the French were unprepared for it, and this left the Poles out on a limb, as the French military authorities took no notice of the Polish situation. What concerned Maczek and other Polish commanders was how the Poles were being deployed across the front, which was in small penny packets. This was something that Maczek did not agree with and he sought the support of Sikorski to prevent it from happening, as it was obvious that the French were quite willing to sacrifice the Poles despite under-equipping them and not training them properly for over six months.

The Poles were not unsympathetic towards the French in their hours of anguish as they sought to deploy every unit available against the German advance but what concerned the Polish commanders was the waste of men and material, which they considered should be used more profitably. However, Sikorski had overestimated his influence amongst the French authorities and even though he beseeched, unrealistically, a postponement of several weeks so that the Polish armoured brigade might be ready to face the Germans, the French commander, Marshal Petain, insisted that the Poles take to the field and help defend France against the German attacks.

Reality was beginning to break through into the Polish camp when, despite all of the Polish misgivings about their deployment and their requirement for extra training, it was finally apparent that nothing could be realistically done to save France. It was finally realised that all plans were futile and that the Germans were dictating the tempo of the fighting, with the French and the allies were reduced to improvised warfare.

After reporting to General Huntziger, commander of the Fourth Army Group, and to General Requin, commander of French 4th Army, fighting near Reims, Maczek received his first battle orders of the campaign. His task was one that was really suited to a large motorized-armoured group – the Poles were to cover the flanks of the French 4th Army and that of the defences on the route towards Paris, which meant paying particular attention to the huge gaps between the two formations. This was an incredible task. The Poles found themselves between the left flank of one of General Requin's divisions, 20th Infantry

32   Stanisław Mikołajczyk, *The Rape of Poland: Patterns of Soviet Aggression*, Westport, Connecticut, Greenwood, 1973, Second Greenwood Reprint, p. 7.
33   Maczek, op. cit. p. 103.

Division and, somewhere out beyond the Poles, 59th Infantry Division. Somewhere on the right flank there was supposed to be another French Army. The Poles twice made contract with the staff of the 59th Division but it seemed that its units existed mostly in the imagination of the French staff. Every time the Poles tried to establish contact with the division in their given positions they encountered Germans. This meant that the Poles were unable to execute their orders, which were to connect the separated flanks of the two armies and plug the gaps between them. The operational goal of protecting the flanks of the army, which was already overstretched, especially to the rear, and along its communication lines, was unachievable, as the Germans were making deep inroads into the French positions from the west. Eventually the Poles realised that they could only make a single practical move, by guarding the flanks and the rear of the 20th Infantry Division, and this is what they did.

In a crucial moment during 20th Infantry Division's withdrawal from the marshlands of St. Gond, the Poles were able to prevent the division being cut off by German advance units striking at Champaubert-Montigivroux. The battle was short and was confined to an action between Polish and German armour, with two squadrons of tanks under the command of Lieutenant-Colonel Zgorzelski acting as a guard from the north. The biggest shock was attacks by Stuka dive-bombers, who twice returned and bombed the length of two Polish tank battalions, the Polish anti-aircraft platoon as well as the Polish staff, who had been travelling in two cars. The Polish anti-aircraft shot down one of the Stukas and then continued to obstinately defend against the German dive-bombers.

The first Stuka attack caught Maczek unawares inasmuch as cars, armour, the anti-tank battery and anti-aircraft battery were assembled in a lightly wooded area which provided little, if any, cover from aerial observation or attack by aircraft. The Poles moved to the French infantry lines, which were already crowded. Their arrival only made the situation worse, as the positions in the woods became more confused, with equipment becoming blocked in and passage for vehicles towards the forest becoming increasingly difficult.

The Polish tanks acting as a group could intimidate the enemy, while the crews were safe enough from shrapnel bursts, although they still needed to find a safe harbour from serious attacks from heavier weapons such as the Stukas, acting in their tank busting role. One of the German assaults had landed a direct hit on one of the trucks supplying the anti-tank guns; the truck went up like a torch with strong reports from the exploding ammunition. The German dive-bombers continued to attack for about an hour before they finally ceased.

The effect of the Stuka attacks was stupefying. The attacks seemed so accurate and precise; the effect of the airplanes in their nosedives, dropping vertically with screaming sirens fitted to them made the attacks seem almost personal – Polish troops reported that it felt that they came towards each individual and nobody else.

This short battle had the effect of slowing the activities of nearby German armour, as was discovered by reconnaissance units from 20th Infantry Division, who, over a twenty-four hour period, took on the dangerous task of searching the area to the south from the marshes around St. Gond. It was thanks to the reconnaissance work by 20th Infantry Division that the Poles were later to find themselves in the unoccupied partition of France, away from the Germans, and eventually many from the Polish division were able to escape from Europe and make their way back to the United Kingdom and resume their fight against Germany.

The situation was rapidly changing for Maczek and the Poles; they were still charged with the operation task of protecting the rear of the French 4th Army but the Poles were also beginning to consider how they were going to leave France, as it was blatantly obvious that the war on mainland Europe seemed lost. It was difficult to decide what to do but the presence of large advanced German motorized-armoured units made it quite obvious to the Poles that the present offensive was coming to an end, if not over already.

There was plenty of evidence of the presence of the Germans as 20th Division were coming into contact with German reconnaissance patrols, mainly to the south, as they reached ever deeper into southern France. Routes for evacuation were not only compromised by the presence of these German patrols but the routes were also blocked with military equipment and by civilian refugees fleeing the fighting and the impending German occupation. Maczek tried his best in this very trying situation and was determined that he and his men would not accept their fate in the same resigned way that the masses of refugees appeared to have done so.

Maczek and his staff, via the French communications officers with Colonel Duchon, searched for contact with French commanders to request orders and co-operation. Through Colonel Duchon the Poles received orders to concentrate their brigade on the River Seine. Throughout the following twenty-four hours the Poles received communications from the commander of XXIII Corps. Afterwards the Polish Brigade settled with 2nd Infantry Division along a passage via the Seine towards the west. At Bar-sur-Seine an intact bridge had been discovered. The bridge had been bombed by the Germans but they had failed to destroy it and so on 15 June 1940 the Poles crossed using it and headed towards a forested area, hoping it might mask their moves.

There were French commanders who were still willing to make a stand against the seemingly unstoppable German advance. The commander of 42nd Infantry Division had an idea to punch a way to the River Loire and make a stand there but Maczek dismissed this as some flight of fancy. Even so, Maczek was happy to see that there were at last some attempts by the French to resist the Germans and that a large-scale counterattack was being contemplated. Then, the news of the loss of Paris reached the Poles and the French.

Despite this news, Maczek did not consider that the war was over. There was still a lot of unoccupied country left as one headed westward towards the Pyrenees and towards neutral Spain, while overseas France had its empire. Many considered that the French would be able to continue the war from their colonies. The commander of the French 42nd Infantry Division set out happily and was content that the Poles were willing to co-operate with him. They sought to turn the situation around after co-ordinating with Corps, seeking detailed instructions, directions and orders.

The Poles moved into the Chaource Forest with one aim – to keep their tanks and vehicles fuelled, but the problem was that the Polish brigade no longer had access to its supply column. Fuel was irregularly received from the nearest depot (the German tanks ran on petrol and simply helped themselves from French petrol stations) however with the Germans advancing this system had broken down, with the result being that the Polish fuel supplies were virtually finished. Maczek noted that by the second half of June 1940 every source of supply was either in German hands, had been bombed by the Germans or destroyed by the French as they retreated. Vehicles sent out by Maczek to obtain fuel came back empty or, more often than not, failed to return; officers and NCOs sent out to look for fuel either returned empty-handed or failed to return.

Orders came from Corps to the Polish Brigade – they were told to operate as an advance guard, and were to move to Montbard on the Burgundy Canal, where they would be assured passage to the West. However the Poles also had to take a reality check and look at the task before them. They estimated that they had 60 kilometres to march with a predicted series of short fights ahead, with a minimal amount of fuel in reserve; this assessment actually left the Poles with a sense of optimism as they realised that they could, after reviewing the fuel situation, take a number of tanks and vehicles with them. Colonel Duchon argued against this but fuel was taken from various vehicles, enough for what was required and those remaining tanks and vehicles, surplus to requirement, were destroyed. In the same manner every drop of fuel was either used or destroyed – nothing fell into the hands of the enemy.

The Polish Brigade moved westward, by now essentially a strong reinforced tank company with two motorized cavalry squadrons, combat engineers, plus anti-tank and anti-aircraft units attached. It thrust out towards the left, forcing its way, with great effort, towards the Burgundy Canal. There was no attempt at reconnaissance after two platoons of motorcyclists were sent out and not seen again. The presence of German patrols seeking fuel and supplies made any further attempt by the Poles to send out reconnaissance patrols absurd.

Already at a distance from Montbard French vehicles, military and civilian, were returning repeatedly in panic away from the direction of the advancing German motorized units that were already in Montbard, complete with artillery. The withdrawing French artillery battery was under the command of Captain Jean Borotra, the famous tennis ace and later lesser-known minister in Petain's government, who gave Maczek useful and accurate information regarding the situation before them. Borotra was later arrested by the Gestapo and incarcerated in a concentration camp, but survived the war and lived to the ripe old age of 95, dying in July 1994.

Borotra's information seems to have allowed Maczek to form a plan to seize Montbard. By now the Poles were a small band of brave men facing a numerically-superior enemy. The Poles were devoid of field artillery and it was conventional wisdom that tanks could not attack at night and could not operate in forests or in urban areas. But Maczek saw this differently – for one thing he and his comrades had nothing to lose, and remembering Warsaw the Poles had a score to settle with the Germans. Maczek decided to attack the town at night with violence and impetus, linking the motorized squadrons and using the element of surprise that the Poles possessed, and hoping that the town would fall to them. This is an example of Maczek at his best: unconventional tactics, perhaps learning something from the Germans, perhaps in today's parlance 'shock and awe', but doing what was totally unexpected especially from the German point of view. Plus, most importantly, Maczek was able to convince and inspire his men that not all was lost and that there was always hope.

Maczek recalled, years later, that he did not really know from where the words came from but he thanked God that on the road before Montbard they did come, and so, with the last of the fuel and the final chance of battle, God willing, they prepared to fight and move westward.

As Maczek had hoped for, an armoured assault on Montbard totally surprised the Germans. The Polish armour swiftly rushed the road with no casualties and pushed to the first buildings of the town and began to link up with under the energetic command of Majors Zgorzelski and Eysmont, supported by Lieutenants Niepokojczyski and Kamil

Czarnecki.

The Poles traversed the twisting road up close to a captured German 8.8cm artillery piece, now ablaze. Lieutenant-Colonel Majewski with his Adjutant, Captain Stefanowicz, Maczek's Chief of Staff Lieutenant-Colonel Skibiński and Captain Stankiewicz, took part in the fighting. The battle was fierce with tanks, artillery and hand grenades all adding to the roar of battle; Maczek recalled a 'parasol of bullets and shells', but the Polish attack was so fierce and unexpected that the Germans were disorientated and swiftly the Poles were able to push them back. The tactics of shock and awe were to become a trademark of Maczek and his men.

The Poles pushed deeper into the town, taking prisoners as they went and continuously fighting. Then came reports about the capture of an undamaged bridge on the canal – the canal still remained in German hands. Then followed the most desperate news from the Polish communications officer via corps headquarters – the French division was not coming to the Polish position but had changed their direction southwards towards Dijon.

Presently there was a sound of a detonation. It was the Germans blowing up the bridge over the Burgundy Canal, a measure taken to prevent the bridge falling into Polish hands. Maczek considered that the German fear was a great compliment to the Poles as it reflected that the enemy considered that the Poles were attacking in great numbers as a result of their fierce attack, rather than being aware of the much smaller numbers really involved in the Polish assault. As Maczek said, it was a great satisfaction that the Germans were moved to take such action owing to the actions of his men.

It soon transpired that the Germans had failed to destroy the bridge and fierce fighting broke out once more in the area of it. This caused a further problem, as it seemed to rule out any chance of the Poles escaping to the west via the Burgundy Canal, given the disproportionate difference in the German and Polish strengths. It was 2 o'clock in the morning and as it was June – Maczek thanked heaven that nights at that time of the year are short.

Maczek began to reconsider his options, as he was still determined to get his men and himself out of France and to the UK in order to continue the fight. He wondered just how the canal was to be forced given that the Poles lacked the necessary equipment to do so, especially artillery. He felt that there was a chance of a feint by moving south in the hopes of outstripping the Germans in order to cross the canal and then heading west. It was lucky that there was thick fog that morning, veiling the Polish withdrawal from Montbard to the forest, which included the evacuation of the wounded led by Major Ejsymont. In the forest the Poles reorganised themselves as they prepared a small vanguard for future operations.

The situation in the region was changing rapidly to the advantage of the Germans. The Poles sought a route out but every exit in the canal valley was already in German hands and so the Poles began to look at Dijon as they desperately continued to find an exit from the area. Meanwhile the remnants of the Polish brigade had to abandon vehicles as one by one they began to run out of fuel.

Sadly for the Poles it was realised that Dijon was occupied by the Germans, with the route into the town already being chocked with German tanks and vehicles. From the north, however, the number of German units advancing southwards were already on the wane and it was noticed by Maczek's men that there were some areas devoid of the enemy, and thus that these areas offered a chance to escape.

Maczek's group now consisted of around 500 men carrying their personal arms. Tanks, vehicles, anti-tank and anti-aircraft guns were already useless owing to a lack of ammunition and fuel. A further problem was what to do with their wounded, especially as there had been a further attack by the Germans, although thanks to the swift actions and calm mind of Captain Neklaws there were no further casualties. A few prisoners were even taken, and then the Poles headed towards unoccupied France.

The final decision to order the destruction of equipment was difficult but necessary and in keeping with good practise in order to prevent it being of any use to the enemy. The night of 17/18 June 1940 was spent destroying equipment and then in the morning, 18 June 1940, Maczek and his men set out on foot to march into unoccupied France. Despite their setbacks since September 1939 Maczek noted that he and his men were in good spirits when they set out for God knows what in unoccupied France. There were still problems ahead, such as how to feed and water 500 men, and it was obvious that they would have to go across country to avoid the enemy as a large number of Polish soldiers moving along main roads would of course attract the attention of the enemy, and so, armed with a single Michelin map of France and protected by a statuette of Our Lady of Lourdes which Maczek's wife had once given to him, Macek and his men set out.

On the march, travelling with Maczek, were Lieutenant-Colonel Skibiński, Captain Stankiewicz, a French military officer, Lieutenant Bonvalet and Maczek's driver, Lance Sergeant Kopchański.

The Poles crept through the forest while from the main road, the 'Route Nationale' from Dijon, there were sounds of vehicles, although the Poles could not decide if there was German armour amongst these noises. The road which the Germans were travelling along crossed the proposed Polish route and so the Poles had to think how they were going to get across it. Even though there were occasional breaks in the German convoys which might have given the Poles a slim chance to dash across the road it was risky, therefore they waited until dusk before attempting such a venture.

German vehicles stopped close to the Poles who listened to the German voices, making quite clear just how unlucky the Poles were. Once again the Poles had to bide their time. As summer nights were short it became obvious that the Poles had to do something soon as the present situation could not continue for much longer. Amazingly the Poles finally just ran across the road and hoped that the German confusion would aid them in getting away.

Maczek had cleared the road and had landed in a thicket with an entanglement of branches and brushwood. This did not give him much distance from the road but he swiftly realised that he was alone. Maczek remembered that he had been in a similar situation during the Polish-Soviet War, twenty years earlier, while fighting Budyonny.

It was a long march, probably three hours in the direction which Maczek considered to be correct, but he was constantly alone. Maczek's major concern was that he would lose his way but during the following night he was at first reunited with Ludwik Stankiewicz and then the rest of his group. Once more they began their march. A routine was established, days were spent in the forests while open spaces and urban areas were traversed by night. The soldiers found the march reasonably easy but were handicapped by the fact that they did not have a relief map of the area, being limited by their Michelin tourist map, but even so they persevered. The Poles continued onwards, moving ever closer towards the unoccupied zone. The days were warm and dull. The Germans, who were on a constant lookout for escaping Allied soldiers, had to be avoided. After eighteen days of wandering the Poles found themselves in Clermont-Ferrand in unoccupied France. Once there straight from his march Maczek reported to the French military authorities, but as was the case in Hungary it was certain that the French, under German pressure, would intern the Poles, so they decided that they needed to endeavour for a little longer and try to reach Britain alone.

There were various ways of getting Poles out of unoccupied France and so on 14 July 1940, the French National Holiday, Maczek in disguise, wearing civilian clothing, and with others went to Marseilles looking for a way to Britain, freedom and a chance to continue to fight. It looked as if every way had been closed to Maczek as the British had already completed a naval evacuation of Polish personnel from the occupied zone in the north – Maczek had literally missed that particular boat. Therefore it became necessary for Maczek to leave France illegally. To this end the Polish Consulate in Toulouse had to issue passports and visas. Whilst Spain was becoming quite impossible as a destination, there were other possibilities, such as the exotic locations of Latin America, the Congo or China.

At this time Marseilles was a colourful location, with many French soldiers who had escaped from the occupied north. There were also many Poles from 1st and 2nd divisions under the commands of Generals Duch and Prugar-Keling respectively, as well as other Polish units including elements of the 10th Motorized Cavalry Brigade. Maczek left France under a false name, as the Germans were looking for him. He was able to leave for Algeria on a ship which was taking demobilised Arabs from the French Army to Oran. From Algeria Maczek was able to cross into French Morocco. All of the time Maczek kept missing ships that had evacuated French personnel to Britain. He did receive news of his family, which made him reluctant to leave for Britain, but he knew where he believed his duty lay and so continued to head for the UK.

After a few weeks Maczek was able to get a berth on a ship heading for Lisbon in neutral Portugal. From there, thanks to the intervention and diplomatic skills of his friend Colonel Mally, the Polish military attaché in Lisbon and a veteran of the 1920 Polish-Soviet War, Maczek flew from Lisbon to London. Maczek landed in Bristol on 21 September 1940. A new life was about to begin for him. Later, in Britain, when soldiers discussed the escape of Maczek and his men it was asserted that their service set a very important principle for other Poles to follow.[34]

---

34   Maczek, op. cit. pp. 110-126.

8

1940: Into Britain

Maczek arrived in Britain in September 1940. This was an important month because as he was endeavouring to escape to Britain so that he could continue his war against Germany, with the hope of eventually returning to his native Poland, Britain had also been engaged in its own bitter life and death battle, the Battle of Britain, which had followed hard on the heels of the Battle for France.

The Battle of Britain, was fought between 10 July and 31 October 1940. The climax of the battle was reached on 15 September 1940, when the Germans lost 56 aircraft. Maczek arrived in the UK six days later. The British victory in the Battle of Britain only became apparent at the end of October 1940. The German failure meant that Germany was forced to postpone its plans to invade Britain, for at least the time being. As we now know it was actually abandonment, as Germany invaded the Soviet Union instead during June 1941. The German invasion of the Soviet Union was to be the eventual undoing of Hitler's plans to dominate Europe and Eurasia. Therefore the Battle of Britain should be seen as the first step towards the eventual defeat of Nazi plans to impose its terrible form of genocidal imperial rule on the world.

Nevertheless, when Maczek arrived in the UK it was a time of invasion fever, as the British people were uncertain of what actually lay ahead – to date the war had been nothing but a series of defeats and withdrawals. However, since the British defeat and withdrawal from France during May and June 1940 the British had acquired another government led Winston Churchill, a man who seemed to represent a different attitude to that of Neville Chamberlain.

With the war entering into a different phase, Churchill was a great war leader but he was no fool, and despite his rhetoric he was very aware that the Germans could land at any time. To this end he sought allies and in 1940 one of the most important were the Poles who had arrived in the UK in relatively large numbers, albeit with a reputation of being politically and militarily unreliable. An example of this was during November 1940 when Churchill and the Polish leader, Sikorski, exchanged letters regarding plans that Sikorski might take command of Polish troops, who were then stationed in Scotland, in the event of an invasion.[1] This illustrates the differences between Poland and Britain and their understanding of civil-military relations. The British understood that the military should be under the control of democratically elected civilian politicians who took advice from their Chiefs of Staff, whilst officers led their troops into battle. The Polish idea was more complicated as civilians were kept away from the military, servicemen considering that that civilian politicians knew nothing of soldiering and therefore had no right to interfere in such matters. Furthermore, with some justification, civilian politicians were not trusted by Poles – the Polish Army was the most trusted national institution.

The image of Sikorski, who held the offices of Polish Prime Minister and Minister for

---

1   PISM, A.XII (Papers of [Polish] Supreme GHQ) A.XII.1/52a-c, Churchill to Sikorski, 4 November 1940; Sikorski to Churchill, 21 November 1940.

War, leading his troops into battle, was a somewhat romantic one, and one which caused the Western Allies to distrust the Poles as romantic fools. Yet Churchill was being somewhat hypocritical in his attitude as he had every intention of fighting the Germans himself if they were to land and advance as far as London whilst in 1944 he had to be blackmailed into not landing with Allied forces in Normandy on 6 June 1944, D-Day.[2] The arrival of Churchill at No. 10 Downing Street as British Prime Minister must have been like a breath of fresh air when, during August 1940, he proclaimed in the House of Commons that the war would be waged until victory.[3]

This was the sort of talk to impress the Poles, even though they were not his target audience. A more pressing problem for Sikorski was that he wanted to expand the nucleus of his forces which were arriving in the UK from overseas. Most of the Poles, quite naturally, wanted to return to Poland in triumph and to their restored frontiers, but there was a problem with their main ally Britain, who refused to declare war on the Soviet Union. The British guarantee to Poland only defended Poland against German aggression and not against Soviet aggression and therefore was unwilling to take Poland's side in the undeclared war between Poland and the Soviet Union. This meant that Poles realised that war against the Soviet Union would have to come somehow, or at least the Nazi-Soviet pact would have to be broken; in either case a Polish Army in exile would have to be raised in order to return Poland to the Poles – one cannot talk of the restoration of Polish democracy as there had not been any to restore; that rare Polish beast had been extinct since 1926.

When he tried to recruit Poles from the Americas to 'liberate' Poland Sikorski was dismayed to discover that very few were interested in the plight of Poland or the Poles.[4] A grievous loss to Sikorski and to the Polish Army was that of the 2nd Polish Division, who had suffered 500 dead and wounded during the fighting in France, whilst 12,000 men had made their way to internment in Switzerland.[5] The question of manpower was one of the most frustrating problems for the Polish leadership and for commanders such as Maczek as they constantly tried to ensure that their numbers were adequate in order to ensure that they would be able to return home. Darker forces would prevail to ensure that this would not happen, with Maczek having to wait for nearly fifty years to see Poland regain its independence after 1989.

A clue to the thinking behind the re-establishment of the Polish Army can be found in the 'Program of Ideology for the Upbringing of the Polish Army on Imperial British Territory' as laid out by Dr. I. Modelski, who also happened to be a Brigadier-General in the Polish Army; the document is dated 14 October 1940.

1. The Polish Army was to represent the country as national heroes.
2. The Polish Army should be a symbol of the honour of every soldier and citizen.
3. The Polish Army is a Christian army.
4. The Polish Army fights for world freedom and democracy.

2   Roy Jenkins, *Churchill*, London, Macmillan, 2001, pp. 744-5.
3   *Dziennik Polski* (London) *'Wojna aż do Zwycięstwa'* 21 August 1940.
4   PISM, A.XII.1/1, Charles Bridge No.4. British Mission to Sikorski, 14 October 1940. Bridge noted that 17% of the US Army was of Polish background while if one measured the number of Poles living in the USA the relative number of Poles should have only have been 3%. The world famous Polish pianist, Ignacy Paderewski, used the same figure in a letter to the American President, Franklin Delano Roosevelt, in a letter dated 30 November 1940, ibid.
5   PISM, A.XII.1/52a-c, Sikorski to Churchill, letter dated 20 December 1940.

5. The Polish Army is a cadre army for a future Polish Army – Every soldier is a future commander and worth its weight in gold for the nation.

6. The Polish Army presents itself as traditional knights as in the case of the Legions, the experiences of 1920, the September 1939 Campaign, the campaigns of 1940 (Norway [the Podhalian Brigade] France [1st and 2nd Divisions – General Maczek] and the Battle of Britain).

There is a footnote which claims that the allegations of anti-Semitism in the Polish Army were planted by fifth columnists to stifle Anglo-Polish co-operation.[6]

A few comments are necessary as Modelski's programme highlights most of the problems of the Polish Army since 1918 while revealing that it had learnt nothing since that date. The symbolic nature of the Polish Army had always been its main problem, as it had caused it to be backward looking while brooking no discussion of its activities. It is a matter of opinion that the Polish Army fought for world freedom and democracy given that Poland was not a democracy. What did the Polish Army understand by world freedom given that it was an extremely exclusive organisation? Point 3 stated that the Polish Army was a 'Christian Army' therefore totally denying the role of the Jews in Poland; furthermore Christianity in Poland usually meant, and still means, Catholicism and not Orthodox Christianity or Protestantism, which were both found in the Polish Second Republic but routinely discriminated against. Point 6 once more harked back to the past – military failure looms large but is illustrative about the attitude of the wartime Polish Army, focusing on heroic failures. The link to the Battle of Britain is somewhat tenuous as even thought Polish pilots fought in the latter stages of the campaign, many other nationalities fought in it from beginning to end; quite simply, it was largely a British victory.

The most important point is number 5: that the Polish Army is a cadre army for a future Polish Army. The experience that Polish troops were to gain by serving alongside Western Allies would have been of great value if Poland had not been overrun by the Soviet Union but it was not to be and eventually the experience of the Polish troops was lost as they settled down to exile while most senior officers began to fight the futile battles of exile and powerlessness.

In his monograph on Maczek Szudek makes the point that when he arrived in the UK during September 1940 he was the most experienced 'commander of armour' to be found in Britain at that time.[7] This would appear to be true, as whilst fighting in France the Allies had not deployed armour in large formations, despite writings during the inter-war period by military tacticians that argued the case for the above; it was only the Germans who had seen fit to use their armour in large formations. In the West it was only Maczek who had any idea of the deployment of massed armoured units, even if he had been denied the opportunity and material to do so.

By September 1940 the British were not only fighting for their very survival, they also lacked equipment as much had been left in France, either destroyed or captured. Regarding armour Britain was in a desperate state with a lack of tanks and of tank commanders with

---

6   PISM, A.XII. 3/3.

7   Przemyslaw A. Szudek, 'The First Polish Armoured Division in the Second World War' in *Themes of Modern Polish History Proceedings of a Symposium on 28 March 1992 In Honour of the Centenary of General Stanisław Maczek*, Peter D. Stachura (ed), Glasgow, The Polish Social & Educational Society, 1992, pp. 35-59.

battle experience.[8]

Maczek was to remain frustrated in the UK for the next 18 months or so regarding any ambition that he might have entertained in commanding a renewed Polish armoured formation. The French Campaign had left the severely weakened Polish Army with a puny armoured brigade which had no tanks at all. This weakened and tank-less brigade was sent to Scotland to defend the Scottish coast from Montrose to Dundee with its HQ in Forfar. And there they stayed for most of 1941.[9]

However this air of frustrated respectability could not be said to be happening in other parts of exiled Polish circles. Here, the Polish Army when not kept busy, reverted to its favourite plaything: politics. To this end a military coup occurred in London during July 1940 when the Polish President-in-Exile, Władysław Raczkiewicz, dismissed Sikorski as Prime Minister. Raczkiewicz considered that Sikorski as Prime Minister and Commander-in-Chief of Polish Armed Forces had too much power and was determined to reduce it by splitting the two offices. There was a further reason: Raczkiewicz had been a supported of the post-1935 Polish military regime and had served as a minor minister in that regime; Sikorski had been an enemy of the regime.

Raczkiewicz appointed August Zalewski, who had been closely associated with the former military regime, as Prime Minister. However during the evening of 18 July 1940 while Zalewski was trying to form a Cabinet, the Chief-of-Staff, Colonel Klimecki and two other senior officers arrived unannounced at the Polish Embassy in Portland Place, London. Klimecki told Zalewski to renounce the premiership and threatened to resort to 'any means' including the 'most drastic'. As they spoke more armed officers arrived at the embassy.[10]

This is a classical example of military intervention in domestic politics and typical of the Polish inter-war military regime. It did nothing to enhance the Polish Government-in-Exile's reputation as the democratic successor to the inter-war regime. Zalewski decided against forming a government but was to remain influential in the politics of the Polish exiled government for the remainder of the war and until his death in 1972.

The British Government was perfectly aware of the situation which had unfolded at the Polish Embassy and was remarkably calm about the entire episode. Savery, in a note to Frank Roberts at the Foreign Office, complained about the 'Mexican behaviour of certain high Polish officers' but nothing else. The Polish crisis passed and Sikorski was back in office within 24 hours of being dismissed. Indeed within two days Roberts noted 'Savery rang, crisis over'.[11]

This is not to suggest that the British Government or the Foreign Office (FO) did not understand what was at stake within the exiled Polish administration. Weekly Foreign Office political intelligence summaries reveal that the British authorities were aware of the power struggle between Raczkiewicz and Sikorski. The FO concluded that it was most important that Sikorski won this struggle, as he commanded Poland's most important

8   Ibid. See also J. Lee Ready, *Forgotten Allies. The Military Contribution of the Colonies, Exiled Governments and Lesser Powers to the Allied Victory in World War II. The European Theater*, (Jefferson, North Carolina, McFarland, 1985, p. 17.
9   Szudek, op. cit.
10 PISM, PRM 37c/10, 18 July 1940.
11 NA, FO 371 24474/C8090/252/55, 30 July 1940.

asset: the Polish Army.[12]

The fact that Sikorski's supporters seized power on his behalf points towards power and not legitimacy but it also proved that Sikorski had the corporate support of the Polish Army, even if he was not a popular general, while civilian politicians did not have any real support from within exiled circles, which were dominated by the Polish military. Sikorski, who was a political nobody and an obscure general in 1939 had, by 1943, gained such kudos amongst the Allies that Churchill was to remark to Stalin, who was trying to remove Sikorski, 'if he (Sikorski) should go, we should only get somebody worse'.[13] Churchill's remark revealed that there was a genuine shortage of political and military talent amongst the exiled Poles, even in 1943. This was due to the political immaturity experienced in Poland owing to military rule there between 1926 and 1939 which did not allow political or military talent to develop, as only those loyal to Piłsudski could flourish and hold positions of power. This legacy could not be shaken off within 12 months. Therefore it made political sense to Polish officers to end any suggestion of weak, civilian government as they would have interpreted the situation with the use of armed force. The fact that they were in exile and abusing another's hospitality was of little consequence to the officers concerned.

The British ignored the Polish actions at Portland Place because quite simply politics of such a shallow nature were of little importance when Britain was facing a German invasion and when it was primarily concerned with how many troops could be put into the field to face any such enemy landings; the Poles represented the largest contingent of foreign troops, not including those from the Commonwealth or Empire. On 25 July 1940 there were 14,000 Polish troops available to Britain.[14] However there was a legacy of distrust, because even if Churchill was willing to stand alongside Sikorski in their individual hours of need it should be noted that the British Foreign Secretary, Lord Halifax and the Minister of War, Anthony Eden, did not trust Sikorski at all.[15] They both considered Sikorski to be a 'Pilsudski-ite' and therefore not a democrat. Furthermore they seriously debated whether he could be trusted to obey British orders in the event of Polish troops being deployed against a German invasion of Britain. Eventually Victor Cazalet, a Conservative Member of Parliament and British Liaison Officer to Sikorski, was entrusted to make Sikorski aware, without causing any offence, that he was to obey British orders in such a situation. Cazalet was successful in his mission but was left wondering what promises Churchill may have made to Sikorski 'for the present or for after the war'.[16]

Regarding the Polish troops in Scotland there was a problem – morale. By July 1940 the Polish Army had been defeated twice and had been ejected from the European mainland. It had been decimated and forced to seek refuge in Britain. The question of morale was not only one of politics but also of physical conditions as the men were living in tents in Scotland; Sikorski was urged by Generals Paszkiewicz and Kukiel, both Sikorski loyalists, to go to Scotland to visit his men and try to restore morale.[17] However he refused to go as

12　*Great Britain. Foreign Office Weekly Intelligence Summaries* (Hereafter *FOWPIS*) Introduction, Clifton Child, Millwood, Kraus, 1983, *FOWPIS*, Vol. 2, July-December 1940, Nos. 39-64, no. 42, 23 July 1940, pp. 4-5.

13　NA, CAB 66 War Cabinet Memoranda, CAB 66/36 WP (43) 175, 26 April 1943.

14　Martin Gilbert, *Winston S. Churchill, Vol. VI, Finest Hour, 1939-41*, London, Heinemann, 1983, p. 678.

15　NA, FO 800 Halifax Papers, FO 800/321 HXXVI/32, Eden to Halifax, 9 October 1940.

16　NA, FO 800/321 HXXVII/33, Halifax to Eden, 11 October 1940; FO 800/321 HXXVII35, Cazalet to Halifax, 24 October 1940.

17　PISM, PRM 26/2, Paszkiewicz to Sikorski, 3 July 1940; PRM 37a/1, Kukiel to Sikorski, 19 July 1940.

Valentine tanks loaded on rail flatcars. As well as armoured vehicles some softskin transport can also be seen in the background. This image was probably taken during 1941-42, when the Poles were stationed around Kelso. During this period they participated in anti-invasion exercises in the area, 65th Tank Battalion, 16th Armoured Brigade, I Polish Corps. The flatcar belonged to the LMS (London Midland & Scottish Railway). (Jan Jarzembowski)

he was aware of the political storm which was building up in London and he did not want to be absent if anybody tried to remove him, as the case proved to be.

The British were well aware of Sikorski's problems in Scotland because when he did finally arrive at the end of July 1940 Frank Roberts noted that, according to Major Perkins of British Military Intelligence, the 'atmosphere on General Sikorski's arrival was 'distinctly frigid' although over the three day visit it 'got better' and that Sikorski left Scotland 'reasonably popular'.[18] The question of Polish morale in Scotland is important for the Maczek story. As the war progressed against Polish interests, Maczek set about training his men in Scotland. As Szudek observes, the time spent prior to the formation of the Polish 1st Armoured Division was not wasted as Maczek imposed a rigorous programme of individual training as preparation for the day came when Polish soldiers would be able to undertake their duties as part of a future Polish armoured formation.[19] Second Lieutenant Jan Suchcitz describes Maczek's guiding principal for educating his men in both France and Scotland as being based on the pre-war Polish system of military training. Maczek maintained that the Polish soldier was to be schooled in the spirit that he was the servant of his nation; he must serve it and give it his protection. This principle was later applied to the

18   NA, FO 371/24474/C7639/1252/55, Report by F.K. Roberts, 30 July 1940.
19   Szudek, op. cit. p. 36.

Another view of Valentine tanks on rail flatcars. Most of the crewmen in the foreground appear to be wearing leather jackets, probably of French issue from their period in France in 1940. However, the soldier in the centre of the group appears to be wearing a British gas mask. (Jan Jarzembowski)

people he liberated including the French, Belgian and Dutch. As Suchcitz noted, Maczek's attitude was that the Polish armoured formation was to observe principals in war that were termed at the time as 'gentlemanly' and today would be considered as the 'observance of human rights'.[20] A further example of Maczek's influence once he arrived in Scotland was that his orders and influence prevented the continuation of the name and uniform of the Polish armed forces being blackened by public drunkenness and lewd behaviour. He managed to restore pride in the Polish Army in Scotland and gave them something to do and targets to work toward. Polish morale in Scotland improved as his targets made them feel that they had something to achieve and that they could put the defeats of the previous twelve months behind them and move forward.[21]

Plans were being prepared in London for the establishment of a Polish armoured division, however the Poles were to experience the limits of their ability to work unilaterally – as they were now under British command any formation of an armoured formation would have to be established to the same establishment as an equivalent British formation.[22] The formation of a Polish armoured division according to the British record was first considered on 7 November 1941, and it was reckoned that 10,000 Polish troops from the Soviet Union

20   *The Soldiers of General Maczek in World War II*, Zbigniew Mieczkowski, Warsaw-London, Foundation of the Commemoration of General Maczek's First Armoured Division, 2004, pp. 21-2.
21   *Dziennik Polski*, 20 December 1940.
22   PISM, A.XII.1/1, 'Re-organisation of Polish Land Forces', 8 April 1941.

Infantry Tank Mk III, Valentine II, of the 65th Tank Battalion, 16th Armoured Brigade, I Polish Corps. These vehicles were delivered 21 November 1941. (Jan Jarzembowski)

A Polish corporal inside his tank, Scotland, November 1941. He is wearing British battledress. The tank is probably a Churchill with the driver's position behind the open hatch. The soldier's right hand seems to be resting on the butt of the forward firing BESA machine gun. (Jan Jarzembowski)

Infantry Tank Mk III (Valentine II). Note the mixture of French personal equipment and uniforms, including tankers' helmets and the pistol holster in foreground. The markings are, left to right: PL (Poland), 16 (bridge classification tonnage number), 072 (65th Tank Battalion) and circle/wing (I Polish Corps). 65th Tank Battalion, 16th Armoured Brigade, I Polish Corps (1 Korpusu Polskiego), Scotland, mid-1942. (Jan Jarzembowski)

would be required in addition to those already in the UK.[23]

In late October 1941 Sikorski tried to explain to Churchill his plan for bringing the Polish Army Corps in Scotland up to the strength of an armoured division with one or two infantry divisions with a full capacity for independent action, but at that time Sikorski lacked the necessary troops and so asked for 8,000 Poles who had been recently released from Soviet captivity as part of a so-called amnesty which allowed for Poles seized and imprisoned by the Soviets following their invasion of eastern Poland during September 1939. The Poles had largely planned to be used as slave labour in the Soviet Far East.[24] Churchill avoided the issue and eventually Sikorski allowed for the bulk of the newly released Poles to stay in the Middle East, from where they eventually took part in the Italian Campaign. Churchill expressed his gratitude to Sikorski for allowing this and explained to him that it would be better (for whom?) in the long run, but he did throw a sop to Sikorski by asserting that there was a plan to bring 5,500 Polish troops to the UK to join the Polish 1st Armoured Division. Churchill noted that Sikorski was willing to disband the 1st Polish Brigade, if necessary, in order to make up the necessary numbers for the Polish armoured division.[25]

Sikorski's military successor, General Kazimierz Sosnkowski, was eventually forced to

23   NA, WO 32/9767 (Polish Armoured Division Formation of:) Major-General A.E. Nye, 4 February 1942.
24   PISM, A.XII.1/52a-c, Sikorski to Churchill, 28 October 1941.
25   Ibid, Churchill to Sikorski, 5 May 1942.

A Polish Valentine crew being briefed. Note the mixture of uniforms. French leather jackets are in evidence, however the soldier on the right is in British battledress. The crewman to his right appears to be holding a French tank crewman's helmet. The ranks are signified as follows - two bars - corporal, a star - junior lieutenant, two stars – lieutenant. Observe also the Michelin man figure on the tank behind the men, a souvenir from France. 65th Tank Battalion, 16th Armoured Brigade, I Polish Corps, Scotland, mid-1942. (Jan Jarzembowski)

do this in 1944 in order that the 1st Polish Armoured Division was able to take part in the campaign to liberate North-Western Europe after August 1944. The rebuilding of Polish land forces was a big deal to the Poles as it was the most important show of Polish strength when it eventually could return to Poland.[26] Meanwhile it was the ever-practical (and honest) Maczek who had to inform Sikorski that it was going to take more than gestures and Nationalism to establish a Polish armoured division to the standard that the British were demanding.[27]

The British held strong views on the formation of the Polish armoured division. These could be termed largely negative although they began in a positive vein as in a meeting of British officers chaired by Major-General Nye in early November 1941 it was noted that a large number of Polish soldiers had experience of tanks, including 600 who had tank combat experience. It was considered at this stage that it would only take three months to train Polish troops sufficiently in order to establish a Polish armoured division.[28] However a minute dated 12 November 1941 observed that the Poles newly freed from Soviet captivity, especially those with any military experience, were in a poor physical state and would

26   PISM, A.XII.22/10, Brigadier-General Paszkiewicz to General Sikorski, 20 October 1941.
27   PISM, A.XII.22/10, Maczek to Sikorski, 20 October 1941.
28   NA, WO 260/15, Formation of Polish Armoured Division, Minutes of Meeting discussing the formation of a Polish armoured unit, 7 November 1941.

Infantry Tank Mk IV Churchill II tanks, 65th Tank Battalion, 16th Armoured Brigade.
15 such tanks were delivered in Scotland in November 1941, but they were disliked
by the Polish crews due to maintenance and reliability issues. (Jan Jarzembowski)

take months of recuperation while General Alan Brooke, Chief of the Imperial General
Staff (CIGS) in a letter to Churchill poured further cold water on the timetable for the
formation of the Polish armoured division.[29] This was all the result of a letter that Sikorski
had sent to General Dill on 28 October 1941, in which he expressed his desire to establish
the formation of a Polish Mechanized Corps, which he hoped would comprise a single
armoured division and at least one mechanized brigade. Sikorski enclosed a plan of how
he saw this being developed and a timetable with a completion date for the summer of
1942 as preparation for a meeting to discuss the factors affecting the formation of a Polish
armoured division, which was due to be held on 4 November 1941.[30]

Churchill supported the Poles in this venture even if Brooke did not; furthermore
Churchill considered that the Poles were being unfairly treated by Brooke.[31] But as we
have already seen by Brooke's reply to the Prime Minister; he had not changed his mind
about the Polish timetable and aspirations. As Andrew Roberts observes, relations between
Churchill and Brooke were never easy, given that during arguments with Churchill Brooke
snapped pencils while only four feet away from the Prime Minister on his side of the narrow
Cabinet table, a gesture that could only be interpreted as threatening and intimidating.[32]

Sikorski was not fazed by Brooke's objections to the practicalities of establishing the

29   Ibid, Minute, 12 November 1941; Alan Brooke to Churchill, 21 January 1942.
30   NA, WO 32/9767, Sikorski to General Dill, 28 October 1941.
31   Ibid, Churchill to Sir Alan Brooke, telegram, Serial No. T.1109/1, 18 December 1941.
32   Andrew Roberts, *Master and Commanders. How Roosevelt, Churchill, Marshall and Alanbrooke Won the War in the West*, London, Allen Lane, 2008, p. 58.

Soldiers from the Division on parade in Scotland, perhaps for some religious or oath taking ceremony. All are suitably bare-headed and the kneeling soldier is holding what could be perhaps either a bible or prayer book. (Jan Jarzembowski)

Parade for members of the 1st Polish Armoured Division whilst they were based in Scotland. (Jan Jarzembowski)

General Maczek standing beside a Crusader tank from his Division, c 1942. The Division's insignia of a Polish winged hussar is clearly visible. (Narodowe Archiwum Cyfrowe)

Polish armoured formation and in a letter to him continued to press for the equipment and men necessary for this, even if much of the equipment available was already earmarked for use by the Soviet Union, which had been invaded by Germany during the summer of 1941, as well as other theatres of war, notably the Middle East, while the Japanese had also just entered the war against the Allies. Sikorski asserted that if he received the necessary men and equipment the armoured division would be fully organised by the end of September 1942 and asked when he should make ready the Polish Army Corps for a move from Scotland.[33] Clearly Sikorski was quite certain that he would get his wishes, but a note in the British archival record reveals that on 7 February 1942 the Poles had 32 Valentine tanks and 21 Churchill tanks and that at that time there was no chance of this changing, as tank production had been given over to supplying the Soviet Union as it continued to fight Germany.[34] The German invasion of the Soviet Union during June 1941 took much of the heat off the Western Allies; to this end the British and American Governments did their best to provide the Soviet Union with the means to fend off the German invasion.

Finally, a week before Sikorski gave the order for the 1st Polish Armoured Division to be established, he explained his plan to Brooke. Sikorski told him that Maczek was to be in command of the division and that it was to consist of 10th Cavalry Brigade, 16th

33   NA, WO 32/9767, Sikorski to Sir Alan Brooke (CIGS), February 1942.
34   Ibid, note dated 7 February 1942.

A Valentine II of the 65th Tank Battalion, 16th Armoured Brigade, I
Polish Corps, Scotland, mid-1942. (Jan Jarzembowski)

Another view of a Polish Valentine II in Scotland, mid-1942. (Jan Jarzembowski)

A photo of a Valentine II, 65th Tank Battalion, 16th Armoured Brigade, I
Polish Corps (T1290252) in Scotland, mid-1942. (Jan Jarzembowski)

Armoured Brigade, the Corps Reconnaissance Regiment and other ancillary units. During
the first period Sikorski proposed to organise the divisional headquarters, two tank brigades,
an armoured regiment, reconnaissance, artillery, signal and engineering units. All were to
approximate as closely as possible to the full establishment while the remaining units were,
for the time being, to be organised as cadres. The second period was to begin with the
expected arrivals of troops from the Soviet Union, when the division could be brought up
to full strength. This would have been primarily the establishment of infantry battalions
and support units; Sikorski considered that this should not present difficulties or entail
a long period before completion. The necessary compliment for the full establishment
according to Sikorski amounted to 5,600 men, of whom 80% would have been required
for the infantry and support units. Sikorski concluded by informing Brooke that if all went
well the division would be fully organised by September 1942. He told Brooke:

> I would like to point out that during this period of organisation of the Armoured
> Division the 1st Army Corps will not lose its fighting efficiency. I need not add that
> the present state of the armament of the 1st Corps limits its fighting capacity to the
> defence of less important sectors. I should, therefore be very grateful if you could
> inform me when you consider that I should hold myself in readiness for the possibility
> of moving the Army Corps from Scotland.[35]

On 16 February 1942 Maczek received orders from Sikorski to the effect that Brigadier-

---

35   PISM, A.XII.1/4, Sikorski to Sir Alan Brooke (CIGS), No. 140/GM/42/tj, 6 February 1942. NA, WO
32/9767, Sikorski to Sir Alan Brookes (CIGS) February 1942.

General Maczek was to form and command an armoured division in accordance with the British Order of Battle/Tables of Organisation and Equipment for such a formation.[36]

---

36   PISM, A.XII.1.1/2, 16 February 1942.

9
Preparing for War: 1942-44

Leopold Lorentz asserts that the 1st Polish Armoured Division was born and bred in the UK.[1] It is hard to disagree with this, as the Division owed everything to the British – its training, its equipping and the hosting of the men. However, the one thing that was not born and bred in the UK was Maczek himself. Polish-born, he was the best commander of armour and leader of men that the Poles could ever ask for, and it could be said it was he who made the Division.

The creation of the Division was always going to be a long hard slog. Even if the Poles were to get the virtually unqualified support of the British Prime Minister, Winston Churchill, the British Chief of the Imperial General Staff (CIGS), General Sir Alan Brooke, with perhaps a more realistic military attitude, continued to slow down the pace of the establishment of the 1st Polish Armoured Division. Brooke demanded that he should have some say in the establishment of the Division and that furthermore it was not to be completed at the expense of other military operations, especially the supplying of the Soviet Union with the necessary equipment to fend off the Axis invasion. The fact that the Soviet Union was seen as the highest priority for the British Government and later both the American and British Governments in the war against Germany was one that dismayed the Poles, who considered the Soviet Union to be an enemy and an aggressor.

Even before Sikorski had formally ordered the establishment of the Polish Armoured Division Brooke was already making sure that priorities were being sorted and he ensured that Churchill was aware of his position by informing him that existing British armoured divisions would be completed by 1 October 1942 and then it would be possible to begin the issue of Cruiser tanks to the Polish Division from that date, with a view that the supply of the Division with adequate tanks would be completed by the end of 1942. Brooke considered that the Poles had large numbers of experienced tank men and therefore their training should not take long.[2]

This note from Brooke to Churchill was created only a few days before the Japanese attack on Pearl Harbour and the American entry into the war, not only against the Japanese but also against the Germans, following the reckless German declaration of war against the USA. The German declaration of war on the Americans was particularly foolish as it ensured the open supply of American equipment to the British and Soviets as well as millions of American troops coming to the European theatre of war. For the Poles it meant that eventually they would be well supplied, owing to American mass production.

In February 1942 Churchill observed to Brooke that the Poles had 125 tanks and considered that they could be made effective as a fighting unit as they expanded with new men and equipment.[3] However, with the American entry into the war the direction of it

---

1   Leopold Lorentz, *Caen to Wilhelmshaven with the Polish First Armoured Division*, Edinburgh, Errol, 1949, p. v.
2   NA, PREM 3 (Prime Ministers' Office) PREM 3/351/10, Brooke to Churchill, 4 December 1941.
3   Ibid, Churchill to Brooke, 14 February 1942.

Polish soldiers wearing AFV crew helmets and British Army greatcoats patrolling through a Scottish town, date unknown but c 1942/43. (Jan Jarzembowski)

began to slip away from British control. Churchill reminded Sikorski of this during 1943 when he observed that the question of securing recruits (Polish) for the Armoured Division from Poles captured in North Africa who had been fighting for the German Army was receiving sympathetic consideration but all of the POWs were under American control and that the British Government was waiting for a reply from the American Government on this matter. However progress was being made, as the Polish prisoners were being segregated from the native German ones.[4]

A progress report on the organisation of the Polish Armoured Division stated that 'the big task of forming an old model armoured division is being carried out by the Poles with enthusiasm and efficiency. Unit training with live ammunition had been in progress for some time in the Lammermuirs but when this Division is completely formed, say in three months time, they will require a more extensive training area'.[5] A British report discusses the training and establishment of the Polish Division in February 1943. The armoured units were in southern England, training in the Newmarket area, while the remainder of the Division was in Scotland. The armoured units were equipped with Crusader Mark VI tanks; the infantry battalions and certain administration units were below establishment and there were no reserves to replace casualties. It was remarked that the issue of Sherman tanks to replace the Crusaders would only serve to increase this personnel problem while there was to be no further reinforcements expected from the Middle East. The Polish idea

4   NA, PREM 3/351/14, Churchill to Sikorski, 15 June 1943
5   NA, CAB 66/33/34, Organisation of Allied Naval, Army and Air Contingents. 23rd Report for the Quarter ending 31 December 1942. Minute 47, Note by Chief Liaison Officer with Allied Contingents, 18 January 1943.

General Marian Kukiel, commander of I Polish Corps 1940-42, on
a visit to 1st Polish Armoured Division in Scotland, 1942. Maczek
stands to Kukiel's left. (Narodowe Archiwum Cyfrowe)

of reinforcing their numbers with Polish prisoners from the German Army seemed to be
the only plan that the Poles had for gaining reinforcements. It is interesting to note that
Polish officers considered that the situation regarding the formation of the Division could
not continue as it was and that they agreed with the British demand for the Poles to adopt
the new model of armoured division in order to fight in Europe. They had realised that
clinging to the old model had more to do with politics and the supposed return to Poland
rather than an intelligent strategy to defeat Germany.[6] Meanwhile the question of the
supply of new recruits was a perennial one, revealed in a letter from Lieutenant-Colonel
Borkowski to Lieutenant-Colonel Victor Cazalet, which discussed the two tasks awaiting
Polish forces during the summer of 1944, either in fighting or intense and final preparations
for the fighting to come. The biggest problem was manpower, or the lack of it, owing to the
failure of the Polish recruiting program in North America and now every able-bodied man
was needed; Borkowski even considered the use of wounded men. This was revealed after
Cazalet had requested in a previous letter to Borkowski for two or three Poles to be made
available to work on Cazalet's farm.[7]

The question of equipment continued to rub, as General Sir Alan Brooke explained to
Sikorski. Brooke informed him that he had been in consultation with the C-in-C Home
Forces and had agreed in principle that measures for the formation of the Polish Armoured

6   NA, CAB 66/39/320, Organisation of Allied, Naval, Army & Air Contingents, 10 July 1943.
7   PISM, A.XII.1/8, Lieutenant-Colonel Borkowski to Lieutenant-Colonel Cazalet, 25 March 1943;
     Lieutenant-Colonel Cazalet to Lieutenant-Colonel Borkowski, 23 March 1943.

Division should be initiated without delay, although problems had presented themselves. The question of moving I Polish Corps to England had been studied carefully but there were considerable problems, including accommodation and finding suitable training areas. It was concluded that it would be better to move the Poles to a suitable area in Scotland. The question of equipment was equally as vexing because the provision of tanks as requested by Sikorski was difficult owing to supplying the Soviet Union and other overseas commitments. At that time the Poles had 53 tanks (32 Valentines and 21 Churchills) but a future supply of Valentines had been earmarked. Brooke suggested that the best way to get the Division up and running was to start on a 'Churchill' basis with the view of changing over to a lighter type of tank when the supply situation permitted. It was suggested that if Sikorski agreed to this the Polish Armoured Division would be supplied with a proportion of Churchill tanks from each month's production. It was considered by Brooke that this would at least meet the training needs of the Division from the very beginning.[8]

Maczek took command with the view that the Division was to be made up of 10th Cavalry Brigade, 16th Armoured Brigade, the Corps Reconnaissance Regiment and other auxiliary units. Maczek's task during the first period of training (three-four months) consisted of field and technical instructions of the cadres and personnel for the two tank brigades. At the same time the remaining units of the Division would be formed, while some still remained as skeleton formations.[9] It was during this period that much of the work necessary to form a division would be done, especially the mechanized elements, while the second part of its establishment was dependent on the recruitment of men newly released from Soviet captivity, who would be directed to the establishment of infantry battalions and those service units necessary for the maintenance of a mechanized fighting division. This should all have been completed by September 1942 but remained dependent on personnel arriving from the Soviet Union.[10]

A further problem was the question of how the Poles were willing to organise their Armoured Division. General Paget, following an inspection of the 1st Polish Armoured Division, raised the question of why the Poles were establishing the Division using an old form of organisation. Sikorski agreed that he was long aware that the old type of armoured division was inadequate for operations in the field in view of the latest war experiences (North Africa), with the wrong proportions of infantry and artillery numbers in relation to the armoured units being the main defect. Sikorski explained that the Poles had adopted the old type of organisation for two reasons:

1. In view of Polish future requirements (these later proved to be political).
2. Because according to Sikorski the Poles had enough specialists to fill the establishment of two armoured brigades (the future army for liberating Poland, it would seem).

Sikorski pressed his point as he claimed that the above were of a basic significance to the Poles. He claimed that these reasons had been understood in their time by Churchill, General Paget and Brooke himself. Sikorski asserted that if it was decided that the 1st Polish Armoured Division was to be reorganised it would mean that one of the armoured brigades would have to be disbanded. Sikorski claimed that such a move would be illogical

8   PISM, A.XII.1/4, General Sir Alan Brooke to Sikorski, CIGS/B.M. No. P.M./203, letter, 6 March 1942.
9   Stanisław Maczek, *Od Powody do Czołga*, Edinburgh, Tomar, 1961, p.137.
10   PISM, A.XII.1/4, Sikorski to General Sir Alan Brooke, No.140/GM/42tj, 6 February 1942.

and unwarranted as highly trained tank specialists would have to be retrained as 'mediocre infantrymen or gunners' and morale would suffer if one of these units was disbanded. Sikorski said that he would like to organise the Division perhaps as a new type, different to others. He wanted to exchange a single infantry brigade from Anders' Army and a single artillery regiment from General Kopański's 3rd Division and send back, in exchange, to Italy and the Middle East, 16th Armoured Brigade and its rifle battalion. In both cases the men would be sent without any equipment as this was to be obtained once in theatre. In this way, according to Sikorski, the 1st Polish Armoured Division would be of the new type and General Kopański's division would also be transformed into an armoured division of the new type. This would have been of great value to the Poles, although as Sikorski said:

'However, should important reasons of an operational nature or the shipping situation render the realisation of this plan impossible, we should have to reorganise completely our formations in Scotland in order to obtain the elements necessary for an armoured division of the new type. In this case the 16th Armoured Brigade (minus its rifle battalion) would have to remain in reserve as an autonomous formation'.[11]

The problem for the Polish 1st Armoured Division and the Poles in exile in general was that after 1942 their concerns were of no importance to the British or the Americans. This is illustrated in a letter from Lieutenant-General Nye to Major-General Regulski, the Polish Military Attaché to London. Nye informed Regulski that he had already seen Sikorski and had made it quite clear that the shipping situation made the exchange of an armoured brigade from the UK with an infantry brigade from the Iraq-Iran (Persia) command impossible.[12] But the question of how the Polish 1st Armoured Division was to be established continued to drag on, because the Polish leadership saw it as an opportunity to establish two armoured units which would eventually fight for Poland, and not the single unit that the Allies considered necessary to fight the war against Germany.

Even though a memo dated 27 September 1943 from the (British) War Office confirmed that the 1st Polish Armoured Division was to re-organise itself as a New Model Armoured Division, General Montgomery, C-in-C 21st Army Group, in a letter to the Polish C-in-C, General Sosnkowski, wrote that he was 'disturbed' that Sosnkowski did not propose to bring the 1st Polish Armoured Division up to full establishment at once and that Sosnkowski intended to wait until he had access to the sources of Polish troops in France and Belgium. If any were captured once the Allies landed in France they planned to draw on Poles who had been fighting for the Germans. Montgomery lamented, 'I am sure that you [Sosnkowski] will agree that it is unsound to take into battle against the Germans a division that is not properly organised, and which has not got well trained reserves immediately available to replace battle wastage; such action would lead to no good results. Perhaps you will re-consider your decision? I had intended to move the Division down to the Yorkshire training areas in April, but there seems little point in doing so if it is not going to be properly organised for battle'.[13] In a further exchange Sosnkowski gave in to

---

11   PISM, A.XII.1/48e, General Sikorski to General Sir Alan Brooke, May 1943. The problem of tank/infantry co-operation was still not sorted out by 1944. In the deserts of North Africa British tanks and infantry tended to work independently with poor results. American tank/infantry co-operation seemed to have few problems, as they worked together more effectively. Carlo d'Este, *Decision in Normandy: The Unwritten Story of Montgomery and the Allied Campaign*, London, Collins, 1983, p. 291.

12   PISM, A.XII.1/48e, Lieutenant-General Nye to Major-General Bronisław Regulski, 25 May 1943.

13   Ibid, General B.L. Montgomery, C-in-C, 21 Army Group, 21 A.Gp/1012/CinC to General K. Sosnkowski, C-in-C, Polish Army, Letter, 23 March 1944.

the inevitable: he confirmed to Montgomery that he would equip the Polish 1st Armoured Division at the expense of other Polish units in Scotland.[14]

It had finally been impressed upon the Polish leadership that the Polish cause was irrelevant to the Allies; they either conformed to Allied wishes or they would have no part in the Normandy landings and they needed to participate in order to return to Poland. Montgomery's statement about the Polish Armoured Division finding replacements from Poles captured from the German Army turned out to be correct as General Kopański explained to Montgomery, now Field Marshal Montgomery, that the Poles were having difficulties replacing their casualties with Polish prisoners of war, as the captured men's training was taking longer than had been anticipated.[15] This was in reference to a report that stated up to 22 October 1944 the casualty list for the 1st Polish Armoured Division was 231 officers and 3,228 men killed or wounded of whom 1,456 were specialists, including 121 tank commanders, 204 radio operators, 155 tank gunners and 149 tank drivers; these were the very men that Kopański was referring to.[16]

Questions of the supply of manpower to the Polish armed forces rumbled on, as during 1940 and 1941 there was a lack of NCOs, which had a knock-on effect later when it was realised just how long it took to train men properly, especially personnel for mechanized regiments.[17] A further memo from Sosnkowski points to the age of the officers that were available for the Polish Army: 53% of the officers were 36 to 50 years of age with only 38% of officers being 35 years of age or under. Sosnkowski observed that the entire Polish Army and its promotional system needed overhauling and made comparable with that of the British Army.[18] The chickens of the old amateur and politicised Polish Army of the Polish Second Republic were coming home to roost, and threatened to make I Polish Corps an irrelevance to the Allied cause.

It had been recognised earlier that a normal ratio of officer to men should be one officer to every four men or 19% of officers to 81% of men but the Polish ratio was 22% officers to 78% men thus giving the concept of a cadre army being formed, something that the Poles had already made in their arguments to Churchill. In the brigades the percentage regarding officers and men was normal, if changeable. The figures were: 1st Rifle Brigade – 9% officers and 91% men; 10th Armoured Cavalry Brigade – 8% officers and 92% men; 16th Armoured Cavalry Brigade – 7% officers and 93% men. Age was a concern as 13% of the ranks were over 40 years of age (1,691 men); 80% were 21 to 39 years of age (10,501 men), only 7% or 902 men being 20 years of age or less.[19] Maczek commented on one intake that he received for training. The intake consisted of 1,238 ORs of whom 30% were up to 30 years of age, 45% up to 40 years of age and 25% up to 50 years of age.[20] Surely, this was far too old for their effective use in a combat unit?

Exercises proved that there was a genuine need to reorganise the Polish Armoured Division because as a result of the three day Exercise 'SNAFFLE' held during August 1943, it was realised that even if the Poles had inflicted a theoretical 75% casualty rate

14   Ibid, Sosnkowski to Montgomery, Letter, 19 April 1944.
15   Ibid, General Kopański to Field Marshal Montgomery, 21 November 1944.
16   Ibid. Chief of Polish General Staff, ref: 1396/GNW/tj.44, 22 November 1944.
17   PISM, A.XII.3/8, Memo by General Marian Kukiel, 15 October 1943.
18   Ibid. Memo by General K. Sosnkowski, 20 October 1943.
19   PISM, A.XII.4/1, *Szef Komisji Kontroli Stanów*, General Norwid-Neugebauer, 4 May 1942.
20   PISM, A.XII.22/8, Maczek to GOC 1st Army Corps, 22 October 1942.

on their 'enemy' it was noted that there was insufficient infantry support; insufficient armoured car reconnaissance; a lack of artillery support as well as problems with sappers and communications. It all proved that the Division needed to restructure.[21]

The fear was that even if some of the Poles did have experience in armoured warfare, they were not up to date with the changes occurring in tactics during the war. Things had changed and the Germans had gained invaluable experience from the fighting on the brutal Russian Front where no quarter was given and every mistake was punished not with theoretical casualties marked with chalk but with broken bodies and minds. The Polish Army, as heroic as it was, was out of touch with the modern world, the use of new arms and tactics and had totally failed to understand its position since the fall of France in 1940. The problem was that even if the Poles had been discussing the matter of the reorganisation of their own units, including the Armoured Division, there appeared to be little to do as far as the leadership was concerned, as they continued to see things as a matter of politics and to provide a show of strength for their eventual return to Poland. Of course, there was also the perennial manpower shortage. On 5 February 1944 General Zając reported that on 8 January 1944 the 1st Polish Armoured Division numbered 14,099 men, thus revealing a shortfall of 565 men.[22] However this also meant that the Division was getting closer to its war establishment.

The problem for the 1st Armoured Division began in 1941, with huge numbers of Poles being released from Soviet captivity but the expected reinforcements for I Polish Corps in Scotland never materialised, as the Allies had other needs for them in the Middle East and later Italy; they became II Corps or more simple 'Anders' Army' under the command of General Władysław Anders. A note regarding the possibility of obtaining troops from this source specifically for the Armoured Division was written during 1941 in which the author expressed the desire that there might be several dozen 'good officers' from armoured or mobile units and that perhaps out of the 200,000 troops from Russia there might be around 1,000 to 1,500 men that would be useful for tanks.[23]

Despite the setbacks that the Poles were to endure regarding reinforcements from the Soviet Union a letter originating from the Polish General Staff to Colonel Carlisle informed him that the training of the Armoured Division had begun. The training was occurring at the British tank depot at Bovington in Dorset. This in the main was concerned with the training of officers, while mechanics and fitters were sent to British military workshops and tank engine fitters were sent to the Metro Camel factory in Birmingham, where the engines were manufactured, to study the engines.[24]

A few weeks later, in another letter to Colonel Carlisle, the Polish General Staff continued to press their case for two armoured units, one being the armoured division commanded by Maczek and the other being the tank brigade for Anders' Army. The Poles informed Carlisle that they were preparing 240 officers as cadre replacements for this. The Poles continued to maintain their position for a need for two armoured units in the exiled Polish army.[25]

---

21   PISM, A.XII.4/2, Notes on 3 Day Exercise 'SNAFFLE', 9 August 1943.
22   Ibid. Report by General Zając, 5 February 1944.
23   PISM, A.XII.23/24, 'Notatka w sprawie utworzenia ośrodka szkolenia broni panc. Na bliskim wschodzie' undated but 1941.
24   PISM, A.XII.23/31, letter from Polish General Staff to Colonel Carlisle, 23 March 1942.
25   PISM, Ibid, Polish General Staff to Colonel Carlisle, WO (War Office) 4 April 1942.

August 1942 saw the beginning of the training of Polish tank crews using Allied tactics as witnessed at Exercise 'RED LYNCH', while throughout 1942 and 1943 there were many courses which were all concerned with trying to establish the 1st Polish Armoured Division to the same standard as that of British armoured divisions.[26] It was noted by the Poles that in 1943 there was a further need for training officers and NCOs in order to be ready for eventual combat. It was suggested that this training could possibly take place during April, May and June 1943.[27]

1943 was to be difficult for the Poles, as it was slowly becoming apparent that what they desired was not going to happen and that all that mattered in the war during 1943 was the Middle East and the Soviet Union; both theatres were linked as neither could fall to the Germans – a breakthrough in one would lead to a breakthrough in the other and victory for Germany. In August 1943 General Nye wrote to General Sosnkowski, who had replaced Sikorski following Sikorski's fatal and mysterious airplane crash off Gibraltar the previous month. Nye wrote:

I am glad to note that we are in agreement that there is a need for this re-organisation to conform with the new type of British armoured division. I am afraid, however, your proposal to effect this conversion by the exchange of an armoured brigade with an infantry brigade from the Middle East presents important difficulties as follows:

a.   The consequent re-organisation of the Polish Corps in the Middle East would upset the present correctly balanced force of infantry and armour.
b.   The state of training and preparedness for operations for operations of the Polish Forces in the Middle East would be retarded by your proposed reorganisation and it is unlikely that this would be acceptable.
c.   It would not be practicable to provide the requisite shipping for the transfer of these formations between the United Kingdom and the Middle East at the present time.

Nye put forward the British plan:

a.   To make use of the personnel of HQ 2 Support Group and 1 Support Battalion, both of which units would have been redundant in the new model armoured division.
b.   To take the Highland (Podhalian) Rifle Battalion from 16th Armoured Brigade.
c.   To make use of miscellaneous units as already illustrated by Sosnkowski.[28]

As Szudek observed, the bottom line was that as long as the Poles refused to move on the question of establishing an armoured division along the lines of the British new model, progress would be difficult. The Poles were, in essence, establishing an already obsolete

26   PISM, A.XII.23/31
27   PISM, A.XII.23/36, Lieutenant-Colonel H. Tasiecki to Captain F.C.B. Fleetwood-Hesketh (WO), 15 March 1943.
28   PISM, A.XII 38/8, General Archibald Nye to General Sosnkowski, 19 August 1943. An earlier memorandum of 4 August 1943 was quite clear that the Poles would have to change in order to fit in with the new British model for an armoured unit.

A close-up of two members of a tank crew from the Division, c 1944. To the right is Captain Jerzy Wasilewski. Both wear the British Royal Armoured Corps-pattern steel helmet. (Narodowe Archiwum Cyfrowe)

unit.[29]

By June 1943 progress was finally being made. Maczek and other Poles interpreted this by the fact that the Division was being moved to England. In his Order for the Day, 24 May 1943, Maczek informed his men that in a fortnight's time they were all going on manoeuvres in England, after observing that they had been guests in Scotland for nearly three years. In Scotland the Poles had learnt about British society and had got on well with the Scots people, Maczek emphasised that this attitude was to continue when they moved to England.[30]

Maczek would have seen that being moved to the training ground in England after three years of lingering in Scotland was a positive move as it meant that the British, despite their reservations regarding the establishment of the Polish Armoured Division, were still contemplating using it in future operations and still felt it worth training for such eventualities. It would have been seen as a sign that at last the Poles were about to return to Europe and take the field once more against the Germans. Any considerations regarding the Soviet Union would have to be put off for another time.

Maczek may have had concerns previously about the type of men that he was expected to train as effective tank crews, but somehow he managed to do so. It was realised that not everybody would be fighting from tanks and that a 50-year old private who understood how a tank engine worked was just as important as a 20-year old tank gunner; they both

29   Szudek, op. cit. p. 39.
30   PISM, R. 482, First (Polish) Armoured Division, Orders of the Day, 1943, 24 May 1943.

Major Michal Gutowski (left) and the commander of 1st Polish Armoured Division's 10th Armoured Cavalry Brigade, Colonel Tadeusz Majewski. (Narodowe Archiwum Cyfrowe)

had their place in an armoured unit.

During 1943, as the Poles took part in various exercises in readiness for the eventual invasion of Europe, they began to receive plaudits for their work. Lieutenant-General J.A.H. Gammell, GOC Eastern Command, wrote of the Polish 1st Armoured Division: ' ... it had made an enormous step forward on the road to achieving combat readiness'.[31]

However, as Szudek notes, as preparations were being made for the invasion of Europe, the Allies became more threatening in their attitude towards the Poles. Eventually the British bluntly put their case: the Poles either established an armoured division of the new model or they would not be allowed to take part in the invasion of Europe.[32]

Sosnkowski was forced into a corner; the very reason for the existence of the 1st Polish Armoured Division was the Polish return to Europe and taking the fight to the Germans. Therefore Sosnkowski reluctantly stripped all of the Polish regiments in Scotland, except the Parachute Brigade, to their bare essentials in order to make up the numbers required for the Division. He was then able to inform 21st Army Group that from 1 October 1943 the Division would be reorganised and brought up to full strength less 120 men. This was accepted by the British, and the 1st Polish Armoured Division took its final shape before being deployed overseas.

After exercising in East Anglia during the summer of 1943 the Division returned to Scotland and continued to work up towards combat preparation. Once again the question of the manpower shortage raised itself and was getting worse owing to casualities during

31   PISM, R. 148. 19 August 1943.
32   Szudek, op. cit. p. 38.

A Mk V Stuart and crew of the Division in training. This was the latest version of the M3 Stuart tank. The vehicle is still fitted with side sandskirts. Kirkcudbright range on the northern coastline of the Solway Firth in Dumfries and Galloway, Scotland, occupies an exposed headland 5 km south of the town of Kirkcudbright. Spring 1944. (Jan Jarzembowski)

M5 Mk V Stuarts of the Division. The triangular marking on the side of the tank in the foreground tank denotes 'A' Squadron. (Jan Jarzembowski)

General Montgomery inspected the 1st Polish Armoured Division at Kelso, Scotland on 13 April 1944. This would provide him with an opportunity to assess the readiness of the division, meet its officers and give one of his celebrated inspirational addresses (he is recorded as saying "We will go together, you and I, to kill the Germans") to the assembled troops in the run-up to D-Day. Here he is signing some sort of volume, perhaps an official visitors book celebrating his visit to the division. (Jan Jarzembowski)

Montgomery's inspection, 13 April 1944, Maczek second from right. (Jan Jarzembowski)

Montgomery's inspection, 13 April 1944. Maczek is on the left of Montgomery, to the right, behind him, is Colonel Tadeusz Majewski, commander of the 10th Armoured Cavalry Brigade (*10 Brygada Kawalerii Pancernej*). (Jan Jarzembowski)

Montgomery's inspection, 13 April 1944. Note the dispatch rider's woollen gloves Montgomery is wearing! (Jan Jarzembowski)

Maczek and Monty, 13 April 1944. (Jan Jarzembowski)

Montgomery addressing men of the Division, 13 April 1944. (Jan Jarzembowski)

Montgomery, and to the left a major of the 10th Dragoons wearing the honorary insignia of the cross of St Andrew and the arms of Lanarkshire. (Jan Jarzembowski)

April 13 1944. The officer wearing the Rogatywka (square hat) centre right
looks like General Józef Ludwik Zając, Deputy Commander of Polish I Corps,
later Inspector of Training of Polish Armed Forces. (Jan Jarzembowski)

training and the usual wastage of any organisation. Furthermore it was also necessary to replace 400 'D' category men who were not fit for active service and had probably been originally recruited as some form of crisis measure to make up numbers.[33]

On 10 February 1944 Sosnkowski held a meeting with the C-in-C 21st Army Group, General Sir Bernard Montgomery, and told him that the Division was ready although still 510 men short. He was certain that this deficit would be made up shortly. However the 1,280 men needed for the second replacement once the Poles landed in Europe and took part in any fighting could only be met when areas of northern France inhabited by Poles were liberated. Regarding the Division's equipment, it had 70% of the due establishment armoured fighting vehicles, 60% of signal equipment, 40% of engineers' equipment and 80% of transport vehicles. Montgomery was satisfied with this and said that it was largely in line with that of British divisions. He promised to inspect the Division, which he duly did on 13 March 1944.[34]

Montgomery's relationship with the Division remained frosty. During the March inspection the Poles did not like how Montgomery dressed, as he arrived in his trademark informal concept of a uniform and upset the Division when he asked Maczek what language the Poles spoke amongst themselves, Russian or German! Szudek takes offense when he records Montgomery writing the next day that he had met quite a number of men who had fought against him in the Africa Korps (in North Africa) under Rommel (Montgomery

33 Ibid.
34 Ibid.

wrote 'Romell').[35] Hamilton asserts that Montgomery was praising the Poles but what may have really offended the Poles was that Sosnkowski refused to bring the Division up to strength with reserves; Montgomery instantly crushed him by telling him that if the reserves were not completed he would not take the Poles to Normandy. Sosnkowski instantly gave in and on 19 April 1944 wrote 'I have given orders to complete the Division at the expense of other Polish units in Scotland'.[36]

One should consider that the Poles were being hypersensitive. A month later Eisenhower, dressed in his very correct parade ground uniform, made a visit to the Poles and was better received. The interesting thing is that Montgomery was a successful general with victories and credited with driving the Axis armies from North Africa, in addition he had also fought on the Western Front during the 1914-18 War; Eisenhower was yet to see combat or lead anything but he was able to tickle the collective Polish ego. Nevertheless, if the Poles wanted to go to Europe it should be remembered that Montgomery retained controlled of this.

---

35   Szudek, op. cit. p. 41.
36   Nigel Hamilton, *Master of the Battlefield: Monty's War years, 1942-1944*, New York, McGrew-Hill, 1983, pp. 557-8.

10

To War: August 1944

Second Lieutenant Tomasz Potworowski writes that the 1st Polish Armoured Division landed in Normandy gradually between 29 July and 4 August 1944 with its commander, General Stanisław Maczek, landing on 1 August 1944 (D+56), 56 days after the original landings on 6 June 1944.[1] The Division was landed at Arromanches and on 7 August 1944 moved towards Bayeux and were for the first time accredited as being part of the Order of Battle in Normandy.[2] As he was embarking for France, Maczek made a chance remark to a French officer, Colonel de Langlade, commenting 'you are a lucky man Colonel. If you are killed in France you will die on your own liberated soil. We shall die on friendly soil, but even so, foreign soil and we shall never see Poland again.'[3] This remark sadly turned out to be prophetic for Maczek and for so many Poles after 1944. Even before the 1st Polish Armoured Division had landed in Normandy one of its number, Colonel Jerzy Levittoux, had been killed at the front during July 1944 where he had been in preparation for the Division's entry into operational service.[4]

Szudek sets the tone perfectly with his description of the 1st Polish Armoured Division's preparations for battle. They had arrived with 13,000 soldiers, 381 tanks and 4,050 vehicles in preparation for battle, the first Polish armoured battle since 1940. It was also the first day of the doomed Warsaw Uprising.

On 6 August 1944 Maczek issued Order of the Day No. 40 in which he said that the Poles should 'demand payment for every Polish life' taken by the Germans. However he was also quick to determine that the Poles should not behave like barbarians but instead fight as every Polish soldier had done so in the past, like the knights of a more chivalrous past. Szudek is careful to remind us that this should not be dismissed as mere romantic rhetoric; Maczek meant it, the Poles were to fight hard but fair and not descend into barbarism. Maczek went further: 'We are going into our first battle alongside the best Allied divisions. We know what you are worth, and that is why today, as your commander, I wish you one thing – let the Germans pay heavily in blood for the privilege of fighting you'.[5]

These were fine words to lead troops into battle with and it should be understood that Maczek meant every last syllable of them. As we have previously seen, Maczek was considerate of human rights when fighting and despite the barbarity that the Polish people

---

1   Imperial War Museum Collection (IWM) 06/38/1, 2nd Lieutenant T. Potworowski, *Army Days 1943-1945. Recollections and Reflections of a Polish Soldier in the Time of Katyn, the Warsaw Uprising and Yalta*, Second Printing, 1997. p. 49.

2   NA, WO 205/1099, 21 Army Group TS OVERLORD Daily Maps, 2 August – 1 September 1944.

3   Eddy Florentin, *The Battle of the Falaise Gap*, London, Elek books, 1965, translated by Mervyn Savill, p. 280.

4   PISM, R. 1078, Daily Orders 1st Armoured Division, 1944, Order of the Day, 24 July 1944. Stanisław Maczek, *Od Podwody do Czołga*, Edinburgh, Tomar, 1961, pp.148-9.

5   P.A. Szudek, 'The First Polish Armoured Division in the Second World War' in Peter D. Stachura (ed) *Themes of Modern History. Proceedings of a Symposium on 28 March 1992 In Honour of the Century of General Stanisław Maczek*, Glasgow, The Polish Social and Educational Society, 1992, pp. 35-59.

Men of the 1st Polish Armoured Division at Scarborough, July 1944, shortly before departing for Normandy. (Narodowe Archiwum Cyfrowe)

Officers of the Division at Scarborough, July 1944. From right to left Maczek, Second Lieutenant J. Tarnowski, Captain T. Wysocki, unknown. (Narodowe Archiwum Cyfrowe)

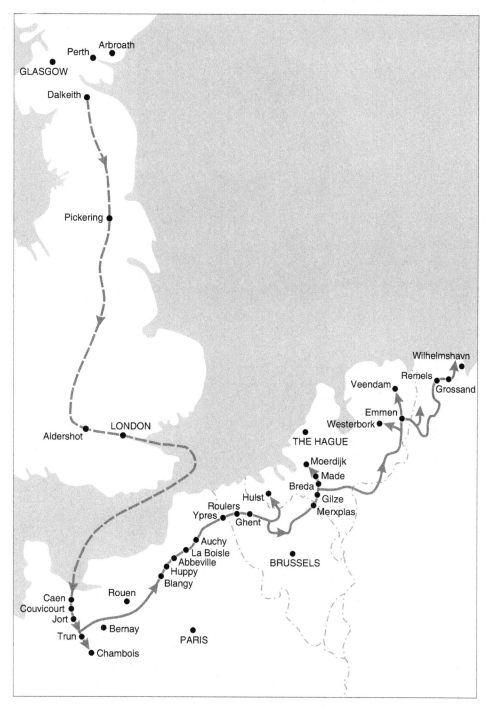

1st Polish Armoured Divsion's Operational Route in North-
West Europe, August 1914-May 1945

A motor vehicle column (mostly Bedford 4x4 trucks) from the Division in Yorkshire, July 1944. (Narodowe Archiwum Cyfrowe)

A fine study of General Maczek with officers from his command, July 1944. To the left is Colonel Kazimierz Dworak, to the right Captain T. Wysocki. Note the Divisional insignia on the officer's left sleeve, recalling the Polish Winged Hussars of the 16th and 17th centuries. (Narodowe Archiwum Cyfrowe)

Superb study of a Cromwell VII tank of the 10th Mounted Rifle Regiment, 1st Polish Armoured Division, Scarborough, July 1944. (Narodowe Archiwum Cyfrowe)

had suffered and continued to suffer at the time of his speech, especially as Warsaw was being destroyed as he spoke, troops under his command seemed to have behaved well, even if the battle for Normandy was at times to descend into slaughter with prisoners being killed both by the Allies and the Germans.[6] Very soon the 1st Polish Armoured Division was to be sped into its own baptism of fire. It was thrown into battle as part of Operation TOTALIZE. This was to prove to be a real blooding for the Poles. In a pencilled note to the 10th Armoured Cavalry Brigade it was observed that there had been heavy fighting throughout the night (8/9 August 1944) which was still continuing and that no doubt the first few days of combat were a shock to many.[7] However in an interview with Polish war correspondent, Maciej Feldhuzen, just before going into battle on 8 August 1944, Maczek was very upbeat about returning to the battlefield. A week later Maczek, after much fighting, spoke to Reuters special correspondent John Wilhelm, telling him that the 1st Polish Armoured Division were 'modern hussars' and wanted to fight the enemy. He went

6   Robin Neillands, *The Battle of Normandy: 1944*, London, Cassell, 2004, pp. 73 & 81.
7   PISM, AV.1/6, Maczek to D-ca, 10 BK. Panc, 9 August 1944.

Cromwell VII tanks of the 10th Mounted Rifle Regiment,
July 1944. (Narodowe Archiwum Cyfrowe)

further, stating that the Poles were very good tank soldiers and once more compared them with 16th Century Polish cavalry.[8]

The operation is often regarded as being controversial as some consider that it was poorly thought out, or that the Polish and Canadian armoured divisions deployed were of little value owing to their inexperience and timidity.[9] Tout observes that given that many Poles had been in combat during 1939 and 1940 it was not strictly true that the 1st Polish Armoured Division was 'green'. Tout considers that the problem was that the Poles had not been provided with any real information concerning the fighting in Normandy despite two months of combat there (June-August 1944). Maczek's Chief of Staff who had been sent

8   *Dziennik Polski i Dziennik Żołnierza* (London) 8 August 1944; 14 August 1944.
9   C.P. Stacey, *The Canadian Army, 1939-1945. An Official Historical Summary*, Ottawa, King's Printer, 1948, p. 198.

Maczek in the turret of a Cromwell VII, July 1944. (Narodowe Archiwum Cyfrowe)

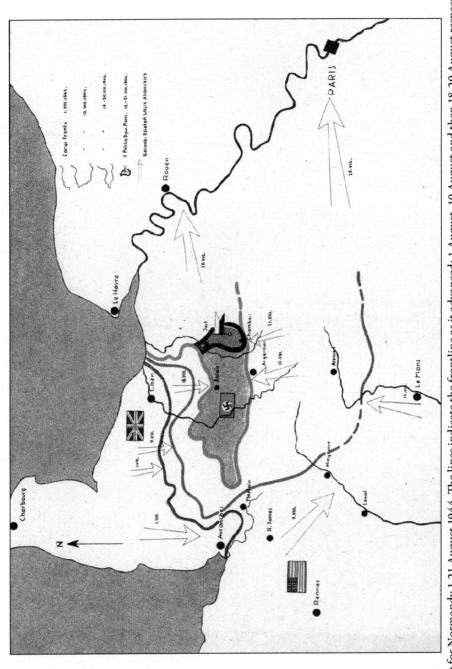

Battle for Normandy 1-21 August 1944. The lines indicate the frontline as it advanced: 1 August, 10 August and then 18-20 August respectively. The thick black line indicates the position of the Division 15-21 August. The thick arrows indicate the direction of Allied advances.

On 9 August 2nd Armoured Regiment approached Couvicourt.
(Wiatrowskiego & Wiatrowski, *2nd Polish Armoured Regiment in action. From Caen to Wilhelmshaven 844 miles*, published in Hannover 1946)

A Sherman Firefly of the 24th Uhlans is unloaded at Arromanches on the Division's arrival in Normandy, August 1944. (Narodowe Archiwum Cyfrowe)

Elements of the 1st Polish Armoured Division unloading at
Arromanches, August 1944. (Narodowe Archiwum Cyfrowe)

out earlier, fact finding, had been killed, therefore it was considered that the first few days
of fighting that the Poles were engaged in was more akin to a full training exercise.[10] Tout
also considers that there were elements of a lack of operational unity between the Poles and
their Allies in Normandy, as he observed that at TOTALIZE the 1st Polish Armoured
Division was totally unprepared owing to language barriers and different codes, which
made them an easy target for the Germans.[11]

A further observation concerns all of the troops who fought in Normandy. Their chief
weakness seems to have been a fault common to many British formations, which was a
ponderous approach to any new problem. As a result of 'overtraining' all of their movements
were organised according to textbooks and training manuals.[12]

It should be noted that intelligence prior to TOTALIZE was poor. There had been
bits and pieces of information available regarding the enemy, such as an order given by SS
General Hauser, dated 21 July 1944, in which noted that German supplies were becoming
difficult to receive and that there was a certain amount of cannibalising of equipment, with
strict savings on equipment by all seen as essential.[13] This should be contrasted with the
ready supply of Allied equipment owing to the mass industrial production afforded by the
USA. There was a serious lack of good intelligence, as an intelligence summary from II
Canadian Corps revealed by admitting that there was a gap in the knowledge of the enemy
forces opposing the Canadian and Polish advance. There were informal reports of both

10   Ken Tout, *A Fine Night for Tanks: The Road to Falaise*, Stroud, Sutton, 1998, p. 109.
11   Ken Tout, *Roads to Falaise: 'Cobra' & 'Goodwood' Reassessed*, Stroud, Sutton, 2002, p. 187.
12   Eversley Belfield & H. Essame, *The Battle for Normandy*, London, Pan, 1983, pp. 128-9.
13   PISM, AV.1/26 Translated of an order given by SS General Hauser, 21 July 1944.

Men from the Division in the Caen area shortly after landing in
France, early August 1944. (Narodowe Archiwum Cyfrowe)

Tiger and Ferdinand tanks.[14] This meant that if there were indeed Tigers in the area it indicated the presence of 101 Heavy Tank Battalion I SS Panzer Corps or 503 Heavy Tank Battalion, left behind when 21st Panzer Division moved west. In addition 1,000 prisoners had been taken from 89th Infantry Division. Even so it was still almost impossible to assess the enemy's immediate composition.[15] The Canadian commander, General Guy Simonds, could not even be bothered at the time to discover the correct spelling of Maczek; he rendered it 'Metchek' in a letter sent at the time.[16]

The problem for the Allies at the start of August 1944 was that the situation in Normandy was beginning to look like a stalemate. Even after six weeks of heavy fighting, the British and Canadian forces were still trying to break through German defences around Caen with no likelihood of an immediate penetration. In contrast American 12th Army Group had already cleared Brittany and had reached the Loire to the south, before beginning to move north and east with what seemed to be relative ease. Furthermore the Americans had captured ten times the territory that the British and Canadian forces had taken from the Germans; the Americans were expanding their captures every day, although it should be recalled that they possessed greater resources than their allies.

Between the two Allied armies lay the German 7th Army. Its commander, Field Marshal Günther von Kluge, had received orders from Hitler to the effect that he was to split the Allies in two and then push them back into the sea. A second Dunkirk was being

14   Ferdinand could be referring to the Ferdinand heavy tank hunter derivative of the Tiger. None saw service in Normandy.
15   PISM, AV.1/26, Orders & Bulletins 2nd Canadian Corps, August 1944. 2nd Canadian Corps Intelligence Summary no. 28, 24 hours period ending 20:00 hours, Brigadier N.E. Roger, 8 August 1944.
16   PISM, Ibid, Simonds to Maczek, 8 August 1944.

offered. However, by this point of the war, the Allies ruled the skies over France, which prevented the Germans from being able to put Hitler's plan into action.

The 1st Polish Armoured Division arrived in France during early August 1944. Montgomery visited the Poles on 5 August 1944 and held a briefing with officers down to squadron-level. This was typical of Montgomery, as he considered that it was better to bypass Army and Corps commanders in order that all combat commanders thoroughly understood his intentions. Montgomery explained his view of the situation to them. He told the Polish commanders that he saw Caen as a pivot or 'a hinge' and that he intended to use the area to wheel south-east in order to strike at the flank of the German 7th Army. To do this 2nd Canadian Infantry Division and 51st Highland Division would open the way in co-ordination with the Canadian and Polish armoured divisions. The two armoured divisions were then to attack the main German line of defence which stood astride the Caen-Falaise road; the Poles were assault the left and the Canadians the right side of the German line.

Montgomery's briefing made a good impression on the Polish officers, unlike his inspection during the spring of 1944, but details of the plan aroused concerns amongst the Poles, especially those who already had armoured combat experience. The Polish 1st Armoured Division was to attack the German line head-on but the Polish left flank was to be completely unprotected. It has been compared with the Charge of the Light Brigade in as much as it was to charge ahead while passing the enemy's waiting guns. One of these experienced officers, Lieutenant-Colonel Franciszek, second-in-command of the 10th Cavalry Brigade, a graduate of the Polish War Academy and battle experienced from the September 1939 Campaign and the 1940 French Campaign, considered that Montgomery's plan went against everything that he had learnt on the battlefield and in the military classroom. Skibiński informed Maczek of his concerns and he agreed with Skibiński, however Maczek considered that Montgomery, whom he considered to be a superior tactician, must have provided protection for the exposed flank with either an aerial bombardment or an artillery barrage, if not both.[17]

Field Marshal Montgomery explained the purpose of TOTALIZE as being that of the Canadian Army launching its thrust southwards in the direction of Falaise on the night of 7 August 1944. The object was to break the enemy's defences astride the Caen-Falaise Road and to exploit it as far as Falaise itself. Montgomery provided some information regarding the enemy defences. 12th SS Panzer Division had hurriedly prepared successive defensive lines covering the approaches to Falaise. About 60 dug-in tanks and self-propelled guns were supplemented with about ninety 8.8cm flak guns given over to an anti-tank role. The defensive positions were manned by elements of 12th SS Division with 89th Infantry Division (newly arrived from the north of the Seine) and 272nd Infantry Division. Located in the rear was 85th Infantry Division.

The plan was to attack under the cover of darkness after a preliminary attack by heavy bombers; the infantry was to be transported through the enemy's zone of defensive fire and to forward defensive locations in armoured carriers. These vehicles became known as 'Kangaroos', and were self-propelled gun carriages specially converted for transporting infantry. To ensure accurate navigation by night the positions and bearings of assault lines were fixed by survey from the leading tanks, directional wireless, Bofors guns firing tracer

17   Szudek, op. cit. pp. 43-4.

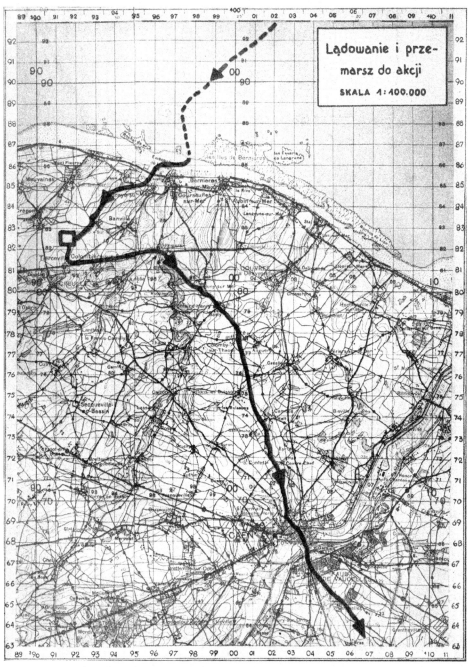

Landing and the march into action. On this and all subsequent maps, the bold line
is always the operational route followed by 1st Polish Armoured Division.

Men and vehicles from the Division in the ruined streets of
Caen, August 1944. (Narodowe Archiwum Cyfrowe)

and 'artificial moonlight'. Once the infantry had penetrated the forward enemy positions it was to debus and fan out in order to mop up the defenders. The night attack was to break thorough the Fontenay-le-Marmion- La Hogue position and exploit it as far as Bretteville-sur-Laize. The following morning the armoured units were to tackle the defences along the Hautmesnil-St. Sylvain Line and move towards Falaise.

At 23:00 hours 7 August 1944 the heavy bomber operation began and thirty minutes later 2nd Canadian and 51st (Highland) Divisions with their armoured brigades advanced. The assault was organised into eight columns of armour, each with four vehicles abreast, which advanced preceded by gapping teams of assault engineers and flail tanks.[18] The enemy was greatly confused by the armoured units driving through their defences. At first light the infantry debussed in their correct areas after a four mile drive within enemy lines and proceeded to deal with their immediate objectives. To the rear of the advance other troops began mopping-up operations, which proved to be a difficult task. By midday 2nd Canadian Division had secured May-sur-Orne, Fontenay and Roquancourt while 51st Division secured Garcelles Secqueville. Soon after Tilly la Campagne was taken.[19]

Szudek makes his own observations of the operation. As he noted, it began with an impressive infantry attack, which as we have already seen, penetrated the German forward defences to a depth of four miles but the main armoured attack was delayed until 13:45

---

18   The flail tanks were modified Shermans utilising equipment designed to trigger landmine explosions safely.

19   Field Marshal, The Viscount Montgomery of Alamein, *21 Army Group: Normandy to the Baltic*, n.p, 1946, pp. 121-3.

hours, 8 August 1944. The 1st Polish Armoured Division attacked in two battle groups, the 10th Cavalry Brigade supported by 8th Rifle Battalion, the British 22nd Dragoons and 2nd Field Artillery Regiment, with 3rd Rifle Brigade supported by 2nd Field Artillery, following. 10th Mounted Rifles moved to the east to try at least to provide some protection for the exposed Polish left flank. Just before moving off heavy bombers of the US Army Air Force arrived to provide 'close tactical support' but it was as disaster, as Maczek described on 13 August 1944: 'at 1330 hours, the Air Force started the bombardment but probably by mistake, instead of bombing the area of Cauvicourt-St. Sylvain, bombed the area south of Caen.' He added: ' ... as a result of this bombardment the Canadian AGRA (artillery) suffered most, losing a great number of men and much equipment but our AA (anti-aircraft) Artillery also lost 44 men (killed or wounded). The situation was extremely difficult as the area was packed with various munitions dumps which exploded for 40 minutes after the bombing as a result of the fires caused.'[20] Ironically, the Germans emerged relatively unscathed.

The consequence for the Poles of the American bombing was that 24th Uhlans and 2nd Armoured Regiment found themselves immediately under heavy fire from the German positions, untouched and well camouflaged. Skibiński, behind the first wave of Polish armour, was impressed with the sight of the Polish and Canadian armoured divisions attacking in formation and then with horror he saw a 'curtain of fire' hitting the left flank of the attacking regiments. The left flank was vulnerable, as both he and Maczek had feared. Skibiński watched the tanks burn; he was right, Montgomery's plan was flawed and Skibiński's reservations were vindicated. To allow the attack to continue Maczek ordered the Podhalian Rifles and part of 8th Rifle Battalion to wheel through 90 degrees and destroy the German guns; eventually they were able to do this. However, caught between heavy fire from the front and the left the Polish attack petered out and the Canadians fared no better.[21]

To look closely at the fighting of 8 August 1944 it is clear that Maczek and Skibiński were correct in their original assertion that Montgomery's plan was wrong. Within minutes 2nd Armoured Regiment had lost 26 out of 36 Sherman tanks. Tadeusz Walewicz, a veteran of the regiment, observes that the Sherman tank was slow and outgunned by the German tanks; the only advantage that the Poles had was that there were a lot of Sherman tanks available owing to American mass productions. Walewicz recalls that at zero hour the order to attack came; the Poles did so along a narrow path which hid well-placed and well camouflaged German 8.8cm guns. The assault was a terrible shock to all but after the initial horror the tactics of the 1st Polish Armoured Division changed. This is confirmed by German reports who, after their mauling of 2nd Armoured Regiment, noted that the 24th Uhlans began to advance with caution and inside a wide hollow to await reports from reconnaissance patrols. Owing to German artillery and tank fire, the Uhlans did not attack but still lost 14 tanks before they returned to safety behind Canadian lines.[22] Simonds tried to make the Poles push on, asking by radio 'why don't the Poles get on?' Maczek tried to explain that it was impossible owing to the superior, carefully positioned, German

20   Brian A. Reid, *No Holding Back: Operation Totalize, Normandy, August 1944*, Toronto, Robin Brass, 2005, pp. 285-6; Szudek, op. cit. 44-5.
21   Szudek, op. cit. 44-5.
22   Evan McGilvray, *The Black Devils' March – A Doomed Odyssey – The 1st Polish Armoured Division 1939-45*, Solihull, Helion, 2005, p. 22.

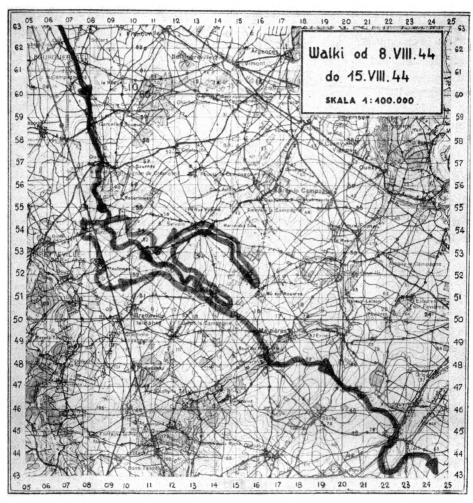

Battles in Normandy, 8-15 August 1944.

tank destroyers, which made any further attacks suicidal.[23] Even if Simonds considered that the Poles were to blame for the failure of TOTALIZE, the more experienced Maczek considered that the Poles had been asked to do too much given the circumstances.[24] Heinz Guderian, the father of German armoured tactics, had long argued that the requirements for a decisive tank attack were suitable terrain, surprise and a mass attack with the necessary breath and depth.[25]

The question of the Polish involvement in the operation continues today, with both defenders and protractors. Graham observes that the Poles were brought into the operation too early as they were originally slated to join at Stage 3 and not Stage 2. Both Maczek (Maczec as Graham renders his name) and the commander of the Canadian 4th Armoured Division objected to Simonds' plan for the armour attack; both were overruled as it was considered that they both lacked the experience necessary to criticise the plan. Graham observes that 'some of the general tactical weaknesses of the Third Division and the Second Armoured Brigade, both experienced but tired formations, and the green Second Division and the Fourth Armoured have been mentioned. None of the four divisional commanders, including Major-General Maczec of the Polish Division, which joined the corps for later battles, may be said to have directed their tactics battles sensitively. The crux of their difficulties was that neither demanded, sought for themselves, nor received accurate and timely information on which to conduct their battles.'[26] This lesson seemed to have bypassed Simonds.

Jarymowycz notes that the immediate problem with Simonds' plan was that it was led by armour and not by infantry and that the armour was too closely packed together, as he writes 'closer than Piccadilly Circus at rush hour'. He quotes one officer who recalled 'I left my tank and walked back to the end of the regimental column, we were closed so tight that my feet never touched the ground, I just stepped from tank to tank.'[27] This narrow front, 1,000 yards, was something that Maczek and Kitching did not like and requested it to be extended in order to give them more room for manoeuvre. Furthermore the Polish startline had heavily wooded areas to their fore. Predictably Simonds refused to amend his orders.[28]

Falaise, like Caen, was a road hub which the Allies needed to take and the Germans needed to hold.[29] Captain Kierz, 2nd Lieutenant Graczynski and 9 ORs were killed while Major Eminowicz and 2nd Lieutenants Małchowski, Worobiec, Kozal, Wileryinski and Czarznowski and 3 others and 89 ORs were wounded. Lieutenants Sikora and Zawalski and 2nd Lieutenants Trela and Werner and 70 ORs were posted as missing.[30] The fighting was carnage.

Initially the Poles were blamed by Simonds for their perceived timidity and lack of experience. Kitching was also scathing, claiming that on 8 and 9 August 1944 the 1st

23   Roman Johann Jarymowycz, 'Canadian Armour in Normandy. Operation "Totalize" and the Quest for Operational Maneuver, *Canadian Military History*, 1998, Vol. 7, pp. 19-40.

24   Horrocks, op. cit. p. 43.

25   Heinz Guderian, *Achtung – Panzer! The Development of Armoured Forces. Their Tactics and Operational Potential*, London, Arms and Armour, 1995, Translated by Christopher Duffy, p. 151.

26   Dominick Graham, *The Price of Command: A Biography of General Guy Simonds*, Toronto, Stoddart, 1993, pp. 142, 150-1.

27   Jarymowycz, op. cit. p. 20.Quoting General S.V. Radley-Walters.

28   Ibid.

29   Neillands, op. cit. p. 15.

30   PISM, AV.1/6, Casualties, 10:00 hours, 9 August 1944.

Polish Armoured Division was of no value to the Canadians. Jarymowycz writes that the experience and 'real fear' of the Polish crews cannot be discounted. As the Poles drove up with the Canadians to form up for TOTALIZE they passed 60 or more burnt out tanks from the previous Operation GOODWOOD.[31] This would have shaken up those who had not seen combat before.[32] One Canadian officer overcame this using aggression when he knocked out 11 anti-tank guns in as many minutes but the Poles failed to do this.[33] Regardless, there appears to have been plenty of pluck and aggression by the Poles who were also trying to deal with bad tactics and inferior tanks.

2nd Armoured Regiment of 1st Polish Armoured Division attacked along a narrow front, the very one which Maczek had complained about. They went in unsupported while the Germans were in excellent defensive positions. The Regiment was equipped with Shermans, which compared unfavourably to German models; once hit they were easily set alight as they were poorly armoured and used petrol, which was highly flammable – the Americans referred to them as Ronsons as in the cigarette light ('one strike and its alight'); the Germans were more blunt, calling them 'Tommy Cookers'. Even Montgomery had doubts about the worthiness of the Allied tanks even if he did query the arguments about the use of armour in Normandy; he did agree that Allied tanks needed larger guns such as the 17 pounder gun as fitted on the Sherman Firefly.[34]

Peter Simonds, the brother of General Guy Simonds, wrote that the tank crews had an incredible numbers of tanks shot out from under them, rather like a cavalryman having a horse shot out from under him. The tank crews (if they survived) would be idle for a couple of hours before being supplied with a replacement Sherman; the Germans found it incredibly difficult to replace tanks. Even if the Germans had superior tanks compared with those of the Allies, the Allies enjoyed superiority in the number of tanks available to them.[35]

The problem of the perception of the Poles being inexperienced and possibly afraid continued as Montgomery wrote in his diary on 8 August 1944 that the 4th Canadian Armoured Division and 1st Polish Armoured Division were making little progress. The nest day, in a letter to Field Marshal Sir Alan Brooke, Montgomery wrote 'so far the Poles have not displayed that dash we expected and have been sticky.'[36] Some of the Allies were stereotyping the Poles as dashing and gallant soldiers but forgot that they were flesh and blood, men like them, and that fear was part of their makeup as with everybody else. Indeed a recent study suggests that the fighting in Normandy was so intense that the killed and wounded ration exceeded that of the British Expeditionary Force of World War One.[37]

---

31   GOODWOOD occurred on 18-20 July 1944, and was a controversial operation even at the time. Its objectives remain a topic for debate.

32   Jarymowycz, op. cit p.31.

33   Ibid.

34   *Montgomery and the Battle for Normandy. A Selection from the Diaries, Correspondence and Other Papers of Field Marshal The Viscount Montgomery of Alamein, January to August 1944*, (ed) Stephen Brooks, Gloucestershire, The Army Records Society, 2008, Letter to Field Marshal Sir Alan Brook, 27 June 1944, pp. 165-170.

35   Peter Simonds, *Maple Leaf Up – Maple Leaf Down. The Story of the Canadians in the Second World War*, New York, Island Press, 1947, p. 168.

36   (ed) Brooks, op. cit. pp. 280-5.

37   Edgar Jones & Stephen Ironside 'Battle Exhaustion: The Dilemma of Psychiatric Casualties in Normandy, June-August 1944' *The Historical Journal* Vol. 53 2010, 109-128.

Furthermore, Montgomery possessed a reputation for being poor relating to foreigners.[38]

Belfield and Essame both assert that three divisions fighting in Normandy – 7th Armoured (Desert Rats), 50th Infantry (Northumberland) and 51st Infantry (Highland) – had all been part of the Eighth Army, fighting in North Africa, Sicily and Italy, but had proved a disappointment in Normandy as perhaps too much had been expected of them. After all, 'an old soldier is a cautious soldier' and many of the above divisions had been in action since 1941.[39]

Horrocks makes the observation that the 'desert veterans' who fought at Normandy did not do as well as might have been expected as they did not receive the necessary training for the transition from desert warfare to the fighting in Normandy; a transition from fighting in the wide open spaces of the North African deserts to the close hedges and sunken lanes of the Normandy countryside, the infamous 'Bocage'. The veteran tank commanders also took unnecessary casualties as they were used to fighting with their turrets open, but were easily picked off by German snipers hidden in the dense Norman hedgerows.[40] Florentin notes that the Allies accepted the loss of four Sherman tanks for the destruction of a single German tank. This so-called advantage resulted in some Allied tank crews having an incredible amount of tanks shot out from under them.[41] The inequality between the German weaponry and the Allied tanks is best illustrated when both Maczek and Witold Deimel (10th (Polish) Dragoons) recounted how an 8.8cm shell fired from 2km distance bored through both turret walls of a Sherman tank and continued out the other side.[42] All of these circumstances conspired against Simonds, who had hoped to be in Falaise within two days instead of the nine it took.[43]

How did Maczek handle the operation? At 02:30 hours, 8 August 1944 he made his plans, which were straightforward and divided into two phases. Phase 1 was that 10th Armoured Brigade was to seize the area south of Estrées-la-Campagne and Hill 140 while 3rd Rifle Brigade was to form a pivot in the area of Cauvicourt. In the second phase 3rd Rifles was to take over 10th Armoured Brigade's position, whilst they were then to capture the Division's final objectives north of Falaise. 10th Mounted Rifles was to provide protection for the left flank throughout the operation using their faster Cromwell tanks, although these were even more vulnerable than the Shermans. The Canadian commander, General Kitching, opted to deploy his field artillery in new positions in captured territory before his armoured brigades advanced while Maczek had his field artillery follow his armour and deploy as and when needed.[44]

Both Simonds and Kitching blamed the Poles for the lack of progress during TOTALIZE after the war but Maczek pointed to ineffective bombing and the lack of artillery support while his leading armoured regiments were engaging enemy positions which were supposed to have been destroyed. A contemporary comment regarding 8 August 1944 ran as follows: 'the ground was difficult for an attack by armour, having small woods and high hedges. In spite of fairly difficult horizons, the ground was very favourable for the

38   Sir Brian Horrocks, *Corps Commander*, with Eversley Belfield & Major-General H. Essame, London, Sedgwick & Jackson, 1977, p. 23.
39   Belfield and Essame, op. cit. pp. 128-9.
40   Horrocks, op. cit. p. 28.
41   Florentin, op. cit. pp. 80-1.
42   Ken Tout, *A Fine Night for Tanks: The Road to Falaise*, Stroud, Sutton, 1998, p. 28.
43   Ibid. p. 104.
44   Reid, op. cit. pp. 284-6.

enemy's A[nti] T[ank] defence. The enemy was not sufficiently neutralized by our own Air Force and artillery, so that the bde could attack without heavy losses (unfortunately the air force passed through our own forces, destroying not only part of the art[illery] but also the am[munitio]n dumped for AGRA [Army Group Royal Artillery]. There is a constant threat to our left flank, which will henceforth menace the div ops and my permanent worry. The Crab regt. (flails) was almost unemployed, since we did not find any mines'.[45]

Maczek certainly had a point, given the patronising and arrogant attitude of the relatively inexperienced Canadian commanders. Keegan notes that the front was too narrow and was blocked off by good German defence work, 12th SS Panzer Division supported by a battalion of Tigers.[46] Second Lieutenant Tomasz Potworowski wrote later that 'General Maczek in a more thoughtful analysis, admits that there was a certain lack of experience in the two armoured divisions entering the battle for the first time, but that the major reason for the limited terrain gains obtained was the depth of the German defences unexpected even at Army Group level. The enemy prepared them methodically as a shield for their westward armoured push against the American forces racing inland on the right of the original zone of the landings. Furthermore our early model Sherman tanks proved no match against the Tigers and Panthers of the very strong SS Hitlerjugend Armoured Division left as a support for the German lines facing the onslaught of the British and Canadian armies of which we were part!'[47] What is also very interesting was that Simonds sacked Kitching on 21 August 1944 for failing to do enough to relieve Maczek's Poles at the seminal battle at Mount Ormel, but this is to get ahead of our story.[48]

The next day saw plenty of heavy fighting but the Germans could not be dislodged; their defences were far more extensive than had been anticipated and the 1st Polish Armoured Division was ordered to break off its attack. The Poles had lost 66 tanks, five self-propelled guns, five 6-pounder anti-tank guns and two 25 pounder field guns deployed as anti-tank artillery. Maczek is one of the few to record the German casualties. The numbers of German dead and wounded are more or less unrecorded but 429 prisoners were taken from the 85th, 89th, and 272nd Infantry Divisions as well as 12th SS Panzer Division. The German equipment losses are logged as being 13 tanks, two 8.8cm guns, seven 7.5cm guns, a single 10.5cm gun as well as fourteen 15cm mortars.[49] The Division's casualties amounted to 656 killed and wounded including one major and two captains. Equipment was replaced the next day but experienced combat officers were not easily replaced, if at all. As we have seen, the Poles shouldered part of the blame for the failure of the offensive, unfairly given the other circumstances such as the 'green' bomber force bombing the wrong target, the poor intelligence and the superior weaponry of the enemy, on the shoulders.[50] After the initial attack Maczek began to develop his own tactics.

Another operation mounted on 14 August 1944 fared no better. Two Canadian infantry divisions were to attack on the Polish left flank. Once more heavy bombers, in larger numbers, were used to flatten the German positions. Once again on a clear day with

45   Ibid. pp. 290-1.
46   John Keegan, *Six Armies in Normandy: From D-Day to the Liberation of Paris, June 6th – 25th August 1944*, London, Jonathan Cape, 1982, p. 253.
47   Potworowski, op. cit. pp. 51-2.
48   John Buckley, *British Armour in the Normandy Campaign, 1944*, London, Frank Cass, 2004, p. 43.
49   Maczek, op. cit. p. 156.
50   Szudek, op. cit. pp. 45-6.

A 40mm Bofors self-propelled AA gun belonging to the 1st Anti-Aircraft Regiment of the Division. The gun was mounted on the Morris C9/B lorry platform. (Narodowe Archiwum Cyfrowe)

Crusader III AA tanks from the Division in France, August 1944. Due to the overwhelming Allied air superiority they saw little service in their intended role. (Narodowe Archiwum Cyfrowe)

A German Marder III Ausf H Panzerjäger, Normandy, August 1944. It
may have broken down, note the tow ropes. (Jan Jarzembowski)

brilliant visibility the Americans bombed the Canadians, causing great loss of life. The
Poles also suffered casualties, especially amongst anti-tank gunners. 10th Mounted Rifles
lost two tanks and had 18 men killed and a further 18 wounded. The attack was called off.
However it was noticed that the German 7th Army, with its three Panzer divisions (2nd
SS, 9th SS and 116th) with 16 other units of divisional size, was beginning to withdraw
east, harried all the way from all sides and from the air. The German escape route was
becoming predictable as their movements were being monitored by ULTRA decrypts
and air reconnaissance. The Germans were marching into a trap which could be closed
near Falaise at a few hours' notice by the II Canadian Corps from the south and the XV
American Corps from the south.

On 12 August General George Patton could see the way that things were going and
requested permission to go to Falaise and destroy the Germans, but the commander of US
12th Army, General Omar Bradley, denied him this for two reasons: firstly, he did not want
to collide with the British and secondly, he was reluctant to co-operate with Montgomery
and so the eighteen mile-wide corridor remained open and the Germans took full advantage
of this. They held the sides of the corridor and the 1st Polish Armoured Division between
15 and 17 August 1944 fought very hard to break through. On 17 August, the Division
stood 15 kilometres inside German lines, completely isolated and unsupported.

Simonds was to find Maczek in the evening of 17 August by his tank on Hill 159 near
Moutier-an-Auge. Simonds had brought a personal order from Montgomery ordering the
Polish division to detach a combat group and seize Chambois, which was situated astride an
important road junction through which it was expected the bulk of the retreating German

A welder strengthening armour on one of 2nd Armoured Regiment's Shermans. (Wiatrowskiego & Wiatrowski, *2nd Polish Armoured Regiment in action. From Caen to Wilhelmshaven 844 miles*, published in Hannover 1946)

forces would pass through. Polish officers were extremely surprised to see Simonds being used as Montgomery's messenger but Szudek claims that it was just another eccentricity of Montgomery's style of command.

The orders given were extremely difficult to execute because they changed the divisional axis of advance. However the regiments nearest the new axis were formed into a combat group commanded by Lieutenant-Colonel Stanisław Koszutski and detailed for the task. The men of the hastily formed combat group were scattered around the battlefield and, as Szudek observes, short of everything including sleep. But, by 0:200 hours, 18 August 1944, they were ready to move out.

2nd Armoured Regiment, 8th Rifle Battalion and an anti-tank squadron moved off into the night and got lost in the darkness of the night. The Germans were also moving under the cover of darkness and at times Polish and German columns became hopelessly entangled. One of the incidents of that night move was that Koszutski's column drove into a village occupied by 2nd SS Panzer Division. A furious fight broke out which was joined by a squadron of Typhoons, who strafed and bombed the Poles and Germans equally. Eventually the Poles captured the position and then discovered that they had taken Champeaux and not Chambois, 10 kilometres north of their objective.

During the morning Maczek received Koszutski's report. Maczek ordered him to proceed directly to Chambois but the signal was not confirmed. Koszutski's radio then failed and he was lost again for the rest of the day. However, Chambois still needed to be taken to fulfil Montgomery's orders. Maczek was more concerned with the essentials rather than mere geographic points. Szudek notes that Maczek had an uncanny knack of tactical priorities but fails to mention Maczek's expertise with a relief map. Maczek quickly noted on a map an elongated ridge called 'Mount Ormel'. The ridge was a little over one kilometre in length and thickened into a large 'head', which made it look like a club. Maczek quickly dubbed it *Maczuga* or 'Mace', not quite an exact one but one gets the idea. Maczek immediately ordered the *Maczuga* or Hill 262 to be seized and held at all costs. This single order from Maczek reveals him as a combat experienced and wise commander, as this one decision decided the Normandy Campaign and its successful conclusion. As Szudek observes, the other commanders and their orders during the battle of the *Maczuga* became so much background noise: the final scene had been set and the Poles were about to settle the fate of the Normandy Campaign. It would seem that only the Germans, along with Maczek, understood the significance of the *Maczuga*.[51]

---

51   Szudek, op. cit. pp. 47-9. For the operational report on the fighting for the period 7 August to 12 August 1944 see, PISM, A.XII.23/30 '*Raport Bojowa Dowodcy 1. Dywizji Pancernej (Walki za okres 7-12. VIII.44r.)*

11

Closure in Normandy

With a single order during August 1944 General Stanisław Maczek decided the fate of the Normandy campaign and sealed the fate of the troops fighting there. If he had failed it might have been possible for the Germans to have counter-attacked and pushed the Allies back into the sea; there was a distinct possibility that the Normandy campaign might have become bogged down and by winter become a very static war, something that Maczek hated. But Maczek's actions, as we shall see, ensured that the German Army was cleared out of Normandy by September 1944 with a significant amount of the enemy killed or captured.

Despite being considered by many Anglo-centric soldiers and historians as being 'inexperienced', Maczek was actually the most experienced commander of armour in Normandy during 1944, while negative observations of reckless operations such as TOTALIZE were justified once German occupied territory was finally overrun, all too frequently at great cost in men and equipment, and the depth of their defences finally uncovered.

Maczek commented that when armoured formations were funnelled through a narrow corridor they were forced to make a frontal attack, which he considered to be the most dangerous procedure. Maczek was also correct in his assertion before the Polish armoured attacks on German positions that in the key areas of the Allied armoured attacks the German defensive system had been continuously strengthened, and once they were overrun it was obvious that these defences were deeper than had been expected.

A V-1 launch site found by 2nd Armoured Regiment. (Wiatrowskiego & Wiatrowski, *2nd Polish Armoured Regiment in action. From Caen to Wilhelmshaven 844 miles*, published in Hannover 1946)

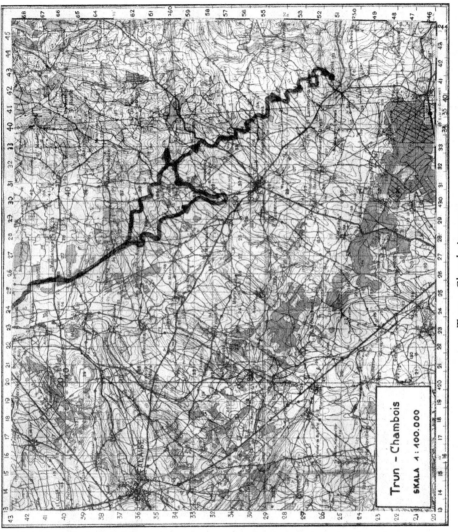

Trun – Chambois route.

All over Normandy German dugouts had been constructed with great care; many had been dug into the sides of the lanes and shored up with timber supports. Allied bombing (when it actually managed to hit the Germans) had had little effect on these defences and furthermore there had been strong German positions scattered all over the terrain. These had been cleverly hidden in woods, orchards, hedges and stone buildings and often had very good fields of fire over open terrain thus giving German tanks and anti-tank gunners a distinct advantage over Allied armour. Maczek also emphasized that the Allies were also handicapped by only having the relatively light Sherman and Cromwell tanks (27 and 30 tons respectively). These had to approach to within 500 metres of the heavier Panther and Tiger/King Tiger tanks (45, 56 and 68 tons respectively) to knock them out. The 8.8cm gun in the Tiger, or in its role as an anti-aircraft gun deployed in the anti-tank role, could easily knock out Allied armour at a distance of two kilometres. The Panther's gun and armament were also markedly superior to those of the Sherman and Cromwell while that of the German PzKpfw IV was certainly their equal. Therefore although the Allied armour greatly outnumbered the German armour, its inferiority made nonsense of this so-called advantage. The Poles lost 66 tanks in TOTALIZE and the Canadians many more; the Canadian commander, General Guy Simonds, considered that Maczek's 'inexperience' was the principle reason for the failure of TOTALIZE. Maczek considered that the main reason was that the tank crews were asked to do too much given the circumstances.[1] Spike Milligan, Irish comedian, writer and veteran of the North Africa and Italian campaigns, once wrote 'we pass several burnt-out tanks, mostly ours; that's the trouble, Jerry had better tanks. We were trying to get away with superiority in numbers, very unfair on our tank crews. We never had any armour to match the Tiger, or the Jag Panther [Jagdpanther].'[2]

Jarymowycz noted that the concept of TOTALIZE was to complement the success of the previous Operation COBRA and destroy all the German armies west of Paris. Despite initial success TOTALIZE foundered because of determined and often desperate counterattacks by the enemy while the Allies once again displayed an inability to put together a breakout doctrine at operational level.[3] English argues that 'without question the tank army remained the weakest link in the Anglo-Canadian Order of Battle' but Jarymowycz disagrees, arguing that the various Allied operations since 6 June 1944 illustrated that when tanks were ordered into battle they displayed aggression to the point of recklessness.[4]

Maczek's method of command in Normandy is worth commenting on, as witnessed after 10th Mounted Rifles' ten hour battle against Kurt 'Panzer' Meyer's tanks on the slopes leading to the River Dives and a valuable crossing at Jort. At Jort Polish sappers had managed to construct a ford enabling the Polish tanks to cross and win the river crossing from the Germans. The date of this victory was 15 August 1944; Maczek arrived in his tank the next day. In his own words he asserted 'it is very rare for an armoured divisional commander, normally confined to his command tank with a whole system of control and coordination, to change from the acoustic to the visual plane on the actual battlefield. It was on the spot in my own voice that I gave the order that morning to the 10th Armoured

1   Sir Brian Horrocks, *Corps Commander*, with Eversley Belfield & Major-General H. Essame, London, Sedgwick & Jackson, 1977, p. 43.
2   Spike Milligan, *Mussolini: His Part in my Downfall*, London, Penguin, 1980, p. 22.
3   Roman Johann Jarymowycz, *Tank Tactics: From Normandy to Lorraine*, Boulder, Rienner, 2001, p. 110.
4   Ibid. p. 325; J.A. English, *The Canadian Army and the Normandy Campaign. A Study of the Failure of High Command*, New York, Praeger, 1991, p. 312.

Cromwell VIIs from the Division in the Falaise area, 15
August 1944. (Narodowe Archiwum Cyfrowe)

Sherman tanks from the Division in the Falaise area, August
1944. (Narodowe Archiwum Cyfrowe)

Officers in a forward observation post, Falaise area, August
1944. (Narodowe Archiwum Cyfrowe)

Brigade to proceed to Louvagny and Barou, and to the 3rd Motorized Infantry Brigade
to proceed to Courcy and mop the forest'. He went on further, 'I appreciate the fact that
everything we have shed our blood for a whole week has this morning become a reality.
Our Division is today the sole unit of the Canadian Army to find itself on the south bank
of the Dives. We have overcome all organised defence. We have regained the freedom of
movement indispensable for cutting off the German retreat.' To Major Maciejowski (CO
10th Mounted Rifles) he said 'you have fought magnificently and you do not realise the
importance of what you have accomplished.'[5] Maczek immediately recognised the value of
the capture of the crossing over the Dives; his soldiers were probably too tired to know or
care at the time but he quite rightly gave them all of the credit for their victory while giving
orders to follow up the victory, thus ensuring that the Germans would have no time to
reorganise. His experience showed through, as other commanders failed to follow through
any advantage that they might have acquired and all too frequently relied on classroom
tactics.

Maczek had received orders to take Chambois at all costs and 10th Mounted Rifles had
been dispatched to do so via Louvagny and Barou to Trun. 1st Armoured Regiment under
the command of Major Stefanowski was sent to Hill 262 while 2nd Armoured Regiment
under Lieutenant-Colonel Koszutski was sent to a position 15 kilometres north-east of
Trun. Simonds warned Maczek that ahead was a single road which was unsuitable for tanks
and 'an enemy which will fight with the savagery of despair'. Maczek replied, 'the value of
the victories of my division will depend upon the difficulties of the operations you entrust
to us'. Maczek then pointed out on the map the quadrant of a circle which would enclose the

5   Eddy Florentin, *The Battle of the Falaise Gap*, London, Elek Books, 1965, translated by Mervyn Savill, pp.
149-152. See also PISM, A.XII.23/30, 17 August 1944, *Dzialanie dla zamkniecia kotla w TRUN*.

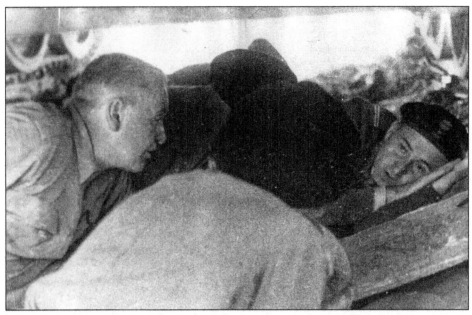

Maczek (at left) conferring under the chassis of a Cromwell VII tank,
Chambois, Falaise area, August 1944. (Narodowe Archiwum Cyfrowe)

German 7th Army, and perhaps thinking of those dark days of September 1939 he smiled and said 'For the first time in years the black shoulder straps are going to advance.'[6] The 'Black Straps' was one of the nicknames that the Germans had given Maczek's armoured brigade in Poland during 1939; it was in reference to the shoulder straps on the jackets; 'Black Devils' was another nickname.

It was during the evening of 17 August 1944 that Maczek received the order to move to Chambois had. Lieutenant-Colonel Koszutski promptly led his battle group to Champeaux, almost 18 kilometres behind German lines, but further north than Chambois. The main reason for this was inaccurate maps, similarity in names, while Polish orders were transmitted by Canadian wireless – all contributing factors. Cadet-Officer Stanisław Gunther of 2nd Armoured Regiment said later that his regiment had used much of their fuel and ammunition during the day's fighting but their orders were to advance at 02:00 hours. New supplies failed to arrive. In spite of this Koszutski realised that his regiment had just enough fuel to get to Chambois, 25 kilometres away but only 50% of his complement of his ammunition. Justifiably, he set out. Thirty minutes later the French guide disappeared. Some say that he deserted the Poles while others claim that he was killed by a sniper. Complete radio silence was imposed while the terrain got worse and worse for the tanks. At the prescribed road junction the Poles knew that they had to take the wider of the two tracks available, but in the dark this was difficult to distinguish and the track that the Poles took narrowed to such an extent that to turn about 60 tanks and 20 various other vehicles would have courted disaster, so they pressed on.

Gunther relates ' ... at a crossroads farther on, there was an almost comical incident: A German traffic controller actually held up two German columns, massed on either side

6   Florentin, op. cit. p. 160.

Elements of the 1st Polish Armoured Division pass a late model German
PzKpfw IV, Chambois, Falaise. (Narodowe Archiwum Cyfrowe)

of us, giving our tanks priority. The darkness and fear were his excuse ... I am convinced that he soon realised his mistake but was horrified by the danger, he saved his own life by allowing us to proceed. After this incident Lieutenant-Colonel Koszutski gave an order to switch the headlights on and progress became more rapid.'[7]

By 18 August 1944 the main Polish force had made little headway towards Chambois. The next day, 19 August, new intelligence reports led to Maczek being ordered to cut through the German positions and seize a hilltop known as either as Point (Hill) 262, from its height, or, as we have already seen, *Maczuga*, the Polish word for 'mace', owing to the shape of the hill. During the previous night Maczek recognised the importance of this hill as he said to Major Czarnecki, Chief-of-Staff, 10th Armoured Brigade, 'you will see two brown dots separated by a bottleneck. It looks like a bone. Or more like a *Maczuga*'. Maczek named it so as he had a 'horror' of map references, instead having a preference for a codename which could be immediately understood by all of his officers. Via the wireless the dialogue between the two commanders continued while in his tank turret each studied the map. Maczek said 'Montgomery has ordered us to take the small cross, I agree. But that's not enough. It's the heights we must seize. Whoever holds the *Maczuga* holds the 'small cross'. Whoever holds the heights holds the valley'. The die was cast while the small cross was another of Maczek's inventions and very much more than a topographical symbol. It was the road junction which would decide the fate of the day.[8]

This position was about three miles north of Chambois and dominated the main route

7   Ibid. pp. 176-7. Evan McGilvray, *The Black Devils' March – A Doomed Odyssey – The 1st Polish Armoured Division 1939-45*, Solihull, Helion, 2005, p. 37.
8   Florentin, op. cit. p. 214.

Knocked out tanks litter Hill 262 after the fierce fighting. To the left, a Sherman from 1st Polish Armoured Division, to the right a German PzKpfw V Panther. (Narodowe Archiwum Cyfrowe)

One of the Division's Shermans *hors de combat* with the bodies of some its crew beside it – Hill 262, Falaise, August 1944. (Narodowe Archiwum Cyfrowe)

to Vimoutiers. At this point about 2,000 Poles with 72 tanks and a number of anti-tank guns were isolated in a steadily diminishing perimeter during the crucial battle for the 'Falaise Pocket'.[9] For 48 hours the Poles defended this position; cut off from any direct support, partly because their exact position was unknown and partly because no force was immediately available to break through the massing Germans.

The position that the Poles found themselves in on the *Maczuga* had developed swiftly and had been unforeseen by both Allied and German commanders. The Germans had anticipated that the retrograde holding action by the armoured groups of II Panzer Corps would be sufficient to hold open a passage long enough, 36 hours at least, to enable elite German troops to escape. Furthermore, the German commander, General Walter Model, had assumed that the Allies would not establish a strong force quickly enough to get astride the escape routes to Vimoutiers in the Trun and Chambois regions. For their part the Allied commanders had confidently expected that the Canadians would soon link up with the Americans and other Poles in Chambois, which would have closed the Falaise Gap. This would have allowed the British divisions coming up from the south, together with the rest of the Canadian, Polish and American troops, to mop up scattered remnants of the German 7th Army.

However Allied intelligence had seriously underestimated the ability of the German commanders to form effective battle groups out of the more fanatical of their men, who were determined to escape or die in the attempt. Furthermore, no serious thought had been given to the tremendous pressure generated by tens of thousands of German troops surging across the River Dives to reach the comparative safety of their comrades only a few miles away. As a result of this underestimation the Germans managed to keep a corridor open across the River Dives, near St. Lambert, a hamlet roughly halfway between Trun and Chambois. The Germans managed this despite the attempts of about 200 men and a few tanks under the command of Major D.V. Currie, who was awarded the Victoria Cross for his action as he and his men entered St. Lambert and remained there, causing huge casualties amongst the fleeing Germans. More Germans filtered across the Dives via other routes while others circumvented the defenders of Chambois. But nearly all of those who had escaped this net then had to try to work their way around the Poles on the *Maczuga*, who were already holding back II SS Panzer Corps' armoured groups attacking the Poles from the opposite direction.

One of the Poles marooned on the *Maczuga* compared their situation to that of a person in the middle of marching ants. At one point 16 Tiger tanks approached the Polish position and were taken on by 12 Shermans, half of which were knocked out. Attached to the Poles was Captain Sevigny, the Forward Observation Officer of a Canadian 5.5 inch medium artillery regiment; Sevigny ordered his regiment of 16 guns to bring down fire almost on his own trench. Dozens of 100-pound shells arrived exactly on target and the German tank attack was crushed.

Sevigny, who had earlier registered several likely targets, also had a panoramic view of the battlefield. Like many artillery observations during this period he directed heavy concentrations of shells which did terrible damage to the Germans, who were mainly in the open. Many of the artillery officers were cut off from their own regiments and had the unusual experience of facing their own guns when directing fire.

According to Sevigny the most crucial day for the Poles was 20 August 1944. In his

9   Florentin asserts that there were 1,900 Poles and 87 tanks. Ibid, p. 237.

pamphlet *Boisjois Cote 262* he gives some of the most appalling detail:

' ... I could not believe my eyes, the Bosches marched against us singing *Deutschland, Deutschland uber alles.* We let them come to within fifty yards, then we mowed down their ranks ... but other waves followed ... the fifth arrived! Not having any more ammunition, the Poles charged their enemy with bayonets ... On this day we had endured eight such assaults ... what fanaticism! One of the wounded near me had the appearance of a child. I read in his pay book the date of his birth, April 1931! He was thirteen. How horrible.'

Sevigny recalled that the same night the wounded Polish officer in charge of this sector called together 15 men still capable of fighting and told them that he did not believe that the Canadians were going to relieve them and that they were now down to five shells to each gun and to the last 50 rounds per man of rifle ammunition. One of the next attacks provided a welcome reinforcement, in the shape of 15 German prisoners who turned out to be Poles, who swiftly changed uniforms and sides and joined the division. Sevigny added that when the Canadian Grenadier Guards fought their way through, helped by a Polish counterattack, the Canadians found that 'the picture at Point 262 was the grimmest the regiment had so far come up against ... unburied dead and parts of them by the score ... they had several hundred wounded who had not been evacuated, about 700 prisoners of war lay loosely guarded in a field.'

One of the prisoners was a German Corps Commander, Generalleutnant Otto Elfeldt, the commander of LXXXIV Corps. The number of Poles was terribly depleted as no food or ammunition or medical supplies had reached them, none of their softskin vehicles had been able to get through the surrounding Germans. Sevigny asserted that the Poles had done the most to thwart the massive German effects to break out of the Falaise pocket and that they endured attacks from both the front and the rear. In the Falaise Gap battle the Polish casualties were about 1,450 of whom 450 were either killed or missing. This amounted to about 20% of their combat strength. The Poles claimed more than 5,000 prisoners, while from 19 to 23 August 1944 II Canadian Corps alone had taken 13,860 prisoners. There are no statistics for the number of Germans who escaped during the battle for Falaise but the highest estimate is predictably the German claim of 50,000, while the Allied estimate is much more conservative at 20,000. Altogether around 40,000 Germans were captured in the 'pocket' while between 10 and 22 August 1944, whilst over 10,000 Germans were killed.

By the end of August 1944 the Allies had destroyed Army Group 'B' (the 7th and 15th Armies) as a coherent fighting force. Army Group 'B' had lost about 400,000 men, of who 200,000 were prisoners of war; 135,000 had been taken between 25 July and 31 August 1944.[10]

It is interesting to note the hostility between the Allied soldiers and the SS in the case of Normandy, particularly 12th SS Panzer Division (*Hitlerjugend*), who had moved into Normandy during March 1944. The Canadians hated the division, as they had shot men who had surrendered. An 'absolute order' was given on 18 June 1944 (D-Day + 12) that no 12th SS were to be taken prisoner. It was a verbal order and never put into writing. It was considered that the 12th SS had no redeeming features and were merely thugs. The 12th SS were mostly men of 18 or 19 years of age, the same age as other German soldiers in Normandy and not children, as frequently alleged. The division, drawn from members of the Hitler Youth or *Hitlerjugend*, indisputably contained elements of hardcore Nazis, and

---

10 Horrocks, op. cit. pp. 50-2.

Destroyed German equipment and vehicles in the Hill 262 area of Falaise.
The reliance of the German forces on horse-drawn transport, even at this
late stage of the war, is evident. (Narodowe Archiwum Cyfrowe)

there were instances of the murder of Canadian POWs. There is no doubt that the Allies
shot captured members of the SS in reprisal.[11] Despite the activities of some of the Allies,
Maczek continued in his desire for 'clean warfare' and that there is no suggestion that the
Poles acted in the manner of some of their Canadian comrades. Maczek sought to see the
war through as a victor and to this end kept his head and saw the *Maczuga* for what it was:
the point from which the local countryside for miles around could be dominated.

The 1st Polish Armoured Division secured the *Maczuga* on the morning of 19 August
1944. A combat group under the command of Lieutenant-Colonel A. Stefanowicz, which
was composed of 1st Armoured Regiment, the Podhalian Rifles and a squadron of tank
destroyers, formed an all-round defence just in time to beat off a strong attack from the
north-east. Once the Polish position had established itself from the direction of Chambois
a dense column of enemy tanks, armoured vehicles of all types, horse drawn carts and
between this mess of vehicles, an enormous group of infantry, came into view. This entire
mass moved slowly and with confidence past the ridge, unaware that it was already in Polish
hands.

Stefanowicz's 50 guns and 100 machine-guns opened up on the Germans. Few
Germans escaped this onslaught, with fires and explosions raging along the road deep into
the night. The German reply came swiftly and consisted of furious and often desperate
attacks which began that night and continued for the next two days. Combat group after
combat group of the German 7th Army threw themselves at the ridge and Maczek threw
into battle all that he had – the 9th Rifle Battalion, a part of the Podhalian Rifles and

11   Robin Neillands, *The Battle of Normandy, 1944*, London, Cassell, 2004, pp. 73 & 81.

Koszutski's force (now located). To the south, on the road to Chambois, the 10th Dragoons and 10th Mounted Rifles received orders to move quickly and link up with the Canadians, who were already supposed to be in Chambois.

However this was not the case, as Chambois at the time was full of Germans, who fought hard. By the evening the town had been overrun by the Poles. Around this time they made contact with the Americans, which gave rise to erroneous reports of the Falaise Gap being closed and the Germans trapped in it.[12] The reality was that on the morning of 20 August 1944 the 1st Polish Armoured Division held three loosely connected areas: on the *Maczuga* were two tank regiments, three infantry battalions and a single anti-tank squadron; at Chambois were 10th Dragoons, 24th Uhlans, an anti-tank squadron and II Battalion/358th US Infantry Regiment, while at Hill 113, about 1.5 kilometres north of Chambois, was 10th Mounted Rifles with two anti-tank squadrons.[13]

These three Polish groups stood defiantly against attacks from the German 7th Army as the Germans tried desperately to escape from Normandy. Each attack became more and more desperate but the Poles remained resolute and refused to move, while the 9th and 10th SS Panzer and 21st Panzer divisions also joined in the attacks on the Polish positions. On 21 August 1944 it seemed that the Poles defending the *Maczuga* might be finally overwhelmed by the waves of German infantry and armour attacks on their position. However at last, from the direction of Trun, tanks from the 4th Canadian Armoured Division finally arrived and the battle was over by 14:00 hours.

Szudek observes that the 1st Polish Armoured Division by far exceeded the role usually assigned to that of a single division. Furthermore he claims that much of this was to do with Montgomery's inefficiency and inability to understand the battle that raged in Normandy. Szudek claims that the victory at the *Maczuga* was due to Maczek's superior tactics and understanding of the situation and it was there that the battle for Normandy concluded.

In terms of casualties the victory was costly for the Division, with it losing 325 killed including 21 officers, 1,002 wounded including 35 officers and 114 missing. These casualties worried Maczek, as when he reported to the Polish Commander-in-Chief, General Kazimierz Sosnkowski, Maczek was swift to add that the Division was ready for further service and was greatly relieved when this was approved.[14] Furthermore, General Henry D. Crerar, the C-in-C of the 1st Canadian Army, did not object to having under his command a division that was nearly 3,000 men short. Crerar, in a letter to Sosnkowski, stated that the 4th Canadian Armoured Division had suffered 20% more casualties than the 1st Polish Armoured Division but was just as ready for combat. The 4th Canadian Armoured Division was ordered to drive southwest to Trun in an attempt to join up with the Americans in a drive towards Chambois. Aerial reconnaissance had shown that there was a tremendous log-jam of German troops and equipment around Trun and St. Lambert-sur-Dives from which they had been able to pull through the Falaise-Argentan neck of the Falaise pocket during the previous 48 hours but the narrow country roads and lanes had slowed the German withdrawal. On receiving his orders to drive his division to the Trun area Maczek decided to do it the hard way in order to get there as quickly as possible. Therefore, instead of taking the long but safer route through the Canadian-held area northwest of Falaise, he

---

12   NA, PREM 3/341/6, Montgomery to Churchill, 18 August 1944.

13   Szudek, op. cit. p. 50; Maczek. op. cit. pp. 167-9.

14   PISM, A.XII.41/3, Brigadier Peto, CLO, Liaison Allied Contingents Memoranda, Polish Manpower, 1 Polish Armoured Division, 30 August 1944.

took the short cut across the River Dives and straight through the German lines!

That night the 1st Polish Armoured Division drove straight to Trun with their headlights blazing and making no attempt to conceal their move. Amazingly, this bluff worked, as German traffic police were taken in by this brazen move and, mistaking them for tanks of either 12th SS or 21st Panzer divisions, directed them straight to the German 7th Army Headquarters. Maczek threw his division around the German Army Headquarters; the German commander, General von Hauser and his staff, found themselves trapped within the Polish armoured circle. The Poles not only had the German headquarters trapped but they were also standing across the last main German escape route from the Falaise pocket. The Polish tanks attacked from all sides as the Germans attempted to break out through the pocket which would have enabled von Hauser and staff to escape. Tanks from 9th SS Panzer Division from outside the pocket attacked the Poles in turn.[15]

Peter Simonds gives an interesting and vivid account of Maczek's head-on tactics regarding movements of his armour across the enemy when 9th SS Panzer Division tried to crash through the Polish armoured ring and re-open the pocket between Trun and Chambois in a drive from Vimoutiers, 21 miles east of Falaise, where it had assembled on getting out of the pocket. The Poles were attacked for two days from all sides with no let up. Aerial support in the shape of *Typhoon* ground attack aircraft assaulted German tanks and vehicles, which had the effect of reducing the ability of 9th SS Panzer Division to attack the Poles. The Poles hung on while the German dead piled up around the Polish position.

German casualties facing the 1st Armoured Division were one general, six colonels, 82 junior officers and 4,976 soldiers (killed, wounded, captured or missing), a total of 5,063. Regarding equipment, the enemy losses were 55 tanks, 44 guns, 14 armoured cars, 38 armoured vehicles and 359 lorries along with uncounted numbers of rifles, small arms and other equipment.[16] Amongst the prisoners taken in Normandy were several thousand Polish conscripts who happily changed sides and were able to make up the numbers of the 1st Polish Armoured Division.[17] Indeed, it is noteworthy that when Crerar visited the battlefield afterwards said that he had ' ... never before seen such devastation on such a scale and it was evident that the whole fury of two SS Corps attempting to breakout of the ring was unleashed against the Poles'.[18]

After Normandy a British Ministry of Information press release gave a view of the end of the Normandy Campaign: 'It was the Poles – actually an Armoured Division – under the command of General Maczek, who, as it is only now officially disclosed, played a leading role in sealing the Allied victory in Normandy, closing on 21st August the gap which was the only remaining outlet for the battered German army east of Argentan. During six days of very heavy fighting the Polish Division took upon itself all the fury of two German SS Corps, taking about 5,000 prisoners, including one general and 140 officers'.[19] The German general captured was *Generalleutnant* Otto Elfeldt, although Elfeldt seems to have spent the rest of his life denying that he was captured by the Poles. The Polish record is quite clear

15 Leopold Lorentz, *Caen to Wilhelmshaven with the Polish First Armoured Division*, Edinburgh, Erroll, 1949, pp. 55-7.

16 Lorentz, op. cit. pp. 55-7.

17 George Forty, *Tank Commanders: Knights of the Modern Age*, Poole, Firebird, 1993, pp. 142-3.

18 Lorentz. op. cit. pp. 51-6.

19 *It Speaks for Itself: What British War Leaders Said About the Polish Armed Forces 1939-1946. Selections from communiqués, speeches, messages and Press reports. Selections of Documents made by Capt. Witold Leitberger, Public Relations Officer, Polish Armed Forces*, n.p. 1946, (Extract) 28 August 1944, pp.110-1.

'Flying cow' insignia on the Sherman Mk IIA of Lieutenant Janusz
Barbarski, 2nd Armoured Regiment. (Jan Jarzembowski)

regarding his capture, as the war diary of 3rd Squadron 10th Mounted Rifles records that
the commander of 2nd Platoon 3rd Squadron 10th Mounted Rifles was 2nd Lieutenant
Antoni Położyński and that on 20 August 1944, 2nd Platoon captured General Otto von
Elfeldt.[20] Indeed Elfeldt surrendered to the pistol of Położyński.[21]

After the war Elfeldt tried to pretend that he had surrendered to a divisional commander,
as he once tried to relate to the British military historian, Liddell Hart.[22] The circumstances
of Elfeldt's capture are very curious, if not bizarre, because his first words to Maczek were 'Sir,
I do not know whether you are my prisoner or I am yours'. At the time the Division was all
but surrounded; the Polish soldier guarding Elfeldt delighted in seeing the general's hands
tremble once he was under fire from his own multi-barrelled mortars (*Nebelwerfer*).[23] On
the same day Położyński was credited with destroying 3 Panther tanks.[24] It was certainly a
very busy day for a man who in exile described how to destroy a German tank – by stalking
it and then getting very close and destroying its bogies. Yet, in five years of meetings and
conversations with this author he never mentioned that he had destroyed the 3 Panthers.
He did describe the capture of the general, as it is fairly well documented.[25] Położyński's
luck finally ran out when he was wounded at Thielt in Belgium on 6 September 1944.[26]

---

20   PISM, C.123 War Diary 3rd Squadron (10th Mounted Rifles) 20 August 1944. A.XII. 23/30, Battle
      Report, Brigadier-General Maczek to General Kazimierz Sosnkowski, 24 August 1944.
21   Franciszek Skibiński, *O Sztuce Wojennej: Na Polnocno-Zachodnim Teatrze Działan Wojennych 1944-
      1945*, Warsaw, MON, 1977, p. 174.
22   Florentin, op. cit. p. 238.
23   Lorentz, pp. 46-7. See also Maczek, op. cit. pp. 176-8.
24   PISM, C.127 10th Mounted Rifles, August 1944 – June 1946.
25   McGilvray, op. cit. p. 19.
26   PISM, C.123, 6 September 1944. After the war Położyński moved to West Yorkshire, married and raised

Alexander Leon 'Manka' Jarzembowski, sergeant-major, Divisional field
post office, Normandy August 1944. (Jan Jarzembowski)

After the *Maczuga* the Canadian commanders were much kinder towards the Poles, as can be seen in a letter from Simonds during October 1944 in which he wrote 'It has been an honour to have had the 1st Polish Armoured Division under my command. I wish to thank you personally and all your soldiers for their invaluable contribution to our success. They have fought most skilfully and courageously'.[27]

The Supreme Commander of Allied Forces, Europe, General Dwight D. Eisenhower in 1948 wrote of Falaise; ' ... the battlefield at Falaise was unquestionably one of the greatest 'killing grounds' of any of the war areas. Roads, highways and fields were so choked with destroyed equipment and with dead men and animals that passage through the area was extremely difficult. Forty-eight hours after the closing of the gap I was conducted through it on foot, to encounter scenes that can only be described only by Dante. It was literally possible to walk for hundreds of yards at a time, stepping on nothing but dead and decaying flesh'.[28]

Montgomery spoke of a similar scene of devastation in the Falaise area. He said that he had never seen such scenes of carnage and this was from a veteran of the Western Front, 1914-18; furthermore he reported that pilots flying at 500 feet could smell the 'stench' of

---

a family. He died on 30 June 2003 aged 89. His memoir *Z Drogi i Przydroża* was published during 1997 but is only available in Polish.

27   *It Speaks for Itself*, Letter from Lt-Gen. Guy Simonds, Acting-General Officer, C-in-C, First Canadian Army to Major-General S. Maczek, General O.C. First Polish Armoured Division, 19 October 1944, p. 114.

28   Dwight D. Eisenhower, *Crusade in Europe*, London, William Heinemann, 1948, p. 306.

dead animals and men.[29]

Later it was considered that the Falaise Pocket should never had been part of the main design of the Normandy Campaign because, as Montgomery said, 'the battle should have never taken place; it was not meant to take place'. Simply it could not have taken place had not the Germans launched such a desperate attack on 7 August 1944.[30]

---

29   NA, PREM 3/341/6, Montgomery to Churchill, 26 August 1944.
30   John North, *North-West Europe, 1944-5. The Achievement of 21st Army Group*, London, HMSO, 1977, pp. 70-1.

12

The Final Months of War: September 1944-May 1945

After the Polish victory at the *Maczuga* and the sealing of the settling of the Normandy Campaign reality began to set in for the Poles. They were somewhat reduced in number and the long envisaged replacements were never to materialize. Furthermore geo-politics were to determine the fate of Maczek and his men, who were not to have any say in the future of their country, although in September 1944 their future did not look as bleak as it was to become. Despite the fact that Stalin's European ambitions were becoming obvious many Poles in 1944 still thought that they could return to Poland in victory.

The immediate problem for the 1st Polish Armoured Division was that it needed to replace the casualties that it had suffered in the fighting in Normandy during August 1944. A Polish report gives the casualties totals as 138 officers and 1977 ORs.[1] This left Maczek 'particularly anxious that the Division shall be allowed to continue up to the Somme'.[2] Maczek's concern was borne out of the fact that there was a definite deficit of 89 officers and 1,111 ORs which he could seen would be difficult, if not impossible, to replace. Maczek considered that if there were to be any more casualties he would consider re-organising his armoured squadrons from four troops to three for the purposes of armoured reconnaissance. The reconnaissance regiments were to have their Stuart tanks replaced with Scout Cars while the anti-aircraft platoons throughout the division were to be abolished and transferred to the infantry.[3] A British report also took seriously the shortages within the Division and how to deal with them; it would seem that by the time of the meeting, the end of August 1944, the Division was being supported by the Canadians and that it was left to see how they fared regarding casualties during the next phase of operations, the move from the Seine to the Somme, which gave the division a two-three weeks' breathing space before any decisions about its future could be made. Overall there was a general sympathy for the Poles and a will to keep the Division intact and not see it reorganised elsewhere.[4]

This was done eventually, as casualties continued. Replacements were becoming available but not at a rate that would immediately recoup the men lost, with 350 men being dispatched from the UK for the week beginning 28 August 1944 and about 700 men to be made ready during the following four weeks. There were also ex-POWs, who had served in the Germany Army, and been taken prisoner by the Allies in France.[5] Brigadier Lloyd

---

1   PISM, A.XII.41/2, 1st Polish Armoured Division position, 29 August 1944.
2   PISM, A.X.II 43/3, Brigadier Peto, Chief Liaison Officer, Liaison Allied Contingents, Memoranda – Polish Man Power, 1st Armoured Division, 30 August 1944.
3   Ibid. PISM, A.XII. 41/2, Memorandum by Lieutenant-Colonel Grudzinski, 6 October 1944.
4   PISM, A.XII.41/7, Minutes of Meeting held by BGS (SD) HQ 21 ARMY GROUP to discuss the Polish Armoured Division, Signed, Captain E.R.R. Fox, Secretary, 31 August 1944.
5   PISM, A.XII.41/3, Minutes of Meeting at Main HQ 21 Army Group, discussion of Replacements of 1st Polish Armoured Division, 24 August 1944.

Over the Seine. (O.I. – K.C., *1st Polish Armoured Division (1 VIII 1944 – 11 XI 1944), France – Belgium – Holland*, published in Breda 1944)

Allied signage, exact location unknown, Germany April 1945. Some of the units referred to are 131 Polish Wing (part of RAF 84 Group, 2nd Tactical Air Force), 411 R.S.U. (RAF Repair & Servicing Unit), 2874 (RAF Regiment Squadron?), 408 ASP (RAF Air Stores Park), 84 GP RAF Police. (Jan Jarzembowski)

An M5A1 Stuart of the 24th Uhlans, Belgium, September
1944. (Narodowe Archiwum Cyfrowe)

Troops from Maczek's Division are greeted joyously by liberated civilians
in the Ghent area, Belgium 1944. (Narodowe Archiwum Cyfrowe)

A Sexton self-propelled gun belonging to the Division, Belgium, 1944. The Sexton mounted a 25-pounder gun-howitzer, and was based on a US tank hull, manufactured in Canada. (Narodowe Archiwum Cyfrowe)

German Sturmgeschütz III Ausf G assault gun with 'saukopf' ('pig's head') gun mantlet; sometimes also used as a tank destroyer. Knocked-out by the Division at Moerdijk, Netherlands, November 1944. (Jan Jarzembowski)

Sherman Mk IIA of Second Lieutenant Wiatrowski, HQ Squadron, 2nd
Armoured Regiment, Netherlands 1944. (Jan Jarzembowski)

minuted that there was a need to screen these prisoners politically and for security reasons
before releasing them to the Poles.[6] A further and major problem was that all of these men
needed to become accustomed to the routine of the 1st Polish Armoured Division, its
method of fighting and organisation, become used to the different tanks and in some cases
become combat experienced.

The experiences of the 1st Polish Armoured Division and their casualty rates at times
become almost an obsession as the Poles strove to keep themselves in the war. Major-General
Regulski observed that since August 1944 the Division had been in almost continuous
operations and that the casualty rate up to 1 October 1944 amounted to 183 officers and
2,143 ORs. The major problem was that the specialists of the armoured brigades were
difficult to replace while the 9th Rifle Battalion had 223 seasoned troops and 518 fresh
but inexperienced troops.[7] These were the problems which beset Maczek as he removed
himself and his division from Normandy and advanced ever eastward towards Germany
and eventually Poland, as they thought. During October 1944 Maczek complained to the
Chief of Staff, General Kopański, that he was not getting replacements and was therefore
unable to replace tanks crews and specialists while equipment was short, which included
communications and tank transporters. There was also a shortage of instructors.[8]

The lack of experienced soldiers in the Division was to make itself felt when, at the
beginning of November 1944, it received an official reprimand from Army Group as a result

6   PISM, A.XII.41/3, Subject Reinforcement Situation – 1st Polish Armoured Division, 21/Agp/3705/27/A/
    Org, Minute 2, Brigadier C. Lloyd, 2 September 1944.
7   PISM, A.XII.42/56, Memorandum – re: Major-General Regulski to Major-General J. Kennedy, 24
    October 1944.
8   PISM, A.XII.41/2, Maczek to Chief of Staff, 4 October 1944.

Shermans from the Division being used as static pillboxes near Kapelsche Veer, Netherlands, 1944. (Narodowe Archiwum Cyfrowe)

This image conveys well the flooded nature of much of the terrain in the Low Countries the Division had to contend with during 1944-45. (Narodowe Archiwum Cyfrowe)

Shermans from the Division on the move near Kapelsche Veer,
Netherlands, 1944. (Narodowe Archiwum Cyfrowe)

Two officers of the 24th Uhlans near Kapelsche Veer, Netherlands, 1944 – Major Romuald
Dowbór (left) and Captain Adam Dzierzek (right). (Narodowe Archiwum Cyfrowe)

Flying cow insignia on a Sherman IIA of HQ Squadron, Second Lieutenant Wiatrowski, 2nd Armoured Regiment, Netherlands November 1944. (Jan Jarzembowski)

Warning signs in the Netherlands, Autumn 1944. (Wiatrowskiego & Wiatrowski, *2nd Polish Armoured Regiment in action. From Caen to Wilhelmshaven 844 miles*, published in Hannover 1946)

One of 2nd Armoured Regiment's vehicles alight in the Netherlands, Autumn
1944. (Wiatrowskiego & Wiatrowski, *2nd Polish Armoured Regiment in action.
From Caen to Wilhelmshaven 844 miles*, published in Hannover 1946)

of slack security in the divisional wireless network which included messages in Polish being
transmitted *en clair*, rather than in code. This was almost unforgivable because even if many
Polish officers struggled to speak English, there were a significant number of Germans who
could speak Polish, as well as Poles who voluntarily served the Germans.[9] It was more than
likely that this problem arose owing to a shortage of technicians, such as radio operators
who understood their trade.

In fairness the Polish commanders were just as alarmed at the type of soldier that they
were inheriting as replacements; the virtual amateur and untutored type who had never
trained in Maczek's excellent school. The problem here was the question of slack patrolling,
after the enemy had raided the southern bank of the River Maas. It was considered that
when Polish patrols met enemy patrols, the Poles tended to react inappropriately (panic!),
whilst patrol reports were incomplete and seemed to arrive at unwarranted conclusions
instead of making a statement of accurate facts. The conclusion reached was that patrolling
and strongpoints were to be beefed up and that fuller reports were to be required in future,
instead of panicky remarks that had passed as reports previously.[10] Equally Crerar wrote
in the Canadian Army newspaper, *Maple Leaf*, on 1 November 1944 of the 1st Polish
Armoured Division that ' ... during recent weeks the Poles have been fighting under
extremely difficult conditions, and have established an outstanding reputation by their
accomplishments.' Crerar also said that 'Every demand ever made on these troops had been
met. Every task has been completed, no matter how bitter the enemy's defences or how
unsavoury the natural conditions. With such officers and men military success and final

9   PISM, AV.1/56, Signal Security, 2 November 1944.
10   Ibid.

A Sherman Firefly belonging to the Division in the Moerdijk area, November 1944. Note the track links utilised as additional armour protection. (Narodowe Archiwum Cyfrowe)

victory can never be in doubt ... in all the fighting of the 1st Canadian Army during the last three months the Polish troops have set the finest of military standards'.[11] Amazing words, given the attitudes of the Canadian commanders earlier in August 1944.

The Poles, as Szudek writes, were ready to fight within a week.[12] But the casualties had obviously taken their toll. In the infantry the companies were reduced to fewer than 100 men; with the armour the tanks were reduced to three platoons but by 31 August 1944 the Division crossed the River Dives via the 'Warsaw Bridge' as they chased the Germans. From there the Poles chased them into Belgium and on 12 September 1944 liberated Ghent and then turned north to clear the coast of the Scheldt estuary. One of the most important tasks for the Division was to locate and capture bridges over water obstacles such as river and canals and so during September 1944 an order from Corps demanded that the 1st Polish Armoured Division should advance and capture a bridge that had been found intact in the Abbeville area.[13] However when the 1st Polish Armoured Division moved towards Abbeville reconnaissance revealed that the bridges over the River Somme there had been blown up by the Germans. This was at 11:30 hours on 2 September 1944; immediately

---

11   *It Speaks for Itself: What British War Leaders Said about the Polish Armed Forces 1939-1946. Selections from communiqués, speeches, messages and Press reports. Selections of Documents made by Witold Leitgeber, Public Relations, Polish Armed Forces*, n.p. 1946, 115.

12   P.A. Szudek, 'The First Polish Armoured Division in the Second World War' in *Themes of Modern Polish History. Proceedings of a Symposium on 28 March 1992 in Honour of the Centenary of General Stanisław Maczek* (ed) Peter D. Stachura, Glasgow, The Polish Social and Educational Society, 1992, pp. 35-59.

13   PISM, AV.I/27 September 1944.

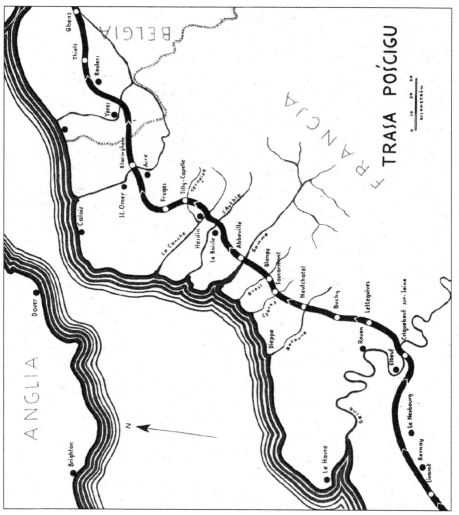

The main route of the 1st Polish Armoured Division into Belgium.

General Stanisław Maczek (right) in the Ghent area, autumn
1944. (Narodowe Archiwum Cyfrowe)

Cromwell VII tanks from the Division in the Ghent area,
Belgium, 1944. (Narodowe Archiwum Cyfrowe)

An M-10 tank destroyer belonging to the 1st Polish Armoured Division, Belgium, Autumn 1944. This photo conveys well the look of a vehicle on active service, serving as the home and sleeping quarters of the crew as well as its combat role. (Narodowe Archiwum Cyfrowe)

An Allied aircraft flies low over 2nd Armoured Regiment's positions in the Netherlands, 1944. (Wiatrowskiego & Wiatrowski, *2nd Polish Armoured Regiment in action. From Caen to Wilhelmshaven 844 miles*, published in Hannover 1946)

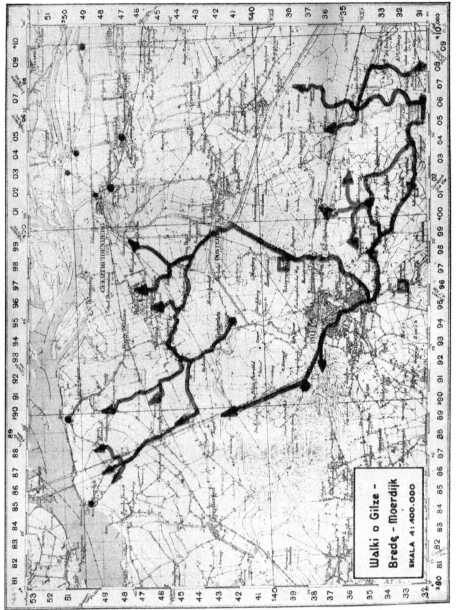

Battles of Gilze, Breda and Moerdijk. Dots indicate extent of planned operations at this time.

Netherlands, the famous land of windmills, as see by a photographer from 2nd Armoured Regiment, Autumn 1944. (Wiatrowskiego & Wiatrowski, *2nd Polish Armoured Regiment in action. From Caen to Wilhelmshaven 844 miles*, published in Hannover 1946)

The view from 2nd Armoured Regiment's positions in the Netherlands, Autumn 1944, giving a good impression of the open terrain encountered in places, vert different to the Normandy bocage. (Wiatrowskiego & Wiatrowski, 2nd Polish Armoured Regiment in action. From Caen to Wilhelmshaven 844 miles, published in Hannover 1946)

Maczek addressing his troops during the ceremony at Breda in which his
Division received the Freedom of the City, 11 November 1944. To the left can
be seen Van Slobbe, the Mayor of Breda. (Narodowe Archiwum Cyfrowe)

the Polish sappers prepared to build a replacement bridge and by 17:15 hours, 3rd Rifle
Brigade under the command of Lieutenant-Colonel Dec had stormed the river and forced
a crossing, which enabled the Division to continue its advance.[14]

By the end of September 1944 the Division had moved to the assembly area east of
Antwerp ready to move into the Netherlands. After fighting in Normandy the Division
found itself operating in an entirely different terrain, which mostly involved river and canal
crossings, in the main lacking any bridges, which the German defenders bitterly defended,
while much of the territory being crossed was marshy and difficult for tanks to traverse.
It was during this wet autumn and winter campaign that superb co-operation between
infantry, armour and sappers was displayed. The heroism of the Polish sappers should
be recorded, as they crossed water obstacles, throwing up bridges and constructing fords
whilst under heavy fire thus enabling the Polish armoured advance to continue. A battle
report sent to Maczek from Zgorzelski of 10th Dragoons on 22 September 1944, written
in the field, reported that the fighting on the Axel Canal had cost 106 casualties in one day
alone, which included four officers. Overall the officer casualty rate was 50% while 430
ORs being killed or wounded reflected a casualty rate of over 50%.[15] However, Maczek was

---

14   PISM, A.XII.23/30, Colonel Dworak, War Report nr. 3, Staff First Armoured Division (Polish), 17
     September 1944.
15   PISM, A.XII. 23/30, W. Zgorzelski to Maczek, 22 September 1944.

A barricade at Breda, Netherlands, 29 October 1944. (Wiatrowskiego
& Wiatrowski, *2nd Polish Armoured Regiment in action. From Caen
to Wilhelmshaven 844 miles*, published in Hannover 1946)

able to report that the morale amongst his men was very good as a result of the success that
the Division was enjoying, despite the casualties they were suffering.[16]

Throughout October 1944 the 1st Polish Armoured Division was engaged in heavy
fighting across this extremely difficult terrain, riven by dykes and canals, each carefully
prepared for defence by the enemy and thus forcing the Poles to fight for every inch of the
territory – their gains were always bloody. A memorandum concerning the 'Western Front'
for the middle of October 1944 reflected that in the armoured and rifle brigades as well as
the dragoons, the officer casualty rates were very high.[17] 30 October 1944 saw Maczek's
greatest triumph of the autumn campaign, the capture of Breda. The people of Breda
are eternally grateful to Maczek and how he captured their town with minimal damage
because, as Captain Stanisław Grabowski, a squadron commander of 1st Armoured
Regiment, observed, there were several ways of taking a town. Montgomery's way was to
lay on an aerial bombardment and 'blitz' the town or shell it and then storm the town.
Maczek's method was to encircle a town and then there was a chance that street fighting
could be avoided, thus he gained renown amongst the civilian population. Captain Tadeusz
Wielgorski, 2nd Armoured Regiment, makes a similar observation, noting that then the
Division captured Breda, all of the regiments and their tanks could have fired and caused
complete devastation. They did not, and that was why Breda 'greeted us so warmly'.[18]

After capturing Breda the Division moved north, chasing the enemy until they trapped

---

16 PISM, A.XII.23/30, Report No. 4, General Maczek, 26 September 1944.
17 PISM, A.XII. 27/13, Colonel Wieckowski to General Boruta-Spiechowicz, Commander 1st Corps, 16
    October 1944.
18 *The Soldiers of General Maczek in World War II* (ed) Zbigniew Mieczkowski, Warsaw-London, Foundation
    for the Commemoration of General Maczek's First Armoured Division, 2004, p. 21.

A sign in a shop window in Breda – "Long live Poland". (O.I. – K.C., *1st Polish Armoured Division (1 VIII 1944 – 11 XI 1944), France – Belgium – Holland*, published in Breda 1944)

"Thank you Poles, for the liberation of Breda." (O.I. – K.C., *1st Polish Armoured Division (1 VIII 1944 – 11 XI 1944), France – Belgium – Holland*, published in Breda 1944)

The Freedom of the City granted by Breda to the 1st Polish Armoured
Division. (O.I. – K.C., 1st Polish Armoured Division (1 VIII 1944 – 11
XI 1944), France – Belgium – Holland, published in Breda 1944)

the Germans against the waters of the Hollandsche Diep. This necessitated ten days of
battle, which included the crossing of the Mark Canal in the very teeth of strenuous enemy
resistance. The battle finished with the capture of Moerdijk on the coast.[19]

In mid-November 1944 the 1st Polish Armoured Division was given its first
opportunity to rest and recoup as it relaxed along the banks of the River Maas with its
HQ at Breda. During this quiet period the Divisional Staff took stock of the campaign.
Casualty rates were compiled and analyzed for the period of 8 August – 15 November
1944. They were quite sobering: 4,478 killed, wounded or missing. This figure included 291
officers, but amazingly only five men had been captured by the Germans in operations after
Falaise. This would rather suggest something of the stubborn and heroic nature of the men
of Maczek's division. The ten week chase across the Low Countries had cost the Division
3,038 casualties. The infantry had borne the heaviest burden with 63% of the casualties,
then the armour with 16.25%, artillery 5.85%, signals 6.75%, sappers 2%, supply 1.45%
and others 2.1%. In addition there was a high number of hospitalised sick: 56 officers and
1,237 ORs. With these figures the number of casualties rose to 5, 771 officers and men.
Against this figure it must be recognised that a large proportion of the sick and wounded,
including men previously hospitalised and thus not part of these statistics, returned to
duty – 1,773 officers and men.[20] However what did this actually mean? Second Lieutenant
Antoni Położyński, who was wounded during September 1944, did return for duty but not
to fight again. Statistics can tell you anything that you want!

At the beginning of the great pursuit on 9 September 1944 the strength of the Division
was 736 officers and 11,950 men. This was boosted by the arrival from the UK of 12 officers
and 350 ORs during September, followed by a further replacement of 12 officers and 277
men during November 1944. Later the number of replacements rose steadily. A meeting
held during December 1944 to consider the organisation and training of the 1st Polish

19   Szudek, op. cit. p. 52-7.
20   Ibid.

Heavily-laden infantry and a Sherman belonging to Maczek's Division
in the Netherlands, late 1944. (Narodowe Archiwum Cyfrowe)

Armoured Division amazingly revealed that there was a surplus of 214 officers while there
was a deficiency of 2,504 ORs. The surplus of officers was due to a recent promotion of 250
cadet-officers. It was considered that there was a further need for training and for more
equipment, to which Maczek and General Kopański (Chief of the Polish General Staff)
agreed. 15 February 1945 was earmarked as the target day for the Division to be fully
operational, while it was agreed that the 214 surplus officers could be used as trainers with
no adverse effect on the operational element of the Division. This was Maczek's suggestion.
He also agreed that the Division would remain available for operations during this period
of reinforcement prior to 15 February 1945 but any such use would retard the date when it
would be fully operational.[21] At the end of March 1945, the Division had received 58 new
officers and 4,496 men as replacements. Most of these soldiers came from POW camps
and from Poles from Polish provinces directly incorporated into the Reich and conscripted
into the German Army. These men were the most valuable and reliable soldierly material
because they had been fully trained and needed a relatively short period of familiarisation
with new arms and equipment.

Replacements for the armoured divisions required specialist training and the Tank
Reserve Squadron proved to be valuable. The squadron organised training courses for tank
drivers (56), wireless operators (85), and tank gunners (75). During the period of operations
the squadron supplied 327 armoured fighting vehicles and replaced 18 officers and 750 men
for fully trained tank crews; an incredible feat for a permanent staff of 3 officers and 46

21   PISM, A,V. 1/63, 21/Agp/1985/4/GSD, Minutes of Meeting held at Main HQ 21 Army Group, 14
December 1944, to consider Organisation and the Training of the 1 Polish Armoured Division.

A fine study of a crew loading
ammunition into a Sherman, Belgium
1944. (Narodowe Archiwum Cyfrowe)

Positions of the Division in the Netherlands, late 1944. In the foreground can be seen a
Bren Gun position, whilst a Universal Carrier rolls past. (Narodowe Archiwum Cyfrowe)

A V-1 that landed on Dutch soil near 2nd Armoured Regiment's positions, Autumn 1944. (Wiatrowskiego & Wiatrowski, *2nd Polish Armoured Regiment in action. From Caen to Wilhelmshaven 844 miles*, published in Hannover 1946)

German dead, Dutch/German border, 15 April 1945. (Jan Jarzembowski)

men. However during the winter break in Flanders Maczek for once, thought about the political situation in which the Poles found themselves in; it was during this period that the future of Poland was settled at Yalta.[22]

It is widely considered, especially by Poles, that of all of the wartime conferences the conference at Yalta (4-11 February 1945) was the most controversial, being frequently compared with the Munich Agreement (1938) which saw Czechoslovakia abandoned to Nazi Germany while at Yalta east-central Europe was handed over to the Soviet Union. Thorpe claims that Churchill was quite ebullient about allowing the Soviet Union to extend its influence throughout the region but Anthony Eden, the British Foreign Secretary, was quite worried and alarmed at Soviet behaviour and intent. He did not believe that they would behave well, merely wanting to extend their world revolution at the expense of anybody who got in the way. Regarding Poland, which was the subject of the agenda at Yalta at seven out of eight plenary sessions, Stalin and the Soviet Government were determined that Poland should be strong but under Soviet control, and that it should receive territory in the west at the expense of Germany.[23] This was poor, if any, compensation for the Polish eastern territories annexed by the Soviet Union during their joint invasion of Poland with Germany during September 1939. It was quite clear that by 1943 the Soviet Union had no intention of returning these territories and had already brutalised the Polish population with mass murder and deportations to the far-flung reaches of the vast Soviet interior. Maczek's home town and region was one of the annexed areas. At the time of the conference the Red Army was making huge advances across Poland, having already 'liberated' the remains of the Polish capital, Warsaw and the second largest city in Poland, Łódź. The Permanent Under-Secretary at the Foreign Office, Sir Alexander Cadogan, remarked in a letter to his wife that ' ... if we couldn't get a decent-looking Polish settlement, none of our other high-falutin' plans for the World Organisation and suchlike would make much sense ... ' However, in a further letter, despite trying to drum up a sense of success Cadogan is not really convinced by the agreement on Poland, which in reality gave the Soviet Union a freehand there, writing, 'We have got an agreement on Poland which may heal differences, for some time at least, and assure some degree of independence to the Poles.'[24] This was a major departure from the original British assertion that they had gone to war to defend Polish independence. Indeed, once General Anders, the Commanding Officer of Polish troops in Italy, heard of the decisions made at Yalta he declared to Churchill that Yalta 'was the end of Poland'.[25]

Maczek considered the evils that the Germans had visited on Poland: the original invasion, the destruction of Warsaw and the death camps at Auschwitz (Oświęcim in Polish) and Dachau; he wondered whether Germany was the primary enemy or was it the 'ally from the east'? He also thought about a Polish return home but to where? The proposed new Polish eastern frontiers followed the Curzon Line, the British proposal of the early 1920s, which placed his home in the Soviet Union. But, apolitical as ever, he rejected all of his personal concerns and stated that a soldier should not speak of his fate or future,

22   Maczek, op. cit. p. 217.
23   D.R. Thorpe, *Eden: The Life and Times of Anthony Eden, First Earl of Avon, 1897-1977*, London, Chatto & Windus, 2003, pp. 303-6.
24   *The Diaries of Sir Alexander Cadogan, 1938-1945*, (ed) David Dilkes, London, Cassell, 1971, A.C. to T.C. 10 February (1945); A.C. to T.C. 11 February (1945) pp. 707-9.
25   NA, FO 371/47578 N 1079/6/G55, 21 February 1945.

A Sherman Mk V, 2nd Armoured Regiment, attacking near Bourtange,
Netherlands, near the German border, 14-15 April 1945. (Jan Jarzembowski)

26 February 1945 – Maczek is awarded the *Légion d'Honneur* by General
Juin at the Arc de Triomphe, Paris. (Narodowe Archiwum Cyfrowe)

Men from the 2nd Armoured Regiment at the Dutch/German
border, 9 April 1945. (Jan Jarzembowski)

no matter how hard or unfair this might be.[26] Nevertheless, it should be observed that
the Foreign Office were aware that Maczek was unhappy with the high-handed attitude
of Anders towards wartime military-politics and had been openly critical of him, a very
unusual departure for Maczek.[27]

The lengthy period of the Division's wait in Flanders came to an end when at the
beginning of April 1945 they moved 250 kilometres from Breda to the region of Hengelo
in preparation for a new offensive. On 14 April 1945 the Division stood on the Dutch-
German border facing northward in flat marshy land bisected by rivers and canals, very
similar to that of Holland and Belgium, which they had conquered during the autumn of
1944. As had been the case during the autumn the Division's sappers using their engineering
skills and bravery were able to overcome all of the obstacles which they encountered in spite
of determined defensive action by the German defenders. The Allies were well aware that
the Germans were abandoning The Netherlands or 'thinning out from Holland' and that
every incident on patrol regarding the enemy, however trivial, was to be reported; equally,
negative reports were just as important.[28] The main source of intelligence regarding enemy
intentions for the defence of Germany was to be the most basic – routine patrols.

It was during this period that Maczek's men received an urgent request which was
to re-link them to their compatriots in Poland, as it was revealed to them that at nearby

26   Maczek, op. cit. p. 217.
27   Evan McGilvray, *A Military Government in Exile. The Polish Government-in-Exile 1939-1945, a Study of
discontent*, Solihull, Helion, 2010, p. 174.
28   PISM, A.V.1/33, signal from 1 Corps (BR), 17 March 1945.

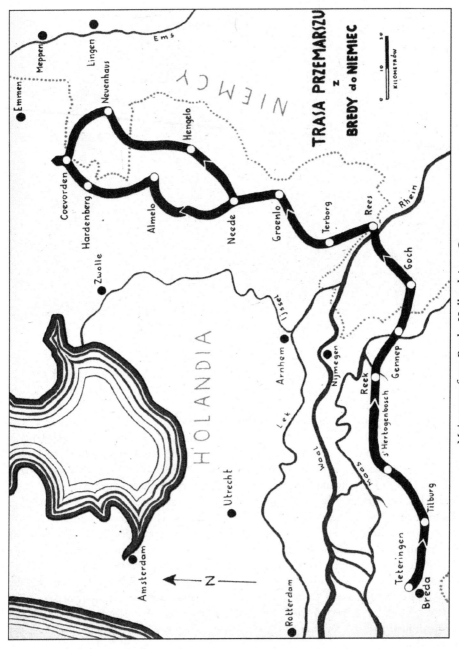

Main route from Breda, Holland, into Germany.

12 April 1945 - Lt.Col. S. Koszustki, commander of the 2nd Armoured Regiment,
receives a report from Lieutenant Maria Milewska, commander of women
belonging to the Polish Home Army who had been liberated by the Division
from their prison camp at Oberlangen. (Narodowe Archiwum Cyfrowe)

A dramatic image of the Poles using a flamethrower in action at Papenburg,
near Oberlangen, Germany 1945. The vehicle is a Universal Carrier, Wasp IIC
flamethrower, possibly belonging to the 10th Dragoons, as there was one such
vehicle in each squadron's scout platoon. (Narodowe Archiwum Cyfrowe)

German dead on the Dutch/German border April 1945. (Jan Jarzembowski)

A mascot on a Sherman V of 2nd Armoured Regiment. Note the spare tank idler wheels secured to the glacis plate, and tracks welded to the sides of the turret and hull to upgrade the armour against anti-tank weapons. The officer with the moustache in the foreground is Second Lieutenant W. Kulesza. German/Dutch border, April 1945. (Jan Jarzembowski)

Close-up of the mascot. (Jan Jarzembowski)

Niederlangen there was camp which contained women who had fought for the Polish underground during the Warsaw Uprising, August-October 1944. It was feared that the Germans might try to use the women as some form of diversionary tactic and that it was crucial that an armoured platoon be sent to the camp and free the women. A platoon from 3rd Squadron, 10th Mounted Rifles was sent to the camp. The women were overjoyed to see the Allied troops, whom they had thought, owing to their uniforms, were British. A woman known simply as Mieczysława described her liberation from *Stalag VI C Oberlangen* by 10th Mounted Rifles. Once the women heard the soldiers speak they realised that they were Polish; the most important thing for the women captives was that the troops spoke to them in Polish. It is interesting to note that one of the liberated women wrote to Maczek on his 100th birthday in 1992, still expressing her gratitude for her liberation so many years before.[29] To conclude this episode the women displayed their military discipline and fortitude when General Maczek later arrived at the camp and the women formally paraded with their commanding officer, Lieutenant 'Jaga' Milewska, of the Polish Home Army, making her formal report that 1,726 women, soldiers of the Home Army in *Stalag VI C Oberlangen* were reporting for duty.[30] The fate of the failed uprising was starkly brought home to the Division that day.

On 19 April 1945 the Division established a bridge over its last major obstacle, the Küsten Canal and reached its final objective: Wilhelmshaven. It was typical of Maczek that during the forcing of the Küsten Canal he delayed the action as long as possible so

---

29   Evan McGilvray, *The Black Devils' March – A Doomed Odyssey – The 1st Polish Armoured Division*, Solihull, Helion, 2005, p. 107.
30   K. Jamar, *Śladami Gąsienic Pierwszej Dywizi Pancernej*, Hengelo, H.L. Smit & ZN, 1946, pp. 301-7.

The advance on Rhede, Germany, 17 April 1945, 2nd Armoured Regiment with the 10th Dragoons. An M5 half –track and a number of dispatch riders can be seen. (Jan Jarzembowski)

Sherman Vs during the advance on Rhede. (Jan Jarzembowski)

Austin K2 'Katie' ambulances from the Division, so called because of the War Office 'K2' designation, Rhede, Germany, April 1945 (Jan Jarzembowski)

A Humber Scout Car from the Liaison Platoon, 2nd Armoured Regiment, with M5 half-track in the background. Germany, April 1945. (Jan Jarzembowski)

Shermans advancing towards Hessel, Germany April 1945. (Jan Jarzembowski)

Polish women prisoners from the resistance movement, *Armia Krajowa* (Home Army), captured during the Warsaw Uprising in 1944 and pictured on 15 May 1945 at Stalag VI C, Oberlangen, Germany, when General Anders visited the Division. They had been liberated by members of the Division the previous month. (Jan Jarzembowski)

Sherman Mk Vs from the 2nd Armoured Regiment advancing towards
Stapelmoorer Heide, Germany, April 1945. (Jan Jarzembowski)

German prisoners captured at Stapelmoorer Heide, Germany, April 1945. Shermans from
the Division are in a Laager formation. One crew appear to be milking a goat (on the
right), hence the goat in foreground turning to look?! The Shermans in the foreground
are Fireflies, with the one on the left having a *trompe l'oeil* (deceive the eye) painted-out
barrel. This was done to deceive the enemy into thinking the shortened barrel meant a
less powerful gun and so more readily exposing itself in combat. Shermans with circular
markings on rear storage bins, C Squadron, 2nd Armoured Regiment. (Jan Jarzembowski)

A Mk 4 Sherman (unit code 52 for the 2nd Armoured Regiment), Germany, April 1945. The white flag was left by surrendering German troops. (Jan Jarzembowski)

Regimental HQ, 2nd Armoured Regiment (52 sign), Germany April 1945. (Jan Jarzembowski)

Originally captioned 'C.O. with Air Liaison Officer Germany, 2nd Armoured
Regiment April 1945', the officer on the left could be the commander of
the 2nd Armoured Regiment, Lt.Col. S.Koszutstki, who handed over the
command to Major Gutowski on 22 April 1945. (Jan Jarzembowski)

A German Jagdpanzer IV/L70 tank destroyer, apparently intact and abandoned
in the area of the Küsten Canal, Germany April 1945. (Jan Jarzembowski)

The unidentified commander of German troops in Hessel, Germany April 1945, organising their surrender. He appears to be a Fallschirmjäger officer. A Sherman IIA is in the background. (Jan Jarzembowski)

Prisoners at Hessel being inspected by Major Michal Gutowski, commander of the 2nd Armoured Regiment. (Jan Jarzembowski)

as to concentrate enough firepower to make sure of success without excessive casualties.[31] On 4 May 1945 10th Mounted Rifles and 8th Rifle Battalion halted on the outer ring of Wilhelmshaven's defensive rings. This position was well prepared and equally well defended. In the evening 10th Mounted Rifles called for artillery support in order to open up a passage into the town but a signal had been received to the effect that an armistice had been arranged from the next morning, 5 May 1945 at 08:00 hours. The artillery opened fire and the bombardment continued unceasingly throughout the night until 07:59 hours.

During the final offensive in Germany the Division lost another 37 officers and 567 men killed or wounded. The Poles took 5,000 prisoners as well as huge amounts of supplies, equipment, arms and naval units. The 1st Polish Armoured Division had been in action for ten months and had suffered casualties to the tune of 304 officers and 4,855 men but it had taken at least four times that number in prisoners (300 officers and 18,300 ORs).[32]

To complete the campaign of the 1st Polish Armoured Division across North-Western Europe Maczek described the surrender of German forces in Ostfriesland at the HQ of II Canadian Corps at Bad Zwischenahn. He recalls how in a large room, General Guy Simonds, the Corps commanding officer, his chief of staff and divisional commanders took their places behind a long table, seated. The lack of chairs for the Germans gave advance notice that the Germans were in for a hostile reception. Maczek sat next to Simonds.

Six German officers entered the room: General Erich Straube, the commanding officer of the German 1st Parachute Army between the rivers Ems and Weser; he was accompanied by the commanding officer of local units of the German Navy, the *Kriegsmarine*, his chief of staff and three officers in command of sectors in Ostfriesland. The German officers entered the room and stood to attention. Maczek looked at the men and reflected how differently they looked from those captured on the battlefield, covered in dust from the fighting and their faces still showing the raw emotion of battle. These men were different – their faces were 'hard and stiff, masks which might conceal everything, or nothing.'

Straube began to speak but Simonds interrupted him saying 'you have not come here to negotiate with us; you are here to listen to the terms of unconditional surrender'. Simonds began to read the terms of the unconditional surrender in a 'hard, clear voice'.

Maczek admits to losing concentration as he thought about the war and remembered with 'intense clarity' General Kutrzeba and Colonel Pawłowski at the capitulation of Warsaw in 1939. Kutrzeba was the Deputy Commanding Officer of Polish troops in Warsaw during September 1939. Maczek mused, was this revenge for that 'tragic moment?'

Maczek's ears began to prick up when he heard Simonds give the orders for the occupation of each area, with the 2nd Canadian Infantry Division being assigned the district bordering the River Weser and the 4th Canadian Armoured Division to the west. Maczek began to think that he was hearing things when he heard Simonds scanning slowly, clearly and on purpose each word: 'Fi-rst Po-lish Division – Wilhelmshaven'.

But, no, Maczek had heard correctly and for the first time, the German officers, still standing to attention, betrayed emotion as Maczek recalled something like a grimace appeared in their eyes. Previously the Germans had studiously avoided looking at him but then, for an instant, the Germans looked at Maczek and his Polish uniform.

Maczek wrote 'surely it was not necessary to remind them that they had unleashed this dreadful war with the attack on Poland and that in the presence of one of the Polish units

31   *The Soldiers of General Maczek*, op. cit. p. 83.
32   Szudek, op. cit. p. 56.

A dramatic image of Shermans from the 2nd Armoured Regiment on Stapelmoorer Heide, Germany April 1945. (Jan Jarzembowski)

Sexton self-propelled gun named 'Jordanow', 2nd Battery, 1st Motorized Artillery Regiment, Germany April 1945. (Jan Jarzembowski)

Sherman Mk IIAs pass a knocked-out German 8.8cm gun on a wheeled mounting on the way to Gross-Oldendorf, Germany, 2 May 1945. (Jan Jarzembowski)

Destroyed German 8.8cm anti-aircraft gun on cruciform mount, Germany April 1945. (Jan Jarzembowski)

Wilhelmshaven 1945 – Maczek with General Klemens Rudnicki
(centre), who succeeded to the command of 1st Polish Armoured
Division in May of that year. (Narodowe Archiwum Cyfrowe)

The last bridge built during the war by the Division, River Leda,
near Leer, Germany, 05 May 1945. (Jan Jarzembowski)

Major Michal Gutowski at the city limits of Wilhelmshaven. He stands
beside a Sherman IIA of the Regimental HQ (diamond sign), 2nd
Armoured Regiment, 6 May 1945. (Jan Jarzembowski)

A German military escort guides the Polish battlegroup through defensive
positions of mines and roadblocks into Wilhelmshaven. The vehicle is a Humber
Scout Car from 2nd Armoured Regiment, 6 May 1945. (Jan Jarzembowski)

The surrender of Wilhelmshaven by the German military commander, *Kapitän zur See* Walter Mulson, to Colonel Antoni Grudzinski (holding map) (second-in-command of the 10th Armoured Cavalry Brigade), at the city limits, a road junction on Bismarck-Strasse and Schaarreihe, 6 May 1945. The offficer to the left of Grudzinski, with moustache, is Major Michal Gutowski, commander of the 2nd Armoured Regiment. (Jan Jarzembowski)

Sherman Mk IIAs of the 2nd Armoured Regiment parked in front of block 2, parade ground, Admiral von Schröder barracks, Wihelmshaven May 1945. (Jan Jarzembowski)

Major Michal Gutowski at the Admiral von Schröder barracks' parade
ground, Wihelmshaven May 1945. (Jan Jarzembowski)

2.Marine-Ersatz-Regiment was under the command of Kapitän zur See Helmut Leissner,
and was sometimes also referred to as *Marine-Ersatz-Regiment Leissner*. Photo taken at the
Admiral von Schröder naval barracks, Wilhelmshaven May 1945. An extensive number of
Kriegsmarine infantry units were formed in the latter stages of the war. (Jan Jarzembowski)

Two rooftop views of Shermans from 2nd Armoured Regiment parked on the parade ground, Admiral von Schröder barracks, Wihelmshaven May 1945. (Jan Jarzembowski)

still fighting, they were now laying down their arms'.

The 1st Polish Armoured Division, fighting in Germany, was to occupy part of Germany. Maczek reflected that this must have been the first time in the history of the long struggle between the Germans and the Poles. Maczek concluded with his admiration for Simonds and how he had conducted the campaign; how he had dictated the surrender terms to the Germans and how he admired him for not choosing the easy way out by assigning the great naval base of Wilhelmshaven to one of the Canadian divisions but to the Polish Division – 'The areas will be occupied by the unit which had received as its last battle order the command to capture it'.[33]

The haul in Wilhelmshaven was incredible: tens of thousands of prisoners including two admirals and a general were taken, while the quantity of captured equipment was staggering – three cruisers, 18 submarines, 205 minor battleships and support vessels, 94 fortress guns, 159 field guns, 560 machine-guns, 40,000 rifles, 280,000 artillery shells and 64 million rounds of small arms ammunition. In addition there were also stores of mines and torpedoes as well as supplies of food for 50,000 troops for a six-month period.[34]

Even if the end of the war for General Maczek and the 1st Polish Armoured Division was that of triumph, peace was to prove to be a disappointment as wartime alliances were quickly forgotten.

---

33   *The Soldiers of General Maczek*, op. cit. pp.86-8; Maczek, op. cit. pp. 235-38.
34   McGilvray, op. cit. p. 113.

13

Betrayal and Exile – 1945-2004

I f, after the war in Europe had finished, Maczek thought as so many Poles did, that he was to return to Poland as one of the victors, he was in for a rude awakening. But given Maczek's intelligence and astuteness he was probably not surprised by the turn of events that were to dominate the remainder of his long life as well as determine that he would live, die and be buried in exile. He would remain reticent after 1945.

The first shock for his men and perhaps for him was that within two weeks of assuming the occupation of Wilhelmshaven he had to leave his beloved 1st Polish Armoured Division when he was promoted to the command of I Polish Corps in Scotland.[1] But what Maczek may not have anticipated was the loss of his Polish citizenship when, during September 1946, he and five other generals along with 75 other senior officers of the Polish armed forces in the West were stripped of their citizenship. A decree issued from Warsaw by the Polish Council of Ministers (a Soviet puppet administration) on 26 September 1946 declared that:

> The following soldiers of the former Polish Armed Forces in Great Britain have lost on the 6th day of September 1946 citizenship of the Polish state by enlisting, without agreement of the appropriate Polish authorities, to serve in the armed forces of a foreign state, by enlisting in the Polish Resettlement Corps which is a paramilitary organisation, being part of the British Army administratively and by undertaking there administrative and recruiting activities in relation to other Polish soldiers with the intent of delaying their return to the Country to the interests if the Polish nation and State:
> Generals
> 1. Kopański, Stanisław
> 2. Chruściel, Antoni
> 3. Maczek, Stanisław, Władysław
> 4. Malinowski, Tadeusz
> 5. Masny, Karol.[2]

And here was the major part of the Maczek story in exile, which was largely characterized by his constant refusal to recognise the Polish Peoples' Republic as anything other than a puppet Soviet regime or quite simply a Soviet colony with the Soviet ambassador in Warsaw acting as some kind of quasi imperial governor-general. After years of vilification, once the communist regime in Poland began to totter, the illegal Jaruzelski regime began to try

---

1 Jerzy Majka, *Generał Stanisław Maczek*, Rzeszów, Libra, 2005, p. 87. Maczek received his command of I Corps in Scotland on 20 May 1945, Tadeusz Panecki et al, *Sztab Generalny (Główny) Wojska Polskiego, 1918-2003*, Warsaw, Bellona, 2003, pp. 196-7.

2 *The Soldiers of General Maczek in World War II*, (ed) Zbigniew Mieczkowski, London-Warsaw, Foundation for the Commemoration of General Maczek's First Armoured Division, 2004, p. 163.

The coat of arms of Beveren-Waas presented, along with the colours, to the 2nd Armoured Regiment, Belgium 2 March 1946 (Maczek is extreme right). (Jan Jarzembowski)

The band of the Division, Beveren-Waas, Belgium, 2 March 1946. (Jan Jarzembowski)

Colour party, led by Major Michal Gutowski
(CO 2nd Armoured Regiment). The standard
bearer is Sergeant-Major Alexander Leon
'Manka' Jarzembowski, Beveren-Waas,
Belgium, 2 March 1946. (Jan Jarzembowski)

to use Maczek's name and deeds as part of their damage control, emphasising how the Polish soldier, in the collective imagination, had always been the saviour of the nation from outside aggression.[3] Perhaps it was one soldier trying to reach out to another. Maczek stoutly refused to recognise these overtures as he quite rightly saw them as abortive attempts to link his name to the Second Republic which he proudly represented, and the illegal pro-Soviet regime in Poland which oversaw Poland between 1944 and 1989.[4] However it would seem that in 1989 Mrs Maczek did respond positively to a letter from the Polish Prime Minister, Mieczysław Rakowski.[5]

It was not unclear to Poles what the situation was in Poland in 1945. Maczek did not desire to return, either for himself or his family, and was somewhat sympathetic towards Colonel Dec when he reported for the last time to Maczek and they discussed Dec's future, perhaps in Poland, while Franciszek Skibiński, who appeared to have embraced the values of communism from a distance, received quite a hostile reception from Maczek, who could see that Skibiński was merely being opportunistic and wanted to further his career even if it was with the communist Polish Army. Within a year of returning to Poland Skibiński was arrested and tortured, including having all of his teeth knocked out. Once Stalinism fell in Poland during October 1956 and a more moderate form of communism took hold in Poland, Skibiński was quietly released and made a general.[6] The decision to deprive Maczek of his citizenship was reversed in November 1971 but as it was the government of the Polish Peoples' Republic and therefore a Soviet vassal, Maczek ignored this decree.[7] Maczek refused to recognise Poland until after 1989 and the fall of communism in Poland.

One of Maczek's veterans, Lieutenant Jan Suchcitz, 10th Mounted Rifles, said that in the remaining fifty years of Maczek's life he sought no honours and remained a firm believer in an apolitical army, taking no part in the folly of politics of the Polish Government-in-Exile in London. He did make the occasional sally into the politics of the Polish Government-in-Exile, such as in November 1961, when he was critical of the manner that the Polish military decoration, the *Virtuti Militari*, was awarded for the 1939 Campaign. For a failed campaign, Maczek considered that too many awards had been made. In 1967, in a letter to General Antoni Grudziński, Maczek was again critical of the mass awarding of the medal, which had the effect of devaluing the award, when it is awarded for genuine bravery rather than time serving.[8] In contrast to some, such as General Anders, he worked modestly in Edinburgh to support his family. He received no pension from either the British or Canadian Governments and it was only the appreciation and generosity of the Dutch people that ensured a safe future for his disabled daughter. It was reported in the Polish press in London during 1995 that Maczek did eventually receive a generous pension

3   Evan McGilvray, 'General Stanisław Maczek and Post-War Britain' in (ed) Peter D. Stachura, *The Poles in Britain, 1940-2000. From Betrayal to Assimilation*, London, Frank Cass, 2004, pp. 59-68.

4   Majka, op. cit. p. 87.

5   JPRS-EER-89-041, 14 April 1989, Rehabilitation of Victims of Stalinism – Apology to Gen. Maczek, Wlodzimierz Krzyzanowski, 'Commander's Return', *Przeglad Tygodniowy*, (Warsaw) 5 March 1989.

6   Piotr Potomski, *Generał Broni Stanisław Władysław Maczek (1892-1994)* Warsaw, Uniwersytetu Warszawa, 2008, p. 339.

7   Zbigniew Tomkowski, *Generał Maczek, Najstarszy Żołnierz Rzeczypospolitej*, Warsaw, Ypsylon, 1994, p. 88.

8   *Kawalerowie Virtuti Militari 1792-1945: Wykazy odnaczonych za czyny z lat 1863-1864, 1914-1945*, (eds) Gregorz Łukomski, Bogusław Polak, Andrzej Suchcitz, Koszalin, Politechniki Koszalinskiej, 1997, pp. 22, 66, 76.

Troops from the Division at Beveren-Waas, Belgium. Note the coat of arms of Beveren-Waas below the POLAND shoulder title on the right sleeve of the soldier second from left. (Jan Jarzembowski)

from the Dutch Government. No doubt this was connected with the liberation of Breda by the Polish 1st Armoured Division and the fact that Maczek did not allow the town to be destroyed during this operation, as had been the fate of other towns and cities across North-West Europe as the Allies advanced towards Germany between 1944 and 1945. There is no detail of this pension in British and Polish archival sources but it was clearly a belated honour as he, as we shall see, worked at humble jobs such as a barman and later a shop assistant right into the 1960s just to provide for his family. However despite these setbacks he was never downhearted and continued in his duties, as saw them, with his veterans.[9] He was always attentive to his Division and its former members, attending reunions and commemorations and he always gladly welcomed visits from his subordinates.[10]

The problem for Maczek and his fellow Poles was what could be considered the craven attitude of the post-war British Labour Government or the fact that this government was faced with what is commonly called *Realpolitik*. Domestically there was a lot of sympathy, especially from the British working class, towards Stalin and the Soviet Union. Some of this was to do with the grassroots of the trade union movement and class warfare while many people also considered, quite rightly, that the Soviet Union had borne the brunt of German aggression after 1941. Could it have done otherwise? However, in Britain it was overlooked that the Soviet Union had taken part in the original invasion of Poland as a partner of Nazi Germany, murdered thousands of Poles, most infamously the murder of the Polish elites at Katyń and other sites, as well as annexing eastern Poland and deporting and enslaving millions of Polish citizens. This was true infamy and the Soviet Union continued to aid Germany right up to the eve of German invasion of the Soviet Union on 21 June 1941.

9   *Dziennik Polski i Dziennik Żołnierza*, 31 January 1995.
10   Mieczkowski, op. cit. p. 22.

The popular British attitude towards the Soviet Union put the Poles at odds with their British hosts. Some Poles hoped that there might be a war against the Soviet Union that would liberate Poland, having seen it annexed by the Soviet Union during 1944-45 under the guise of liberation. Many British people began to see the Poles as 'fascists' and 'Jew-baiters'.[11] It has to be said that at times history was against the Poles given some of the more unfortunate actions of the Second Polish Republic which, after 1926 and certainly after 1935, became more fascist while anti-Semitism by most Poles, even if often denied, was a fact of life and remains so to this day.

In the House of Commons British MPs demanded an answer regarding the activities of officers serving in Polish II Corps, as it had been alleged that some of those serving in Italy had been distributing and broadcasting to other Polish officers and soldiers ant-Soviet and to a certain extent anti-British propaganda printed in the UK.[12] Further allegations were made by MPs, sympathetic to the Soviet Union, who claimed that Polish troops were interfering with public meetings while a statement was made to the effect that in a Polish camp in Scotland there had been hangings and shootings of those Polish soldiers who had served in the West by Polish soldiers who had served in the *Wehrmacht* or as guards at concentration camps, as the soldiers who had served the Allies refused to take part in military training for a war designed against the Soviet Union. All of this was denied by the British Government.[13]

A situation which might have been useful, the granting of British citizenship to those members of the Polish armed forces who had been unwilling to return to Poland, was scotched by the British Prime Minister, Clement Attlee, who in a reply to Captain Gammaris who had proposed the idea, said that this was 'a hope rather than a pledge'.[14]

At all times it was quite clear that the British Government, in spite of the problems which the Poles were beginning to throw up, were not going to force Polish service personnel to return to Poland.[15] The question of numbers was also somewhat confusing as during October 1945 it was claimed that out of 60,000 Polish troops, 23,000 wanted to return to Poland while 13,000 from Italy were willing to return to their homeland yet only a few hundred stationed in Germany were willing to do so.[16] What to do with these Polish troops was also becoming quite a question as one MP stated there were some 1,000 Polish troops kept in a transit camp in Oxfordshire who had nothing to do except 'wander aimlessly about the countryside'.[17]

The debate concerning the Polish Army in the West continued to rumble on. It was recognised that the Polish Army in Poland was largely officered by Soviet officers at senior levels and that there were no Poles above the rank of captain in that army. This situation led to many Poles living in Poland to conclude that the *true* Polish Army was still in Italy and the UK.[18] Thus the Soviet-backed Polish Peoples' Army was unrecognised by the Polish people.

In the UK the problem of how exiled Poles were perceived remained. The Member

11   McGilvray, op. cit. p. 63.
12   *Hansard*, Col. 17, 29 May 1945.
13   *Hansard*, Cols. 707-09, 5 June 1945.
14   *Hansard*, Cols. 23-5, 9 October 1945.
15   *Hansard*, Col. 243, 10 October 1945.
16   *Hansard*, Cols. 1821-2, 22 October 1945.
17   *Hansard*, Col. 1857, 23 October 1945.
18   *Hansard*, Cols. 2755-2800, 7 December 1945.

for Newcastle-under-Lyme stated that the problem remained that the Poles were backward looking and really wanted a war with the Soviet Union, whom he denied had ever invaded Poland, whether in 1939 or 1944.[19] A further problem was that many British people, instead of noting that Poland, despite its faults, had been invaded and occupied by the Soviet Union, instead continued to dwell on the anti-Semitic nature of many Poles. This was true but served to overlook what the Soviets were doing in Eastern Europe, which could hardly be said to include protecting Jewish interests. Indeed Stalin should be viewed as an anti-Semite.

There was an interesting exchange in the House of Commons regarding the Soviet invasion and occupation of Poland during 1944-45 when Captain George Jeger, the Member for Winchester, said that 'if there was a fire in the house of the honourable member and a fire brigade broke into the house to put it out, would he complain of having been attacked by the fire brigade?' Major Tufton Beamish, the Member for Lewes, who had served with the Poles in Italy, replied 'I certainly would if the fire brigade knocked me on the head in addition to putting out the fire ... '[20] This was an excellent riposte, which illustrates just how divided people were regarding the Poles. It is interesting to note that those who actually had experience of the Poles could see that despite the ill-judged actions of pre-war Polish governments, this did not justify the Soviet occupation of their country, the deportation of vast numbers into the Soviet interior and annexation of huge swathes of Poland which, in turn, altered the citizenship of those living in these areas from that of Polish to being Soviet citizens and falling at the mercy of the Soviet system.

As 1945 passed into 1946 the figures for Poles who expressed a wish to leave for Poland were given as follows:

- UK – 36.8%
- Middle East (MEF) – 6%
- Central Mediterranean Force (CMF) – 10.8%
- British Army on the Rhine (BAOR) – 1.2%.

This represented only 17.2% of all Polish servicemen under Western command.[21] Only 0.5% of Polish airmen wanted to return to Poland.[22] The problem was that few British people trusted the men of II Polish Corps, many of whom were considered to harbour pro-Fascist, if not Nazi, sympathies, and certainly anti-Soviet sensibilities, which continued to anger British public opinion.[23] The question of the political activities of the Polish II Corps continued to be examined by British parliamentarians, especially as the Corps was costing the then colossal sum of £2,000,000 per month to maintain. Since the UK's finances were in a dreadful state as a result of having fought a war to defend Poland, it would have been useful if the Corps could be considered trustworthy and loyal to the UK. However, it was obvious that the Corps was agitating against Britain and British interests, while there was evidence that elements of Polish II Corps were involved in terrorism in Poland.[24] These

19   Ibid.
20   Ibid.
21   *Hansard*, col. 12, 22 January 1946.
22   *Hansard*, col. 124, 23 January 1946.
23   *Hansard*, cols. 1336-7, 4 February 1946.
24   *Hansard*, cols. 1127-31, 11 February 1946.

allegations did nothing to serve well the Poles living in the UK, who were quite innocent of the charges laid, as they had nothing to do with II Corps but still they remained tarred with the same brush.

Finally the British Government cut through all of the tangled arguments, claims and counter-claims as forwarded by the various partisan observers and parties with the announcement of the Polish Armed Forces (Repatriation and Resettlement Scheme). This paved the way for the discharge of Poles from the military which Ernest Bevin, the British Foreign Secretary, observed would have happened much earlier if these men had been British but remained certain that this was not a question of discharging the Poles *en masse* overnight. This was the reason for the Polish Resettlement Corps (PRC) being established. The PRC was established so that Poles being discharged from the armed services could go to this halfway house (PRC) for preparation for life in the West. The first step was to bring II Corps from Italy to the UK and away from mischief; their families were to follow later.[25]

However the move of II Corps was one that raised concerns within the British security community as they wanted to be certain that these men were properly vetted. There were a large number of fascists within their number and the last thing that the British wanted was that some of these men would arrive in the UK and link up with British fascists. There was also a fear of the attitudes of right-wing Catholics and their activities. Indeed both the internal and external British security agencies requested that members of II Corps should be vetted before being allowed into the UK in case they harboured pro-fascist attitudes.[26] The most incredible thing was that the eventual arrival of II Corps from Italy was considered by the British security services to have been irregular, they just turned up! As they had arrived in the UK it was decided in the absence of any other policy it would be better that they should be incorporated into the PRC.[27]

It is interesting to note that the British authorities did not really trust Polish II Corps and that that it was probably best if these men were removed from the European mainland and sent out to the wilds of Scotland where they could plot and complain as much as they liked; they had been disarmed and were going nowhere while remaining firmly under British control. It is just sad that under these circumstances Maczek, who had served the British loyally, should not get a pension whilst Anders, who had been most difficult, received such an award. It was a matter of politics.

The establishment of the PRC angered the Soviet Government and the puppet Polish Government and though the British Government tried to prevent Poles from losing their citizenship they failed. The Soviet Government and its Polish vassal considered that those who enlisted in the PRC should lose their citizenship as they were deemed to have accepted military service with a foreign power.[28] This was not true as the PRC was not a military establishment even if its members did wear uniforms, although it could be argued that uniforms made sense as there were plenty of uniforms available after the war but precious little civilian clothing.

The concept of the PRC was delineated by the statement 'enlistment in the Resettlement

---

25 *Hansard*, cols. 299-306, 22 May 1946.
26 NA, KV 4/286, Polish Resettlement Corps, Policy for the Absorption and Control of Polish Forces in the UK, Including Procedure for Discharge and Repatriation, 14 October 1946; 29 October 1946.
27 NA, KV 4/289, Eligibility for Enlistment into the PRC of Liaison Officers in Germany, 14 October 1947, Minute by Mr. Roy.
28 *Hansard*, col. 586-7, 14 October 1946; cols. 883-5, 16 October 1946.

Corps is a necessary stage in the orderly transfer into civil life of members of the Polish Armed Forces ... '[29] Earlier, the Polish communists had broadcast a speech in which the Polish Defence Minister, Marshal Zymierski, made it quite clear that those who joined the PRC would lose their Polish citizenship.[30] Joining the PRC was a logical and practical step for the integration of Poles into British life but the hostility of some sections of British society continued to dog the Poles. William Gallacher, the MP for Glasgow and sympathetic to the Soviet Union, and frequently withering in his condemnation of the Poles, observed that the *Manchester Guardian* was aware that many Poles even after spending time in the PRC left without even learning to speak English.[31] An academic study concluded that the plethora of Polish associations which sprang up in the UK in the first ten years after the war did indeed retard Polish integration into British society given that Poles would speak Polish at these places while Polish language newspapers were made available and that even their children attended Polish school on Saturdays.[32] However this must be balanced by the fact that the British at that time suffered from a 'deeply engrained xenophobia' and that the UK was not a cultural 'melting pot'; even if Poles did learn English they were unlikely to be allowed to become assimilated into mainstream British society and therefore it was not so surprising that Poles looked to their compatriots for company and association.[33] The question of newspapers was even raised in the House of Commons when it was suggested that Poles should not be reading Polish newspapers at all but should learn English from the *Times* or the *Daily Worker*.[34] The Poles seemed to have overestimated their popularity in the UK.

A stated aim of integrating Poles into British society was 'members of the Polish Resettlement Corps are eligible for courses under vocational training schemes on the same terms as British ex-servicemen provided that their allocation to a training vacancy would not deprive a British subject of a training opportunity and provided that the representations of the industry concerned have agreed to the absorption of Polish trainees'.[35] And here was a problem which had been identified during February 1947, the difficulties of senior Polish officers in getting employment.[36]

A further problem was that the British Government immediately after the war felt

---

29　*Hansard*, Cols. 14-15, 24 October 1946.

30　NA, KV 4/286, 17 September 1946.

31　*Manchester Guardian*, 10 April 1947.

32　Jerzy Zubrzycki, *Polish Immigration in Britain. A Study of Adjustment*, The Hague, Martinus Nijhoff, 1956, pp. 118-19, 149.

33　Ibid. p. 154. The author has noticed that Poles who settled in the Leeds-Bradford area on the whole can be divided into two groups: Poles who served as ordinary soldiers and later went into manual work tended to speak more or less fluent English, probably as a result of working alongside the 'ordinary man' who even if there was some initial reserve from the English, were eventually accepted at a working level whilst the Polish officer class appear to have been more 'stand offish' and did not mix as much with the local people and as a consequence their language skills never really advanced. Local Poles also told the author that they did not consider that their exile in the UK was to be permanent; many considered that within a decade they would be able to return to Poland, perhaps after the death of Stalin and the overthrow, somehow, of communism in Poland, if not throughout East-Central Europe. Stalin died in 1953; nothing really happened. Eventually the Poles realised that they were in the UK for good but some of their patterns of life in exile were already established.

34　*Hansard*, cols. 22-3, 17 March 1947.

35　*Hansard*, cols. 1764-5, 25 November 1947.

36　*Hansard*, cols. 1477-1584, Polish Resettlement, 20 February 1947.

that it could not possibly anger Moscow or Warsaw owing to British public opinion and felt therefore that the Polish armed forces in the West could not be maintained. But this was unlikely in any event given that the British at the time were demobilising after the war; why should the Poles remain armed? Therefore the PRC was considered the best vehicle for demobilising the Poles while trying to buy time to try to decide what to do with these men. The numbers involved were huge: 250,000 Poles wanted to settle in the UK which included 100,000 men from the controversial Polish II Corps under the equally controversial and bellicose General Anders. Only about 3,000 Poles wanted to return to Poland.[37]

Anders was taken by surprise with the establishment of the PRC as he was convinced that the British and Americans would go to war against the Soviet Union.[38] In the West on 1 July 1945 there were about 126 Polish generals of whom only 20 wanted to return to Poland; Maczek was in the group of 106 who did not wish to return to Poland owing to the expectation that there might be a war about Polish independence.[39]

The émigré Polish military press in London kept Polish soldiers up to date with events in Poland and also how the debate connected with the future of the Polish armed forces was going within British political circles throughout 1946.[40] But the future for the Poles in the West looked bleak as it was obvious that the Soviets had annexed Poland and despite the British Foreign Secretary, Ernest Bevin, trying to defend the Polish soldiers, the Soviets were winning the war of words.[41] A further concern had to be what to do with the Poles who had fought alongside the Germans, whether voluntary or otherwise as their numbers were vast: 68,693.[42]

Thomas Lane makes the astute observation that the Polish question after the war was basically about Polish II Corps or the so-called 'Anders' Army'.[43] And this was the rub; I Polish Corps, now under the influence of Maczek, was, like his former armoured division, largely apolitical while II Corps under the highly political Anders had been a thorn in the side of the Allies since its members had left captivity in the Soviet Union. Their collective experience of Soviet cruelty and the virtual genocide of the Polish people had coloured their view. Furthermore, most of these men came from territories which even if the Poles and Ukrainians disputed ownership, the Soviet Government had already incorporated into their own territory, leaving the inhabitants as Soviet citizens who could no longer be defended as Poles. The Soviet annexation had been complete in the former eastern Poland; Maczek also came from the same area but as a serving officer of the Polish Republic offered no opinion: his code forbade it. Lane also points to another problem which people such as Anders ignored – that after the war there was no legal basis that the British Government

37   P.H. Vigor, C.E. Chojecki, *The Polish Resettlement Corps*, RMA Sandhurst, Conflict Studies Research Centre, February 1994, pp. 2-3.
38   Keith Sword with Norman Davies & Jan Ciechanowski, *The Foundation of the Polish Community in Great Britain, 1939-50*, London, School of Slavonics & East European Studies, University of London, 1989, p. 194.
39   Potomski, op. cit. p. 338.
40   *Dziennik Polski i Dziennik Żołnierza* (1946) passim.
41   Bevin's defence of the Polish Army was reported in *Dziennik Polski i Dziennik Żołnierza*, 22 February 1946.
42   Ibid, 6 June 1946. There was further debate about Poles who had served in the German Army, ibid. 20 June 1946; 9 October 1946.
43   Thomas Lane, *Victims of Stalin and Hitler. The Exodus of Poles and Balts to Britain*, Basingstoke, Palgrave Macmillan, 2004, p. 188.

could control for keeping the Polish Armed Forces in existence after war's end and the expiry of the Allied Forces Act.[44]

The problem of senior Polish officers gaining employment in the UK was one that was to haunt Maczek in exile. The most obvious way to help Maczek and his family would have been for the British Government to have provided him with a pension. A decision arrived at on 7 February 1947 made a pension of £100 per month available for Anders while Admiral Świrski and General Rudnicki received £75 per month; later General Kopański and Air Vice Marshal Izycki, after their services with the PRC were terminated, also received a monthly pension of £75.[45] Incredibly, Maczek, who out of the Poles, had done the most for the Allies and certainly had not caused disunity in the Polish ranks was to receive nothing and this caused comment from within official British circles.

At the end of 1948 Field Marshal Montgomery raised the question of senior Polish officers who had given distinguished service during the war and would very likely in the near future be seeking employment or some means of support. Montgomery had in mind fourteen such officers including Maczek. Some had already been dealt with, but the case of Maczek was truly one of betrayal and pathos, albeit one which he never complained of. A loose undated minute in the file is extremely revealing as it runs:

> ... General Maczek with the 1st Polish Armoured Division played a large part in closing the Falaise Gap.
> b) these officers at PRC have aided Britain in assisting government policy and resettled their men into the British economy.
> c) These men have lost everything they possessed. Kopański and Maczek have been publicly deprived of their Polish nationality. The majority have spent their spare money in ensuring a good education for their children and as a consequence have saved little or nothing.

It was also observed that those over the age of 50 were unlikely to find employment and that it would not be right that they might have to apply for national assistance.

Of Maczek it was further said ' ... General Maczek had most loyally handled the problem of the resettlement of Poles in Scotland and the liquidation of the Polish commitment in the Scottish Command. He fought most gallantly under Field Marshal Montgomery's command throughout the 1944/45 campaign in France and who, since he has been running the PRC Commitment in Scottish Command, has absolutely no money of his own, and has a wife and two children to educate, also an idiot child whom he has to maintain. He is most anxious to know whether any provision will be made for him. I cannot help feeling that it would be an injustice, after the service rendered to us, to leave this type of man to sink or swim on his own.'

The author of the statement considered that a pension should be made available if a Polish officer was:

a.   Of the rank of Major-General or its equivalent or above.
b.   Had served in the Polish Armed Forces under British command during the war.

---

44   Ibid. p. 184.
45   NA, PREM 8, Prime Ministers' Office, PREM 8/890, Pensions for Senior Polish Officers, 10 November 1948.

c.   Had served in the PRC.[46]

A minute by Barbara Green at the Ministry of Labour and National Service would also seem to largely agree with these findings as she wrote ' … as for the older men, I think that the suggested arrangement is the only sensible way of providing for them, since a Polish officer over 50 [years of age] can scarcely be expected to make his own way in this country.'[47]

It had already been established that Maczek could hardly make his 'way' in Britain as he had been described as being 56 years of age with no special qualifications and that he proposed in the future to farm or run a boarding house but had no money.[48] One might dispute that Maczek had no special qualifications, after all, he was a very successful commander of armour and could have easily lectured in a British military staff college until his retirement but it was not to be as politics ruled the roost in the years immediately after the war. This meant that Anders got his pension and that Moscow had to be appeased, which ensured that all Poles had to be removed from anything vaguely military; Maczek's reticence on political matters meant that he lost out in every arena.

Maczek was not the only Pole who would be victimised by the conditions which prevailed after 1947 regarding the employment of Polish ex-servicemen. It was established in late 1947 that there were about 1,700 Polish ORs in the PRC who were over 40 years of age and were unskilled in any industry and thus unlikely to find any work or training owing to the fact that British people were offered first refusal for any which was available.[49] It must be noted that it was considered by some in British Government circles that the Poles were being difficult by not making men from the PRC available for work in an attempt to retain the Polish Army. Clement Attlee, the British Prime Minister, writing to the Foreign Secretary and the Secretary of State for War, stated that 'I think that the Poles ought to be brought quickly to a more reasonable attitude. Please therefore concert with the Minister of Labour and make suggestions to put an end to the obstructions raised by the Poles.'[50]

In a minute dated 9 September 1946 it was revealed that the British Foreign Office had given an undertaking to Warsaw and therefore the Soviet Union that the Poles in the UK would not be employed on 'warlike duties' but only in civilian duties.[51] This is quite revealing as it was obvious that London was dancing to Moscow's tune while Moscow obviously feared that there might be a nascent Polish cadre army being developed in the West that might be used against them sometime in the future. It was something that the Poles clearly desired and it seems that Maczek was implicated in some form of skulduggery in the dragging of heels regarding the release of Polish ex-servicemen into civilian life. This is revealed in a long complaint made by Brigadier H.R. Hall, Chief Advisor British

---

46   NA, PREM 8/890, Duchy of Lancaster to Attlee, Prime Minister, 13 November 1948. The author obviously was sympathetic towards Maczek's plight while the use of the term 'idiot child' in a pre-politically-correct age was not considered to be abusive but the correct term. In fact Maczek's daughter, Magdalena, appears to have suffered from Down's Syndrome.

47   NA, LAB 18/515, Resettlement of Officers of the Polish Resettlement Corps, Policy and Procedure, Minute, Barbara Green, 22 December 1947.

48   NA, PREM 8/890, 7 February 1947.

49   NA, WO 32/12257, Employment of Polish Resettlement Corps, Employment of Poles in W.D. Establishments, G.W. Lambert, 17 December 1947.

50   NA, WO 32/12257, Prime Minister's Personal Minute Serial Number M.256/46, Attlee to Foreign Secretary and Secretary of State for War, 7 August 1946.

51   Ibid. Minute, 9 September 1946.

Advisory Staff, PRC, H.Q. Scottish Command, Edinburgh, to Lieutenant-Colonel P.H. Labouchere during December 1947. Hall wrote:

I have read Eastern Command's A/33/665 of 9 December 1947 about our draft of 700. This, on the face of it looks a bad show and I shall have something to say to General Maczek about it. There are, however, a few comments that I should like to make.

Polish officers are reluctant to part with their units and like anybody else when ordered to send a draft away, their reaction is to send the worse men. Apart from that, we have relegated nearly all of our best men; the remainder are employed by someone or other. It is obvious that the first people to be sent away would be those hanging about in camps doing nothing. Our Poles are very well dug in Scotland, as they have been here for seven years. They hate moving. Taking into consideration they are by no means our best, I am not at all surprised their morale was low.

The complained of, fall into three categories.

a.   Unfit men. These men have been discharged from Convalescent Depots as employable, something must be done about them and it's no solution to leave them sitting in camps in Scotland. I make no apology for sending these with the exception of one who is stated to be about to enter hospital. I suppose that this is substantiated by evidence?

b.   Men for emigration. In Scotland we try to make would-be emigrants take jobs until they get passage. This is the correct policy, is it not? Men who are due to embark on 15 December 1947 should not of course have been sent. I am afraid both the Poles and the B.A.S. (British Advisory Staff) slipped up over this.

c.   Men stated to have offers of employment in Scotland. If that is really so, it seems an easy matter to relegate them wherever they are. If the Poles have sent somebody down in the process of being relegated by the Minister of Labour, I am very sorry.

But I suspect that several of these Poles could get jobs if they wanted to, but prefer an easy life in the P.R.C. The move to England is just the urge needed to push them into civil life.

Several men are marked as having English (Scottish) wives in Scotland. We cannot keep a man in the P.R.C. for ever because he had a Scottish wife. In one case the man is stated to have an English wife in Oxford! That seems a very odd case for keeping him in Scotland. Nevertheless, the incident is not one of which I am proud. We have some good men left if we could get our hands on them, and I think we shall when we get them all in one unit without hundreds of detachments. Incidentally, relegation here is now most disappointing and I think we may have several more available when we take stock in January.

I am, however, having great difficulty with Maczek over the whole question. He maintains in the face of his own returns, that he can find no more men. He also states that General MacLeod told him that he might keep a ten per-cent reserve in Scotland. However, when we have completed the disbandment of 101 & 104 Basic Units and 1. Polish General Hospital and we get all of our spare men into one unit, I think that we shall dig them out.[52]

52   NA, WO 32/12260, Brigadier H.R. Hall to Lieutenant-Colonel P.H. Labouchere, 13 December 1947.

This appears to be a unique occasion where Maczek actually defies British policy and seems so minor compared with the antics of Anders and others from Polish II Corps. It is interesting to note that Anders and five other generals, not named, could not have been enlisted into the PRC as it would have been inflammatory to the Warsaw Government but Maczek was not regarded in the same light and was used in the PRC.[53]

The end for Maczek's former armoured division came during March 1947 when a discussion was held at the HQ of BAOR to decide on the demobilisation of the 1st Polish Armoured Division and the move back to the UK of volunteers from the Polish Armed Forces in Germany to join the PRC. It was agreed that the 1st Polish Armoured Division would be wound up at 1 minute past midnight on 1 May 1947. Operationally the HQ of the British 7th Armoured Division would assume control of the area occupied by the 1st Polish Armoured Division and the 1st Polish Parachute Brigade. The HQ of the 1st Polish Armoured Division would become non-operational and all responsibility of Polish matters would be assumed by the HQ of the Polish Administration Staff, Germany.[54] That was the end of a truly gallant division which had served the British well in good as well as evil times.

What was Maczek's immediate fate after his demobilisation in 1949? He did not receive a military pension or indeed any pension at all, and so had to seek work in order to provide for his family. At the age of 57 Maczek took to physical work: the only work available to him despite his huge wealth of experience of soldiering. As with so many other soldiers before and after him, he did not fit in – a square peg in a round hole. The military rarely prepares its veterans adequately for civilian life.

A soldier from Maczek's former division gave him a job and, as ever uncomplaining, Maczek rose early every morning and took the bus to work, 30 kilometres from his home in Edinburgh, and returned late home every evening. Later he worked as a barman at the Learmouth Hotel in Edinburgh which was run by an ex-NCO of the 1st Polish Armoured Division. His humbling circumstances failed to depress Maczek and he was always smiling and optimistic. Life was difficult for Maczek and his family but he never asked for help.[55] Mieczkowski relates that when Maczek left the PRC, he did receive an 'insignificant pension' from the British Government which did not help to support his family. Every time his veterans stepped into Maczek's bar they always stood to attention before him in recognition of his rank.[56]

This then leaves us with the question, what was the remainder of Maczek's life like once he left the military and accepted manual work? It was a far cry from his university studies and fighting on the Italian Front and in Eastern Poland when he was in his 20s and then his life as a respected senior officer. Apart from writing his memoirs, which do not go beyond 1945, as far as we know, he became a symbol and an inspiration to his veterans and nothing could be more symbolic than his residency in Edinburgh, far from the internecine politics of exile that at one time divided the Poles in London. In later life, by doing nothing, he was to become a thorn in the side of the Polish communists who ran Poland on the behalf of the Soviet Union.

53   NA, FO 945/686, Polish Forces Official Committee, Sub-Committee on Eligibility for the Polish Resettlement Corps, Minute of 1st Meeting, 5 May 1947.
54   NA, FO 1052/344, Polish Resettlement Corps, Minutes of Meeting held in Chief of Staff's Conference Room, Headquarters British Army of the Rhine, 11:00 hours, 14 March 1947.
55   Potomski, op. cit. pp. 342-3.
56   Mieczkowski, op. cit. pp. 162-66.

Maczek visiting Breda in 1964. (Private collection)

Other countries did not forget Maczek as Maczek's daughter, Renata, related in her schoolgirl account of her family's visit to the Netherlands during the late 1940s where Maczek was feted as he travelled the area.[57] During 1964 Maczek once more was feted by the people of the Low Countries as he was an honoured guest when he and other veterans retraced their route of 1944. In Axel there were four days of celebrations during which Maczek was received as guest of honour; at Ypres, a tablet commemorating the 1st Polish Armoured Division was unveiled while a street in Axel was named in honour of Maczek, 'Generaal Maczekstraat'.[58]

Maczek became the unofficial leader of the Polish community in Scotland. By keeping away from the problems of the Polish Government-in-Exile, which was recognised nowhere in the world, he maintained his dignity and continued to ignore any overture from the Polish Peoples' Republic, which became stronger during the 1980s. Maczek continued to work with his 'boys', who were now on the whole pensioners. By his 80th birthday even the British remembered Maczek, as it was announced that he was to be the guest of honour of the Commander of the Army in Scotland during the Edinburgh Tattoo, to be held later that year. The Dutch, as ever, broadcast a concert in honour of Maczek's birthday while Macek modestly told *The Scotsman* that he preferred to be called Mister rather than General and he did not like being 80!

Maczek's century was cause of great celebration; again cards and notices poured in from

57   PISM, KOL 298/53, Renata Maczek.
58   *Dziennik Polski i Dziennik Żołnierza*, 15 October 1964; 19 October 1964; 24 November 1964.

all over the world and by this time Poland, having shed communism, was once more a free and independent state. Sadly Maczek was too frail to return home and, anyway, Maczek's home was now in the newly independent Ukraine. The tributes on his 100th birthday were testimony to his enduring legacy in the free world; young Belgians and Dutch people, born after the war, wrote to Maczek expressing their gratitude for the freedom that he and his men had delivered, at the cost of themselves.[59]

In the year of Maczek's centenary, 1992, the Polish President, Lech Wałęsa, made Maczek a full general and awarded him a pension.[60] A grand present when you are one hundred!

General Maczek died on 11 December 1994. He was 102 years of age. The Poles, Scots and Dutch mourned his passing. After a funeral in Edinburgh, he was buried in Breda, the scene of one of his greatest victories. His legacy, amongst those who choose to remember it, will be primarily that of his military achievements but that would be to forget his humanity even in war and the evils that visited his country. It would be to forget his sense of duty that extended over the remainder of his life, not only to his veterans, who spoke of him as *Baca* or 'head shepherd' but also his family, especially his daughter, Magdalena. His life in exile was one of obscurity and of difficulty; he never retrieved his position professionally or socially, he was not allowed to. But despite this his men remained devoted to him as he continued to serve them and a country that no longer existed except in their hearts, even if it was to return once more as an independent state before Maczek died.

The old warrior must have died contented.

---

59   (ed) Stachura, op. cit. pp. 66-7.
60   Ken Tout, *A Fine Night for Tanks: The Road to Falaise*, Stroud, Sutton, 1998, p. 122.

Order of Battle of the 1st Polish Armoured Division 16 September 1942

Divisional HQ
HQ
8th Field Court

10th Armoured Cavalry Brigade
HQ
10th Mounted Rifle Regiment
24th Uhlan Regiment
14th Uhlan Regiment
10th Dragoon Regiment

16th Armoured Brigade
1st Armoured Regiment
2nd Armoured Regiment
3rd Armoured Regiment
16th Dragoon Regiment

Army Support Group
HQ Group
1st Artillery Regiment (motorized)
1st Anti-Tank Artillery Regiment
1st Anti-Aircraft Artillery Regiment
1st Rifle Battalion (lorried)

Divisional units
1st Reconnaissance Regiment
1st, 2nd, 10th and 16th Signals Squadrons
10th and 11th Engineer Companies
11th Engineer Park Company
Traffic Movement Squadron
3rd Military Police Squadron

Divisional Service Units
10th and 16th Transport Companies
Transport Company Army Support Group
10th and 16th Workshop Companies
Divisional Workshop Company
6 Light Aid Detachments Type 'B'
6 Light Aid Detachments Type 'C'
Workshop Platoon Anti-Aircraft Artillery
    Regiment
10th and 11th Field Ambulances
Divisional Hygiene Platoon

Order of Battle of the 1st Polish Armoured Division North-West Europe 1944-45

(General Stanisław Maczek)

Divisional HQ
HQ Squadron
1st Traffic Control Squadron
10th Mounted Rifle Regiment (Reconnaissance) (*10 pułk strzelców konnych*) – Maj. J.
  Maciejowski
8th Field Court
Field Post Office

1st Reserve Tank Squadron

10th Armoured Cavalry Brigade (*10 Brygada Kawalerii Pancernej*) – Col. T. Majewski
HQ
1st Armoured Regiment (*1 pułk pancerny*) – Lt.Col. Aleksander Stefanowicz
2nd Armoured Regiment (*2 pułk pancerny*) – Lt.Col. S. Koszustki
24th Uhlan Regiment (*24 pułk ułanów*) – Lt.Col. J. Kański
10th Dragoon Regiment (*10 pułk dragonów zmotoryzowanych*) – Lt.Col. Władysław
  Zgorzelski

3rd Rifle Brigade (*3 Brygada Strzelców*) – Col. Marian Wieroński
HQ Company
1st Highland Rifle Battalion (*1 battalion Strzelców Podhalańskich*) – Lt.Col. K. Complak
8th Rifle Battalion (*8 battalion strzelców*) – Lt.Col. Aleksander Nowaczyński
9th Rifle Battalion (*9 battalion strzelców flandryjskich*) – Lt.Col. Zygmunt Szydłowski
Independent Machine-Gun Squadron (*samodzielna kompania ckm.*) – Maj. M.
  Kochanowski

Divisional Artillery (*Artyleria dywizyjna*) – Col. B. Noel
HQ
1st Motorized Artillery Regiment (*1 pułk artylerii motorowej*) – Lt.Col. J. Krautwald
2nd Motorized Artillery Regiment (*2 pułk artylerii motorowej*) – Lt.Col. K. Meresch
1st Anti-Tank Regiment (*1 pułk artylerii przeciwpancernej*) – Major R. Dowbór [formed
  1945 from smaller units]
1st Light Anti-Aircraft Artillery Regiment (*1 pułk artylerii przeciwlotniczej*) – Lt.Col. O.
  Eminowicz, later Maj. W. Berendt

Divisional Engineers (*saperzy dywizyjni*) – **Lt.Col. J. Dorantt**
10th and 11th Engineer Companies
Bridge Platoon
Park Company

1st Signals Battalion (*1 batalion łączności*) – **Lt.Col. J. Grajkowski**
HQ Squadron
1st, 2nd, 3rd and 10th Signals Squadrons

Workshop Units
Workshop Company 10th Armoured Cavalry Brigade
Workshop Company 3rd Rifle Brigade

Supply Units
3rd, 10th and 11th Supply Companies
Lorried Infantry Company
1st Ordnance Park

Medical Units
10th Light Field Ambulance
11th Field Ambulance
1st Field Dressing Station
Field Hygiene Platoon

Bibliography

Unpublished materials

The Polish Institute and Sikorski Museum (PISM), London
A.V. – 1st Polish Armoured Division.
A.VI – I Polish Corps.
A.VIII – Polish Resettlement Corps.
A.XII – Supreme General Head Quarters (GHQ).
B.I.58 – Depositions 10th Motorized Cavalry Brigade.
KOL.1- Journal of the Activities of the Supreme Commander.
KOL.298 – General Maczek Collection.
PRM – Prime Ministers' Office (Polish).
B. – Individual accounts from the French 1940 Campaign, General Dworak's manuscripts and other individual pieces concerning the Division.
C. – Divisional, Brigade and Regimental diaries.
R. – Divisional, Brigade and Regimental orders.

The National Archives (NA), Kew, London
CAB 65 – War Cabinet Minutes.
CAB 66 – War Cabinet Memoranda.
CAB 80 – Chiefs of Staff Memoranda.
CAB 85 – Allied Forces (Official) Committee.
FO 371 – Foreign Office Correspondence.
FO 800 – Halifax Papers.
FO 945 – Polish Forces Official Committee.
FO 1052 – Polish Resettlement Corps.
KV – Security Service Files.
LAB 18 – Resettlement of Officers of the Polish Resettlement Corps.
PREM 1 – Prime Minsters' Office.
PREM 3 – Prime Ministers' Office.
PREM 8 – Prime Ministers' Office.
WO – War Office.

Imperial War Museum (IWM), London
06/38/1 – 2nd Lieutenant T. Potworowski, 'Army Days 1943-1945. Recollections and Reflections of a Polish Soldier in the Time of Katyn, the Warsaw Uprising and Yalta'. Typescript, bound script. 2nd Printing, 1997.

Theses
Suchcitz, Andrzej, 'A Brief History of the Military Planning and Preparation for the Defence of Poland, October 1938-August 1939', (MA Dissertation, University of London, 1981).

Newspapers
The Daily Telegraph, 1944-45.
Dziennik Polski (London) 1940-1995.
The Independent, 1994-95.
Joint Publications Research Service – East Europe Report 89-041, 14 April 1989.
The Manchester Guardian, 1940-1947.
The Times, 1940-1945.

Printed primary sources
Brooks, Stephen, (ed) *Montgomery and the Battle for Normandy. A Selection from the Diaries, Correspondence and other Papers of Field Marshal, The Viscount Montgomery of Alamein, January to August 1944*, Gloucestershire, The Army Records Society, 2008.

Dilks, David, (ed) *The Diaries of Sir Alexander Cadogan, 1938-1945*, London, Cassell, 1971.

Great Britain Foreign Office Weekly Intelligence Summaries, 10 vols. Introduction by Clifton Child, Millwood, Krauss, 1985.

Hansard, 1945-48.

It Speaks For Itself: What British War Leaders Said About the Polish Armed Forces 1939-1946. Selections from Communiqués, Speeches, Messages and Press Reports, Selections of Documents made by Capt. Witold Leitburger, Public Relations Officer, Polish Armed Forces, n.p. 1946.

Macleod, Roderick, Kelly, Dennis, (eds) *The Ironside Diaries, 1937-1940*, London, Constable, 1962.

Piłsudski, Józef, *Pisma Zbiorowe*, 10 Vols. Warsaw, Krajowa Agencja Wydawnicza, 1937.

Protokoły z Posiedzeń Rady Ministrów Polskiej, 7 Vols. Kraków, Secesja, 1994-2000.

Stacy, C.P. *The Canadian Army, 1939-1945. An Official Historical Summary*, Ottawa, King's Printer, 1948.

Turnbull, Elizabeth, Suchcitz, Andrzej, (eds) *Edward Roland Sword. The Diary & Despatches of a Military Attaché in Warsaw, 1938-1939*, London, Polish Cultural Foundation, 2001.

Woodward, Llewellyn Sir (ed) *British Foreign Policy in the Second World War*, 5 Vols. London, HMSO, 1970.

Printed secondary sources (books and monographs)
Alexander, Martin S, *The Republic in Danger: General Maurice Gamelin and the Politics of French Defence, 1933-1940*, Cambridge, CUP, 1992.

Ascherson, Neal, *The Struggles for Poland*, London, Michael Joseph, 1987.

Babel, Isaac, *Red Cavalry* edited by Nathalie Babel. Translated with notes by Peter Constantine, introduction by Michael Dirda, New York, W.W. Norton, 2003

Beauvois, Yves, *Les Relations Franco-Polonaises Pendant Le 'Drole de Guerre'*, Paris, L'Harmatton, 1989.

Belfield, Eversley, Essame, H, *The Battle for Normandy*, London, Pan, 1983.

Bideleux, Robert & Jefferies, Ian, *A History of Eastern Europe. Crisis and Change*, London, Routledge, 1998.

Buckley, John, *British Armour in the Normandy Campaign, 1944*, London, Frank Cass,

2004.

Carton de Wiart, Adrian Sir, Lieutenant-General, *Happy Odyssey*, London, Cape, 1950.

Cieciala, Anna M, & Komarnicki, Tytus, *From Versailles to Locarno: Keys to Polish Foreign Policy, 1919-25*, Kansas, University of Kansas Press, 1984.

Cornwell, Mark, *The Undermining of Austria-Hungary. The Battle for Hearts and Minds*, Basingstoke, Macmillan, 2000.

Corum, James, S, *The Roots of Blitzkrieg: Hans von Seeckt and German Military Reform*, Kansas, University of Kansas Press, 1992.

Davies, Norman, *White Eagle, Red Star: The Polish-Soviet War, 1919-1920 and 'the Miracle on the Vistula'*, London, Pimlico, 2003, reprint.

Davies, Norman, *God's Playground. A History of Poland. Volume 2: 1795 to the Present*, Oxford, Clarendon Press, 1981.

Deighton, Len, *Blitzkrieg: From the Rise of Hitler to the Fall of Dunkirk*, London, Triad Granada, 1981.

D'Este, Carlo, *Decision in Normandy: The Unwritten Story of Montgomery and the Allied Campaign*, London, Collins, 1983.

Deszczyński, Marek Piotr, *Ostantnio Egzamin Wojsko Polskie Wobec Czechosłowachiego, 1938-1939*, Warsaw, Neriton, 2003.

Dominick, Graham, *The Price of Command: A Biography of General Guy Simonds*, Toronto, Stoddart, 1993.

Eisenhower, Dwight D, *Crusade in Europe*, London, William Heinemann, 1948.

Elster, Jon, (ed) *The Roundtable and the Breakdown of Communism*, Chicago, University of Chicago Press, 1996.

English, J.A., *The Canadian Army and the Normandy Campaign. A Study of the Failure of High Command*, New York, Praeger, 1991.

Figes, Orlando, *A People's Tragedy: The Russian Revolution, 1891-1924*, London, Pimlico, 2004.

Florentin, Eddy, *The Battle of the Falaise Gap*, translated by Mervyn Savill, London, Elek Books, 1965.

Forty, George, *Tank Commanders: Knights of the Modern Age*, Poole, Firebird, 1993.

Garlicki, Andrzej, *Józef Piłsudski, 1867-1935*, edited and translated by John Coutouvidis, Aldershot, Scolar Press, 1993.

Garlicki, Andrzej, *Józef Piłsudski, 1867-1935*, Warsaw, Czytelnik, 1988.

Gilbert, Martin, *Winston S. Churchill, Vol. VI, Finest Hour, 1939-41*, London, Heinemann, 1983.

Guderian, Heinz, *Achtung Panzer! The Development of Armoured Forces. Their Tactics and Operational Potential*, translated by Christopher Duffy, introduction and notes by Paul Harris, London, Arms & Armour Press, 1995.

Gunsburg, Jeffery, A, *Divided and Conquered. The French High Command and the Defeat of the West in 1940*, London, Greenwood Press, 1979.

Hamilton, Nigel, *Master of the Battlefield: Monty's War Years, 1942-1944*, New York, McGraw-Hill, 1983.

Hargreaves, Richard, *Blitzkrieg Unleashed: The German Invasion of Poland*, Barnsley, Pen & Sword, 2008.

Horrocks, Brian Sir, *Corps Commander*, with Eversley Belfield and Major-General H. Essame, London, Sidgwick & Jackson, 1977.

Jamar, K, *Śladami Gąsienic Pierwszej Dywizji Pancernej*, Hengelo, H.L. Smit & ZN, 1946.

Jarymowycz, Roman, Johann, *Tank Tactics: From Normandy to Lorraine*, Boulder, Lynne Rienner Publishing, 2001.

Jenkins, Roy, *Churchill*, London, Macmillan, 2001.

Jędrzejewicz, Wacław, *Piłsudski: A Life for Poland*, New York, Hippocrene, 1982.

Kacewicz, George, V, *Great Britain, the Soviet Union and the Polish Government in Exile (1939-1945)* The Hague, Nijhoff, 1979.

Karski, Jan, *The Great Powers & Poland, 1919-1945, From Versailles to Yalta*, Lanham, University Press of America, 1985.

Keegan, John, *Six Armies in Normandy: From D-Day to the Liberation of Paris, June 6th – 25th August 1944*, London, Jonathan Cape, 1982.

Kieniewicz, Stefan, *The Emancipation of the Polish Peasantry*, Chicago, University of Chicago Press, 1969.

Klimecki, Michał, *Polsko-Ukraińska Wojna w Lwów i Galicję Wschodnią 1918-1919*, Warsaw, Volumen, 2000.

Kośminder, Tomasz, *Planowanie Wojenne w Polsce w Latach 1921-1926*, Tórun, Adam Marszałek, 2001.

Lane, Thomas, *Victims of Stalin and Hitler. The Exodus of Poles and Balts to Britain*, Basingstoke, Palgrave Macmillan, 2004.

Lorentz, Leopold, *Caen to Wilhelmshaven with the Polish First Armoured Division*, Edinburgh, Errol, 1949.

Łukomski, Gregorz, Polak, Bogusław, Suchcitz, Andrzej, (eds) *Kawalerowie Virtuti Militari, 1792-1945: Wykazy odnaczonych za czyny z lat 1863-1864, 1914-1945*, Koszalin, Politechnika Koszalinskiej, 1997.

Mackiewicz, Stanisław, *Colonel Beck and his Policy*, London, Eyre & Spottiswoode, 1944.

Macmillan, Margaret, *Peacemakers: The Paris Conference of 1919 and its Attempt to End War*, London, John Murray, 2001.

Maczek, Stanisław, *Od Podwody do Czołga: Wspomnienia Wojenne 1918-1945*, Edinburgh, Tomar, 1961.

Majka, Jerzy, *Generał Stanisław Maczek*, Rzeszów, Libra, 2005.

McCauley, Martin, *The Soviet Union, 1917-1991*, London, Longmans, 1994, Second Edition.

McGilvray, Evan, *A Military Government in Exile. The Polish Government-in-Exile 1939-1945, a study of discontent*, Solihull, Helion, 2010.

McGilvray, Evan, *The Black Devils' March – A Doomed Odyssey – The 1st Polish Armoured Division, 1939-45*, Solihull, Helion, 2005.

Megargee, Geoffrey, *Barbarossa, 1941: Hitler's War of Annihilation*, Stroud, Tempus, 2008.

Michta, Andrew A, *The Soldier-Citizen: The Politics of the Polish Army After Communism*, Basingstoke, Macmillan, 1997.

Michta, Andrew A, *Red Eagle: The Army in Polish Politics, 1944-1988*, Stanford, Hoover Press, 1990.

Mieczkowski, Zbigniew, *The Soldiers of General Maczek in World War II*, Warsaw & London, Foundation for the Commemoration of General Maczek's First Armoured Division, 2004.

Milligan, Spike, *Mussolini: His Part in my Downfall*, London, Penguin, 1980.

Mikołajczyk, Stanisław, *The Rape of Poland: Patterns of Soviet Aggression*, Westport, Greenwood Press, 1973, Second Greenwood Reprint.

Mirówicz, Ryszard, *Edward Śmigły-Rydz: Działalność Wojska i Polityczna*, Warsaw, Instytut Wydawniczy Związków Zawodowych, 1988.

Montgomery, Viscount of Alamein, Field Marshal, *21 Army Group: Normandy to the Baltic*, n.p., 1946.

Neillands, Robin, *The Battle of Normandy: 1944*, London, Cassell, 2004.

North, John, *North-West Europe, 1944-45. The Achievements of 21st Army Group*, London, HMSO, 1977.

Panecki, Tadeusz et al, *Sztab Generalny (Główny) Wojska Polskiego, 1918-2003*, Warsaw, Bellona, 2003.

Pepłonski, Andrzej, *Wywiad w Wojnie Polsko-Bolszewickiej, 1919-1920*, Warsaw, Bellona, 1999.

Peters, A.R. *Anthony Eden at the Foreign Office, 1931-1938*, Aldershot, Gower Publishing, 1986.

Pipes, Richard, *Russia Under the Bolsheviks, 1919-1924*, London, Harvill Press, 1994.

Polonsky, Antony, *Politics in Independent Poland, 1921-1939*, Oxford, OUP, 1972.

Potomski. Piotr, *Generał Broni Stanisław Władysław Maczek (1892-1994)*, Warsaw, Wydawnictwa Uniwersytetu Warszawa, 2008.

Prazmowska, Anita, *Britain and Poland, 1939-1943: The Betrayed Ally*, Cambridge, CUP, 1995.

Ready, J. Lee, *Forgotten Allies. The Military Contribution of the Colonies, Exiled Governments and Lesser Powers to the Allied Victory in World War II. The European Theater*, Jefferson, McFarland, 1985.

Reid, Brian A, *No Holding Back: Operation Totalize, Normandy, August 1944*, Toronto, Robin Brass Studio, 2005.

Ripley, Tim, *The Wehrmacht. The German Army in World War II, 1939-1945*, London, Fitzroy Dearborn, 2003.

Roberts, Andrew, *Master and Commander. How Roosevelt, Churchill, Marshall and Alanbrooke Won the War in the West*, London, Allen Lane, 2008.

Romeyko, Marian, *przed i po maju*, Volume I, Warsaw, MON, 1976.

Roos, Hans, *A History of Modern Poland. From the Formation of the State in the First World War to the Present Day*, London, Knopf, 1966.

Rothschild, Joseph, *East Central Europe Between the Two World Wars*, Seattle, University of Washington Press, 1990.

Rothschild, Joseph, *Pilsudski's Coup d'etat*, New York, Columbia, 1966.

Schindler, John R, *Isonzo: The Forgotten Sacrifice of the Great War*, Westport, Praeger, 2001.

Simonds, Peter, *Maple Leaf Up – Maple Leaf Down. The Story of the Canadians in the Second World War*, New York, Island Press, 1947.

Skibiński, Franciszek, *O Sztuce Wojennej: Na Polnocno-Zachodnim Teatrze Działan Wojennych, 1944-1945*, Warsaw, MON, 1977.

Stachura, Peter, D, (ed) *The Poles in Britain, 1940-2000. From Betrayal to Assimilation*, London, Frank Cass, 2004. Foreword by Stanisław Komorowski.

Stachura, Peter, D, (ed) *Themes of Modern Polish History. Proceedings of a Symposium on 28 March 1992. In honour of the Century of General Stanisław Maczek*, Glasgow, The

Polish Social and Educational Society, 1992.

Stawecki, Piotr, *Polityka Wojskowa Polski, 1921-26*, Warsaw, MON, 1981.

Strachan, Hew, *The First World War. A New Illustrated History*, London, Simon & Schuster, 2003.

Sword, Keith. (ed), *Sikorski: Soldier and Statesman. A Collection of Essays*, London, Orbis, 1990.

Sword, Keith, with Norman Davies & Jan Ciechanowski, *The Foundation of the Polish Community in Great Britain, 1939-50*, London, School of Slavonics and East European Studies, University of London, 1989.

Taylor, A.J.P. *Bismarck, the Man and Statesman*, London, NEC Mentor, 1968.

Thompson, Mark, *The White War. Life and Death on the Italian Front*, 1915-1919, London, Faber & Faber, 2009.

Tomkowski, Zbigniew, *Generał Maczek, Najstarszy Żołnierz Rzeczypospolitej*, Warsaw, Ypsylon, 1994.

Tout, Ken, *Roads to Falaise: 'Cobra' & 'Goodwood' Reassessed*, Stroud, Sutton, 2002.

Tout, Ken, *A Fine Night for Tanks: The Road to Falaise*, Stroud, Sutton, 1998.

Vigor, P.H., Chojecki, C.E. *The Polish Resettlement Corps*, RMA Sandhurst, Conflict Studies Research Centre, February 1994.

Villari, Luigi, *The War on the Italian Front*, London, Cobden-Sanderson, 1932.

Wandycz, Piotr, *Soviet-Polish Relations, 1917-1921*, Cambridge, Harvard University Press, 1969.

Whiting, Charles, *The Poor Bloody Infantry, 1939-1945*, London, Guild Publishing, 1987.

Wiatr, Jerzy J, *The Soldier and the Nation. The Role of the Military in Polish Politics, 1918-1985*, Boulder, Westview Press, 1988.

Wiles, Timothy, (ed) *Poland Between the Wars, 1918-1939*, Bloomington, Indiana Polish Studies Center, 1989.

Williamson, David G, *Poland Betrayed: The Nazi-Soviet Invasion, 1939*, Barnsley, Pen & Sword, 2009.

Wittam, John, *The Politics of the Italian Army, 1861-1918*, London, Croom Held, 1977.

Wyszczelski, Lech, *Polska Myśl Wojskowa 1914-1939*, Warsaw, MON, 1988.

Zaloga, Steven J, *The Polish Army, 1939-1945*, London, Osprey, 1983.

Zamoyski, Adam, *The Battle of the Marchlands*, New York, Columbia University Press, 1981.

Zubrzycki, Jerzy, *Polish Immigration in Britain. A Study of Adjustment*, The Hague, Martinus Nijhoff, 1956.

Journal articles

Biskupski, M.B., 'The Military Elite of the Polish Second Republic, 1918-1945: A Historiographical Review' *War & Society* Vol. 14 (1996) pp. 49-86.

Drzewieniecki, Walter, M, 'The Polish Army on the Eve of World War II' *The Polish Review* Vol. 26 (1981) pp. 54-64.

Gasiorowski, Zygmunt, 'Did Pilsudski Attempt to Initiate a Preventative War in 1933?' *The Journal of Modern History* Vol. 27 (1955) pp. 135-151.

Jarymowycz, Roman Johann, 'Canadian Armour in Normandy. Operation 'Totalize' and the Quest for Operational Maneuver' *Canadian Military History* Vol. 7 (1998) pp. 19-40.

Jones, Edgar, Ironside, Stephen, 'Battle Exhaustion: The Dilemma of Psychiatric Casualties in Normandy, June-August 1944' *The Historical Journal* Vol. 53 (2010) pp. 109-128.

Poliakov, V. 'Pilsudski' *The Slavic Review* Vol. 14 (1935-36) pp. 44-52.

Conference Papers

Professor Martin S. Alexander (University of Wales at Aberystwyth) 'The Surrender of France in 1940: Men and Command', Paper given at *Why Fighting Ends: A History of Surrender*, International Conference, Weetwood Hall, University of Leeds, 25-28 June 2009.

Internet

Thomas Nelson Page, *Italy and the World War* (1920) Chapter XIV 'Conditions When Italy Entered the War' http://net.lib.byu.edu/estu/wwi/comment/Italy/Page05.htm, accessed 22 April 2009.

'Constitution of the Republic of Poland (1921) http://-personal-engin.edu~zbigniew/constitutions/k1921.E.html, accessed 31 January 2003.

Index

Index of Military Units

All units are Polish unless noted as follows:
[A]   Austro-Hungarian
[B]   British
[C]   Canadian
[F]   French
[G]   German
[S]   Soviet
[US]American

CPSIA information can be obtained at www.ICGtesting.com
Printed in the USA
BVOW06s1348210915

418556BV00012B/8/P

9 781910 777381